Praise for Cathy Duffy's *Government Nannies*

While maintaining a high level discourse, Mrs. Duffy clarifies a very complex issue with humanity in a way that puts humanists to shame. This brilliantly-argued book exposes the profoundly radical social engineering concealed inside the rhetoric of Goals 2000 and Outcome-Based Education. Scrupulously fair-minded, Mrs. Duffy reveals the worldview of state planners who worship predictable order over freewill dynamism and a state-regulated security over liberty. I recommend *Government Nannies* wholeheartedly.

John Taylor Gatto
Former New York City and New York State Teacher of the Year
and author of Dumbing Us Down, The Exhausted School,
and The Empty Child (forthcoming book).

"*Government Nannies* provides a timely review of dangerous new bureaucratic attacks on individual liberty and the family itself. Seizing upon the public's justifiable demand for educational reform, social engineers have crafted eight educational goals and an 'outcome-based' system of evaluation that have profound implications for parental rights, political freedom and professional success. Cathy Duffy exposes this deliberate and destructive hoax in her important book, *Government Nannies*. Current and prospective parents, principled educators and others committed to defending the American heritage of freedom and the family should take careful notice of this massive expansion of federal power and act accordingly.

George Roche
President, Hillsdale College

"*Government Nannies* is a frightening look, not into the future, but into social policies being imposed by government bureaucrats today. If you think outcome-based education is an obscure bureaucratic fad that doesn't affect you and your family, you need to read this book. As a parent and home education leader, I am alarmed at the degree to which our government is part of the problem in the unfolding crisis in our culture."

David Mason
Director, Congress Project, The Heritage Foundation

"Under the cover of misleading goals, hazy jargon, and professional smiles, the nationalization of children in America proceeds apace. Cathy Duffy's *Government Nannies* is an eye-opening account of this Matriarchal State in action. I salute as well her call for a "separation of school and state," and her faith in an educational renewal rooted in the dedication and love of families themselves."

Allan Carlson
The Rockford Institute

The First Amendment makes clear that Federal involvement in education is unconstitutional. The language in the Bill of Rights is intended to prevent Federal assistance to any establishment of religion. Cathy Duffy's book helps remind us that education inescapably flows from religious premises, and that our tax dollars are now being used to advance an anti-religious agenda through Goals 2000 and Outcome-Based Education.

Howard Phillips
U.S. Taxpayers Alliance

GOVERNMENT NANNIES

THE CRADLE-TO-GRAVE AGENDA OF

GOALS 2000

AND

OUTCOME-BASED EDUCATION

BY

CATHY DUFFY

NOBLE PUBLISHING ASSOCIATES
GRESHAM • OREGON

NOBLE PUBLISHING ASSOCIATES

 P.O. Box 2250

GRESHAM, OREGON 97030

(503) 667-3942

Government Nannies
© 1995 by
Cathy Duffy

The Foreword
© 1995 by
John Taylor Gatto

Printed in the United States of America

ACKNOWLEDGMENTS

I would love to use this space to thank the hundreds of people who have helped me gather, sort, and evaluate information as well as those who helped fine tune its presentation. However, because I deal with so many controversial issues, I think it better to "protect the innocent" who might prefer not to be associated with all of the positions I present. Still, I do want to single out one group for special mention—the numerous dedicated and unpaid researchers who read, study, and write at home because the issues are too important to wait for a special interest group's attention. Many of them have generously shared their research with me and with thousands of others who are much the wiser for their efforts. I would also like to add a public note of appreciation to the wonderful people at Legacy Communications and Noble Publishing Associates who demonstrate by their actions what the word "teamwork" means.

TABLE OF CONTENTS

ACKNOWLEDGMENTS iii

FOREWORD ix

INTRODUCTION xxvii

1. GOVERNMENT NANNIES/ AT-RISK FAMILIES 1

Your Concerned Government/ Goal 1/ The Whole Child/ At-Risk/ Preschool Services/ One-Stop Shopping for Services/ Developmental Delays, Excuse for Family Intervention/ And What Do You Do in Your Home?

2. NEED SOME—FORCE ALL 27

Healthy Tomorrows/ The Ohio Plan/ Initial Targets/ Screening and Assessment/ New Districts/ Goals 2000 Across America/ Parents As Teachers Programs/ Unsubstantiated Child Abuse and Social Services/ State Family Policy/ Should We Have a State Family Policy?

3. GOALS 2000—HOW LARGE IS YOUR VILLAGE? 47

Who's to Blame?/ Would You Buy a Used Car from the Education Department?/ If Schools Were Businesses.../ Centralization, a Plan or a Cop-Out?/ Big Brother Can Do It Better

4. OUTCOME–BASED EDUCATION 69

Will the Real OBE Please Stand Up?/ What's a World Class Standard?/ Assessments/ Assessment Score Reliability/ Does It Work?/ Confusion in the Ranks/ Who's In Control?/ Whose Agenda?/ The Emasculation of Local School Boards/ Teachers and Administrators are Forced to Jump Aboard

5. GOAL 3(COMPETENCY? WHAT DOES IT MEAN?) 103

Outcomes/ Takeover by the Feds/ Government-Approved Feelings/ Social Engineering/ Conforming Diversity/ School Wars

6. PRISONERS OF THE SYSTEM 129

Spending More Time in Prison?/ Values and Mental Coercion/ A No-Win Situation for Public Schools/ Children Caught in A Double Bind

7. THE HEALTH EDUCATION CONNECTION 153

Comprehensive Health Curriculum/ School-Based Clinics/ Parents Lose Control/ From the School to the Clinic to the Welfare Office/ The Nunno Family

8. THE SCHOOL TO WORK TRANSITION 169

Oregon Leads the Way/ People As Human Capital/ Enforced Attendance/ What Choices Do We Have?/ OBE and Certificates of Mastery/ Learning Centers/ Employment Barriers?/ Government Tells Business How to be Efficient/ High Skill/High Wage Fairy Tales/ Collusion between Government and Big Business/ Education for the Workforce

9. THE COMPUTER CONNECTION 193

     SPEEDE/ ExPRESS/ Privacy Disappears

10. NATIONAL STANDARDS, ENFORCEMENT AND MONEY . .205

     Accountability to the Feds/ Kentucky/ Court-Assisted Takeover/
     England's Experience/ It Will Only Cost.../ Local Level Budget
     Busting/ Prophecy or Common Sense?

11. RISK, RESPECT AND RESPONSIBILITY 231

     Is Choice in Education the Answer?/ Indirect Regulation/
     Enlarging Government Dependency/ Regulation of Colleges and
     Universities/ A Socialist By Any Other Name.../ Separation of School
     and State/ Revolution or Resolution?/ Freedom to Risk/ What About
     the Underprivileged?/ What Next?

Bibliography 261

Index 265

FOREWORD

by
John Taylor Gatto

You are holding an important book in your hands, one which should dispel any lingering notions that "Goals 2000" or any of the official "Outcome-Based Education" strategies are merely ways to return the government schooling machine to its accustomed track. Like a good detective or prosecuting attorney, Cathy Duffy has marshalled an army of facts and cases; and she lets the documentation lead her where it must—into a strange world which social engineering has made for our children. Schooling in this century, particularly over the years since the Russian space program provided an

John Taylor Gatto is a former New York City and New York State Teacher of the Year; author of *Dumbing us Down*, *The Exhausted School*, and *The Empty Child* (forthcoming book).

excuse for the federal government to sit at the policy table, has become an exercise in the concentration of power and the domination of our minds by advocates of a socialist world view.

Until recently, the progress of this scheme was slow and nearly invisible. At first it proceeded structurally, enlarging schools, removing control in important ways from local school boards and transferring it to state departments of education, placing curriculum decisions in the hands of remote agencies. But in recent years the thing has become bolder, openly attacking family loyalty, belief in God, cultural attachment, and other keys to personal meaning as intolerable obstacles to the realization of the covert design. Outcome-based education, for instance, as it has been conceived in foundations and academic centers, is a way to break the resistance of a child's mind to "scientific" indoctrination in attitudes and beliefs deemed desirable by unseen policy makers. Where in the past such resistance could only be punished by a bad grade, with OBE the offender can be subjected to constant peer pressure to conform, and can be held in confinement until his will surrenders. In the most ambitious conception, those not possessing acceptable attitudes will not be employable!

It should not take a George Orwell to discern what the future holds for all of us. If we are not vigilant in the defense of liberty and vigorous in the attack on this alien conception, we shall become a hive society, an anthill nation.

Let me tell you a little of how all this came about to prepare the ground for Mrs. Duffy's case:

The government began to compel us all to send our children to school in 1852 in Massachusetts; from that state the compulsion spread slowly south, west, and north—far too slowly to support the false contention that forced schooling was popular anywhere.

But in 1818, 34 years before the first compulsory school laws, Noah Webster estimated that over five million copies of his *Spelling Book* had been sold in a country of under twenty million population. And when you consider that every purchase decision had to be made freely by an individual or a family and that there were no federal, state or city tabs on which to run bulk purchases, it would seem to suggest that most people don't have to be tricked or compelled to learn; most people in a natural setting will do it on their own because they want to. Each *Spelling Book* purchase decision was made privately. In each case someone forked over some cash to buy a book. According to the American Library Association, only one adult American in every 11 does that any more; so you can see we must have been *radically* literate by modern standards in those by-gone days.

Between 1813 and 1823, Walter Scott sold five million copies of his novels in the U.S., equal to about 60 million books today; James Fenimore Cooper's books (think of *Last of the Mohicans*) also sold in the millions. Pick up a Cooper or a Scott at your local library, and you will discover both authors write complex, highly allusive prose, not easy reading even by a college student today.

In 1812 Pierre DuPont de Nemours published *Education in the United States*, a book in which he expressed his amazement at the phenomenal literacy he saw. Forty years before passage of our first compulsory school laws, DuPont said that fewer than four of every thousand people in the new nation could not read and do numbers well. Looking around himself and comparing America with the Continental traditions he had left behind, he saw a world in which nearly every child was skilled in argumentation (the old-fashioned term for "critical thinking") because of the widespread habit of involving young children in disputes about the meaning of ambiguous Bible passages, or so that seemed the explanation to Mr. DuPont.

It appears that before 1852, when Massachusetts got compulsion schooling, the American people were educating themselves quite well; sometimes they used traditional schooling, sometimes they invented new kinds of schooling, and sometimes they substituted for formal schooling—as Benjamin Franklin did—as they best saw fit. "As they best saw fit" they understood to be the prescription for a free country; "as the authorities best see fit" the formula of a dictatorship.

Our early catch-as-catch-can entrepreneurial forms of instruction offered abundant choices of useful ways to grow up, useful ways to read, write, and think. Historically, schooling was about literacy, and that is why it succeeded so well; literacy isn't very difficult to achieve for children when they perceive that the adults about them think that it's important.

Kids Like to Learn

The secret to our amazing mastery of literacy in those far-off days has its foundation in the fact that reading, writing and numbers are easy to learn in spite of what we hear today from the reading, writing and numbers establishments whose bread and butter depends on convincing taxpayers the opposite is true. A few private schools and private individuals still understand that basic truth and manage to instill literacy correctly—at a fraction of the cost of most public schools. A big part of the secret lies in keeping the instruction intimate.

While there are larger-scale examples, my own early years show how easy it is to learn to read and do arithmetic well without compulsion schools. In 1941, when I went to first grade at the age of five in Swissvale, Pennsylvania, a borough of Pittsburgh, I could read complicated books without a coach.

And I understood enough of those books to read with enthusiasm. The last thing I read at home before I went to school to learn "Twinkle, twinkle, little star" was Matthew Arnold's 19th century epic poem about Persia, "Sohrab and Rustum." I liked Sohrab and wondered, I recall, what delights first grade was going to hold.

If you find that hard to believe—or exceptional, I want to suggest the reason for that lies in the elimination of the historical memory—and its replacement by something called "social science"—by the policy makers who have controlled 20th century schooling. Remember that for the first 200 years of U. S. history, most schools wouldn't *accept* children who couldn't read and count; so they must have learned those things where I did—at home.

The miracle woman who taught me to read was Frances "Bootie" Zimmer, who graduated from Monongahela High School in 1929, a woman from a little coal-mining, steel mill town in western Pennsylvania. Bootie never got a college degree, but nobody despaired about that in those days because daily life seemed to run very well without too many college graduates around.

Here was Bootie's method: She held me in her lap and read to me while she ran her finger under the words. That's not the phonics method, and that's not the whole word method; that's the just plain reading method. It's hard to make a living out of peddling it. From the time I was two years old, she read to me every single day from increasingly difficult books, none of which seemed hard to me because I was having so much fun. She read real fairy tales, not sanitized ones, real history books and newspaper stories, and real grown-up works including some tales from Boccaccio. What she avoided like the plague were scientific readers of any sort, the books with

364-word pseudo-scientific vocabularies and lots and lots of pictures. Pictures have nothing to do with learning how to read well, and too many of them will guarantee that you don't.

Here I've presented you with a very great mystery: we had a perfectly literate country before the advent of government schooling in 1852; what on earth has happened since? Why aren't we a literate society in our present well-schooled era if we once were in a lightly-schooled one?

A look at the course 20th-century schooling has deliberately taken will make it clear we are not in the presence of a simple mistake in social engineering. What has happened was meant to happen. We are in the dead zone of a powerful ideological agenda, an agenda so passionately and grimly supported by its proponents we might almost view it as a religion.

History is essential to a proper understanding of the present situation. Can you understand who you are without knowing your own history? Similarly I think it impossible to know what the schools really are and in what direction they are tending without knowing where they came from, who are the midwives, and who the guardians. Otherwise, you are compelled to regard your classroom problems as a mechanic might, tinkering to fix them, demanding money to reach ends which are beyond the reach of money, or, worst of all, entertaining seriously the newest government schemes of school reform, outcome-based education and national testing, as cures for the disease of bad schooling instead of booster shots of the virus.

How We Got Into The Present Mess

The structure of 20th-century American schooling is modeled on a system invented in early 19th-century Prussia after Napoleon's amateur soldiers beat the professional soldiers of Prussia at the Battle of Jena in 1806. When your business is renting soldiers to other countries, losing a battle like that is not taken lightly. Almost immediately afterwards, the philosopher Johann Fichte delivered his famous "Address to the German Nation" in which Prussians were told that the nation was going to be shaped up through a new Utopian institution of forced schooling in which everyone would learn how to take orders. Prussia is such an important country in terms of its influence on the development of American institutions that I wish we had some time to discuss it.

The formation of Prussia was the result of the last Crusade of the Catholic Popes which did not go to the Holy Land but to the northeast of Europe to pacify the pagan Prussians. Almost half the combatants on both sides in the American Revolution were German mercenaries, and many of those were Prussian, including our brilliant cavalry officer, the phony "Baron" Von Steuben. While our Revolution was being contested, Prussian women had to register at the local police station each month when their menses stopped. That was Prussia in 1776; forty-three years later it gave the world the first successful national government forced schooling scheme.

Modern forced schooling started in Prussia in 1819 with a clear vision of what centralized schooling could deliver:

1. Obedient soldiers for the Army,
2. Obedient workers for the mines,
3. Subservient civil servants for the government,
4. Subservient clerks for industry,
5. And citizens who thought alike about major issues.

This Prussian system was intended to create an artificial national consensus on matters worked out in advance by leading German families and the heads of institutions.

A small number of very passionate American ideological leaders including Horace Mann of Massachusetts, Calvin

Stowe of Ohio, Barnas Sears of Connecticut, and others visited Prussia in the first half of the 19th century, fell in love with the order, obedience, and efficiency they saw there, attributed the well-regulated, machine-like society to its educational system, and campaigned relentlessly upon returning home to bring the Prussian vision to these shores. At the same time, through the Utopian socialist colonies springing up all over the United States in this period, the Prussian ideal of an idyllic childhood free of care and responsibility as the best preparation for a lifetime of taking orders was being tested, refined and promoted. Pestalozzi and Froebel were the two theorist-practitioners Prussian schooling followed in this regard, and Robert Owens' utopian socialist colony at New Harmony in western Indiana was privileged to host Pestalozzi's principal English-speaking interpreter as its own schoolmaster.

Prussian policy-makers had learned by experimentation that it was easier to apply behavior-shaping techniques to children who knew very little and were only modestly literate than it was to shape those young people who had been trained early in thinking techniques. Froebel's "kindergarten" with its early removal of the child's parents and culture from the scene, and its replacement of serious learning with songs, games, pictures and organized group activities was remarkably effective in delivering compliant material to the State. In the United States the Prussian training methods were actively spread by Elizabeth Peabody of Boston Peabody prestige, and others equally well-placed. Miss Peabody was the sister of Mary Peabody, the second Mrs. Horace Mann.

The ultimate goal of Prussian schools was to unify the country under centralized leadership, not to teach literacy. By 1852 our first forced schooling appeared; the goal of important leadership in the northern U. S. was to mold those hordes of immigrant Irish Catholics whose emigration was being encouraged to provide a cheap labor supply to the burgeoning factory system of the Northeast, and settlers for the West. These newcomers were to be bent to a national consensus based on the New England cultural model, a plan which necessitated the destruction of the southern tidewater cultural model—a detail accomplished soon after we got forced schooling by the defeat of the South in the Civil War.

To reach synthetic consensus, as Prussia had demonstrated, children would have to be removed from their parents, and from inappropriate cultural and religious influences, too. The *tabula rasae* could only be written upon away from prying eyes and competing influences; school would provide the isolation chamber in which to do that. In making this form of isolated school experience, policy-makers were following the best model of Jean Jacques Rousseau who had set it down in his book, *Emile*. Prussia had followed the same model.

So at the behest of Horace Mann and other leading citizens, without any national debate or discussion, we adopted Prussian schooling or rather, most had it imposed upon them. Yet there was still another obstacle in reaching Prussian perfection; the traditional form of school size, shape and governance militated against it. The one- and two-room schoolhouses, highly efficient as academic transmitters, breeders of self-reliance and independence, intimately related to their communities, almost exclusively female-led, and largely unadministered, had to be put to death.

Remember, academic prowess and self-reliance were no longer the purposes of schooling—at least on a policy level; during the first 50 years of our new school system, the Prussian purpose, which was to create a form of what we would call

today "welfare-state socialism," gradually forced out the traditional American purpose: to prepare the individual for an
independent life. The factory economy could not use independent people, and neither could the strong-state society
which influential men were struggling to bring into being.

The Prussian purpose was collective; the American purpose as it had come down through our early history, individu-
alistic. Prussia was a rigid class society; America had fluid
classes and an easy disrespect for authority. In Prussia the purpose was realized by a three-tier school system. The lowest tier,
which comprised 94% of the students, was called the
Volksschulen, the "people's schools"; here "socialization" was
the goal, the production of a cheerful, compliant, cooperative
proletariat, only lightly connected to family, culture, and
religion. Thinking was reserved for about one kid in sixteen,
and was apportioned among two further types of schoolhouse. The highest form of thinking, dialectics and various
forms of analysis were reserved for the Academies which
handled about one half of one percent of the children, the
other five and a half percent were educated at Realschulen—
these were to be the service class for the policy-makers —
engineers, architects, doctors, lawyers, high academics,
writers, and propagandists.

In Prussia intellectual development for the masses was
regarded with managerial horror, as something which caused
armies to lose battles. That attitude was transferred across the
Atlantic along with Prussian school structures and procedures,
reinforcing the strong New England distrust of the poor.

I hope you recognize I have just described for you the
world of systematic schooling as it is practiced almost everywhere in the United States of America.

The Prussian Educational Method

Three major ideas were transferred almost intact from Prussia and slowly worked themselves into the 20th-century framework of American national schooling. The first was the very sophisticated notion that state schooling exists not for the benefit of the students and their families but for the benefit of the state. In this idea the will of children has to be broken in order to make use of them later as plastic material. If the will can be broken, all else should follow.

Children were not to be taught to think but only to memorize facts unrelated to their lives. Memorization is an essential glue to give continuity to families, communities, and religions; but if its use can be perverted by the massive introduction of nonsense-memories, artificially bolstered by making the testing of these phantoms the raison d'etre of going to school, a personal vacuum can be created or at least approached. An empty child. A blank tablet. And in strong-state, command economy theories, it is only such a population which allows itself to be scientifically managed.

Children who "think" weaken the grasp of central authority; children must be discouraged from pursuing their own natural interests and family interests for the same reason. In Prussian schooling, teachers following instructions passed down the chain-of-command to them, defined what children's interests should be. This logic of management created the need to eliminate the familiar one-room schoolhouse because it vested too much responsibility in the children themselves and in un-monitored female managers.

The second important idea in Prussian method was extreme fragmentation of wholes into "subjects," into fixed time periods, pre-thought sequences, externally imposed questioning, synthetic "units," and the like. This simplified many of the problems of leadership. Thought broken into fragments can be managed by a poorly trained, poorly paid teaching force; fragments can be memorized even by a moron. Fragments memorized and disgorged create the appearance of mathematical precision in testing; fragments tested deliver beautiful distribution curves of supposed achievement, pretty bell curves.

The third idea adopted from the Prussians was that the government is the true parent of children, the state is sovereign over the family. By 1989, a little over 100 years ago, the crop from these Prussian seeds was ready for harvest. In that year U. S. Commissioner of Education William Torrey Harris assured railroad magnate Collis P. Huntington that American schools had been "scientifically designed" to prevent "over education." The average American would learn to be content with his humble role in life, said our commissioner, because he would not be tempted to *think* about any other role.

By 1896 John Dewey was saying that independent, self-reliant people would be an anachronism in the collective society of the future; in modern society, said Dewey, people would be defined by their associations, the groups to which they belonged, not by their own individual accomplishments. In such a world people who read too well or too early are dangerous because they become privately empowered. They know too much, and they know how to find out what they don't know all by themselves, without consulting experts.

Dewey said the great mistake of historic pedagogy had been to make reading and writing constitute the center of early schoolwork. He advocated that the de-coding method of teaching reading (which we call "phonics" today) be abandoned and replaced by the whole-word method (which at various times we've called "look-say"), and this was advised not because Dewey thought the latter was more efficient (he admitted that it might be less efficient), but because learning to read hard books produces independent thinkers, thinkers who can't be "socialized" very easily.

By socialization Dewey meant what a whole generation of activists who appeared between 1890 and World War I meant, conditioning to a program of social objectives administered by the best social thinkers in government. Socialization was a giant step on the road to state socialism, and it was a vision radically disconnected from America's populist past, its historic hopes and dreams of independent families, independent religions, and independent livelihoods.

Somewhere around the turn of the 20th century, making people "dumb" for their own good became the point of our national exercise in forced schooling: 1870-1900 had hammered home the political framework of forced schooling to create "dumbness"; 1900-1930 had established the industrial methodology of accomplishing this; 1930-1960 was the period when the socialization methodology became entrenched; and 1960 to the present is where the psychologizing of a well-schooled proletariat has been the principal subject of schooling.

I know you will find all this hard to believe, yet the track of the Prussianization over the past 150 years is quite clear. Beginning in the late 19th century and continuing right through today, a small band of very influential people, substantially financed by money provided by the large private foundations like Carnegie, Rockefeller, and Ford, have introduced what might be called "modified scientific socialism" into American institutional education. To do this, they learned how to gain control of the machinery of government, and then, in direct violation of the letter and spirit of both our Constitution and Bill of Rights, began to destroy the mecha-

nisms of local control of schooling, vesting control in a continually centralizing, highly radical, and very undemocratic
form of governance. Supporting these revolutionary developments was an increasingly complete control of the public
oversight mechanisms of journalism, which provided a cloak
of invisibility over what was happening.

This small band of influential people had determined privately that this was the best course for the American state,
and so with no public discussion and little wasted motion,
they pointed our nation down the statist road. We were going
to become a multi-tiered class society like Germany (or
Japan); and that is, in fact, what we are well on the way to
becoming.

Choice and Competition in Education

The movement toward big state socialism is not a historical curiosity but a powerful, dynamic force in the world
around us. One of the favorite words of education bureaucrats
is "socialization," a term made prominent by John Dewey,
leader of the Fabian socialist movement in the America of his
time. The training ground for a socialist world society has
been our schools and continues to be our schools, though a
complex counter-movement is under way to deconstruct and
decentralize government schooling, returning it to families,
local groups, neighborhoods, and communities.

Centralized schooling is at present countering the threats
to its continuation with demands for even more control over
children's lives and even more money to pay for the extended
school day and year such control would require. The tech-
nique being used to motivate compliance is a drum beat of
manufactured fear, fear of foreign competition which we are
told threatens our entire economy. What is never mentioned

by this panic strategy is that the American economy grew to its position of world dominance under the direction of a relatively unschooled population, and that our current dominance after the collapse of Russia is greater today than it has ever been in the past.

No, the calls for increased doses of centralized government schooling serve a different master than intellectual development. I note with interest the growth of day care in the United States and frequent calls to extend schooling downward to include four- and three-year olds. Kindergarten was created to be, and was quietly celebrated as, a gentle way to break the monopoly influence of mothers on their own children.

I haven't yet supplied you with a sensible motive for the growth of this indecent interference in the intimate lives of families and cultures and churches, a sensible motive which might explain the compliance of millions of otherwise hardheaded citizens in the dismal record of schooling and its increasingly aggressive shakedown of the taxpayer. Why hasn't this failed institution been allowed to collapse?

The answer lies in the transformation of schooling from a simple service to families and communities into an enormous, remotely-controlled commercial enterprise. Schools are the single largest employer in the United States, the largest mediator of contracts. This low-visibility phenomenon of school as a big business provides it with powerful political friends, advocates. and many other useful allies. This explains in large part why no amount of failure ever changes things for very long in schools. School people are in a financial position to outlast any storm and to keep short-attention public scrutiny thoroughly confused by constant promises to reform.

A glance at the short history of American public schools, barely a century old as a widespread government monopoly, reveals the standard pattern: periodic public outrages followed in every case by an enlargement of the monopoly. The net effect of public clamor has been to diminish, not enlarge, the range of worthwhile alternatives. Surely this is the richest of all ironies and a testimonial to the interests served by schooling exactly as it is.

I spent 30 years inside public schools, some considered good, some bad; from that experience it seems certain to me that management is unable to clean its own house. That, unfortunately, goes even for local management because too much authority has been parceled out to distant overseers. All significant change ideas are marginalized and degraded, and all watchdog mechanisms co-opted. This will not change until we have full free-market choices of how to grow up, as was the case for most of our national history.

The recent arguments for national testing, national teaching licenses, and national curriculum are a clever way to head off potential competition before it forms. If the government is allowed to pre-empt the standard-making function and to reduce standards to its own anti-intellectual, lowest-common-denominator prescription, then the centralized schooling system itself can be *allowed* to come apart because the State will instead be able to reach into private schools, religious schools, and home schools with its message. If the past has anything to teach us, it is that we cannot allow this to happen. What is needed is the kind of wildly swinging free market we had for the first 200 years of our national history.

Up to now, we have been sold a bill of goods and have believed a fairy tale. We have been led to believe that a body of theory and practice exists at the teacher college level which accurately prescribes the way all children learn, and what learning is of most worth. Nothing could be further from the truth. By pretending this fantasy was true, we have cut our-selves off from the accurate information and efficient innovation only real markets can provide. Fortunately our national situation has been so favorable through most of our history that the margin of allowable error we enjoy has been vast.

But the future is not so clear, although I have implied that our position of advantage is so great over other nations it would be difficult to squander. It is in the arena of emotional and spiritual capital, in the simple satisfactions with life, in finding joy in living, that our relative position has been slipping for years. Violence, divorce, suicide, alcoholism, crime, loneliness, narcotic addiction—all these are tangible measures of poverty in education. Surely schools, as the institutions monopolizing the day times of childhood, can be called to account by the people. The final judges in a free society are not experts but plain people.

And the courtroom of plain people is a free market. Over 50 years ago my mother, Bootie Zimmer, chose to teach me to read well. She had no degrees, no government salary, no outside encouragement; yet her private non-expert choice to make me a fluent reader was the key to a good and adventurous life. Give plain people back their right to choose, and the school nightmare will vanish in a generation.

And now I shall turn you over to Cathy Duffy, whose fairmindedness puts any "humanist" I ever met to shame. Remember as you read that she is defending your right to control your own mind. If that is radical, you live in a world Thomas Jefferson would despise.

INTRODUCTION

Historians have a far easier task than the field marshal on the eve of battle. The historian has the advantage of time and distance as well as access to sources of information that the tactician in the field lacks. The field marshal has to make the best decisions possible with all the information available to him. He also contends with an ever-changing playing field.

I feel much like the tactician in the thick of battle as I attempt to take aim at the massive, moving, multiplying, federal octopus of government-nanny programs. The legislation is still being written as we go to press. No one will know what some of the legislation actually means until it makes its way through the court system. Most schools have begun to implement various parts of the program, but few have a clear idea of what they are doing.

Little analysis has been done, this work being one of the first such efforts. That means that I must draw upon "current events" for much of my information. Newspapers, magazines, reports from research and philanthropic foundations, bulletins, tapes, video presentations, and personal interviews are the best sources for up-to-the minute facts. The immediacy of the issue also precludes the leisure that the historian has to check five sources for verification or to wait for results to confirm observations. Like the field strategist, I have to take my best shot at the moving target. Despite the difficulties, I have tried to confirm reports and seek original documentation whenever possible. The historian ten or twenty years from now should expect to have more complete proof and documentation than is available at present. Although I have done my best to document the evidence, I do not intend this book to be the last word on the subject, but rather an opening salvo.

Some might think that I am being an alarmist in my assessment of Outcome-Based Education and Goals 2000. The truth is that I have taken a fairly conservative approach, bypassing information for which I personally cannot produce documentation (even though I know that it exists), granting people the benefit of the doubt, and striving to be fair to all. Probably some will even fault me for not being alarmist enough.

In my research, I spoke with numerous people on all sides of the issues, and I discovered an uncomfortable truth. Some of the people doing some of the most objectionable things are not evil people. They sincerely believe that they are doing the right thing. As far as I can tell, they are motivated by a sincere concern for others, although I am not naive enough to deny that most people function from an assortment of mixed motives.

I have discovered that people whom I believe to be "sincerely wrong" generally view life from a different world view at some level. They differ from me in one or more of the major philosophical issues such as what they believe about man, God, government, the purpose of life, and the purpose of government. A good example would be those who view children as empty buckets, waiting to be filled. They believe that children only learn in response to external stimuli. They deny self-formed aspirations, spiritual motivations, and conscience. Children must then be molded, shaped, and controlled by reward and punishment. We no longer trust children to learn anything simply for the sake of learning, but instead we motivate them with fear about short or long-term consequences.

Those holding to the empty bucket view would then see the government as responsible to see that those buckets get filled. They also view the reward/punishment, stimulus/response philosophy as the key to social programs. If we continue tinkering with programs, we will eventually come up with the right formula for eradicating poverty, ignorance, and crime. Thus a philosophical world view translates into a belief about the role of government.

Conflicting world views are the heart of the problem. As I see it, the future of our country hinges upon resisting the encroachment of the world view that advocates government as "savior." You need not be religious to have problems with that belief. Anyone who values freedom and autonomy—and even those who are unaware of their independence—becomes a victim when society decrees that all must relinquish a certain amount of both of these rights for the good of the whole.

My concern and purpose for writing this book is to stimulate more people to value their freedom and autonomy enough to stand against the encroachment of benevolent government-nanny programs that would keep us all as perpetual children.

CHAPTER ONE

GOVERNMENT NANNIES/AT RISK FAMILIES

Nancy Smith relaxes in her hospital bed, relieved after the delivery of her first child, a healthy little girl. Joe Smith, perching on the edge of the bed, beams at his wife, as if the accomplishment was mostly his. We don't blame him. He's a typical new father who loves his family.

There is a courtesy knock on the door; then a matronly woman walks in. "Congratulations, Mr. and Mrs. Smith. I've just come from the nursery. Your Amanda certainly is a beautiful little girl."

"Well...thank you...um...are you on the hospital staff?" asks Nancy.

"Oh, I'm sorry! I forgot to introduce myself. I'm Ms. Davis from the Healthy Beginnings Program. I just love working with brand new babies!" Ms. Davis practically glows in anticipation.

"What kind of work do you do, Ms. Davis?"

"Oh, you know, there are so many young couples who are nervous about their first child. I'm just like a grandmother who helps out a little bit." The lines around her clear blue eyes deepen with her smile. "It's so sad that most families are so scattered that there is no one around to help out our young mothers. So that's why I'm here. I just want to be a helping hand."

Nancy, sensing that this is more than a courtesy visit, shifts into a sitting position. "That's very sweet of you. I appreciate the offer, but my mother is planning to come stay for a few days until I'm back on my feet. And Joe's mother lives close by. She works days, but she'll be around as much as she can. I'm sure we'll be fine," she explains.

Ms. Davis beams patronizingly at Joe and Nancy. "Oh, there's so much to learn about parenting. It's really not as simple as it was in the old days. There are so many dangers facing our children now; we have to be extra careful that they get a good start. Do you know that the latest research has sadly shown us that parents in this last generation learned some terribly negative ways of interacting with their children? They just didn't know better, and some of the books they read...well they were no better than a bunch of old wives' tales."

Joe, slightly miffed, answers, "My parents seemed to know what they were doing. They did a good job with me and my brothers."

Ms. Davis's face briefly flashes a contemptuous look, but she quickly softens to her grandmother mode. "I'm sure they did, but there's simply no way that a non-professional can keep up with the latest developments in the field. Researchers are discovering more and more about proper parenting every day. There's so much to learn." She spreads her hands with finality. "We do all of that for you. We keep up on the latest information from the experts so we can help all of our families to be successful."

"Successful?" wonders Nancy to herself, deciding not to pursue it. After all, Ms. Davis appears so nice and so concerned.

"So," Joe asks, "just what kind of help can you give us?"

Ms. Davis, smiling broadly, pulls the visitor's chair closer to the bed and removes her clipboard from her briefcase. "We tailor our services to meet the needs of each family, so, if you'll just help me with a little background information, we can figure out what we can do for you. Let's begin with Joe. What sort of work do you do?"

"I have my own landscape maintenance business. It's great because my time is sort of flexible."

Ms. Davis scribbles quickly on her clipboard, then continues, "How much do you earn per week?"

Joe, taken aback by the question, thinks, "What business is it of hers how much I earn?" But he answers, "It depends on my accounts. Some of them are regular, but sometimes we have special jobs, so it varies quite a bit."

Ms. Davis jots down, "undependable income," then continues with her questions. Nancy starts folding and unfolding the top edge of the bed sheet as the questions make her increasingly uneasy. Joe stands up and looks out the window as the questions get more and more personal. "What do you do with your free time?" "How much time do you spend watching television each day?" "How many books do you read?" "Do you have good relationships with your relatives?" "How's your sex life?"

Finally, Joe decides that Ms. Davis is just too inquisitive, and he turns to confront her. "Ms. Davis, I'm not sure where this is going, but we don't want to answer any more of these questions."

Used to being rebuffed, Ms. Davis is ready to change the subject. "Oh, that's okay. We've got enough to start with. Your P.E. can fill in any missing details on her first visit."

"P.E. What's that?" Nancy asks wearily.

"That's your parent educator. We assign one to every new family so that they will always have someone to turn to for help and advice."

"But we don't need anyone else. I already told you that our folks are nearby, and they can't wait to help us with Amanda," protests Nancy.

"Well, my dear. Maybe you don't realize it now, but you really will need some help. After all, your husband does not make very much money, so you will definitely need to take advantage of some of the wonderful programs we have to help low income families. We can help with her vaccinations, make sure she's developing properly, and even aid in nutrition. After all, we want Amanda to be a healthy, strong little girl, don't we?"

Miffed and a little embarrassed, Joe counters, "I think we can take care of ourselves. I know that our parents will help us if we really need anything. But we have already figured out our budget, so we know we'll be okay. I don't think we want to use any of those programs you mentioned."

Ms. Davis, having encountered independent, defensive parents before, smoothly replies, "I'm sure you will change your minds. After all, you wouldn't want to harm Amanda because of your pride. I can see that you can really use some good advice. You just don't understand how crucial getting the right care during these early years is for children."

Joe and Nancy are feeling a little beleaguered by this time, so they mumble something that passes for reluctant agreement. Ms. Davis rises from the chair, concluding her visit. "You don't need to sign up for any programs today. We'll just see how things go. Your P.E. will be visiting in two weeks, and you can talk it over with her. I'm sure you'll just love her. Take care of our sweet little Amanda for me. Bye."

Your Concerned Government

Even though Nancy and Joe's story sounds far-fetched, this scenario is already happening in several states. Missouri and Hawaii are in the forefront. Social workers are more subtle than Ms. Davis with most families, but often enough, they are quite forceful, particularly with low income families and those with poor English skills who are easily intimidated.

The social workers are not abusing their power in these cases. They are simply doing their job. And their job assignments come from the state and federal governments. While most of us weren't looking, our government redefined its role. Cradle-to-grave care from your concerned government is the new plan. The policies cover all areas of life, from health to death, leisure time behavior to careers. But some of the most intrusive policies are the ones that have as their targets our children. Parents and families are no longer assumed to be competent enough to handle their responsibilities on their own. The government decided to join us as partners in parenting. Pieces of legislation to this effect have been passed already at state and federal levels, but the big transition is yet to come.

The plan centers around Goals 2000, President Clinton's agenda for "education reform." Education reform *is* part of the plan, but Goals 2000 goes much further, out of the classroom and into the home, beyond instruction and into indoctrination. In reality, it provides the framework for a cradle-to-grave takeover of America's families. The heart of Goals 2000 is a set of eight national goals; these goals are:

1. All children will start school ready to learn.
2. The high-school graduation rate will increase to at least 90 percent.
3. American students will leave grades four, eight, and twelve having demonstrated competency in challenging subject matter, including English, mathematics, science, foreign languages, civics and government, economics, arts, history, and geography; and every school in America will ensure that all students learn to use their minds well, so they may be prepared for responsible citizenship, further learning, and productive employment in our modern economy.
4. The nation's teaching force will have access to programs for the continued improvement of their professional skills and the opportunity to acquire the knowledge and skills needed to instruct and prepare all American students for the next century.
5. U.S. students will be first in the world in science and mathematics achievement.
6. Every adult American will be literate and will possess the knowledge and skills necessary to compete in a global economy and exercise the rights and responsibilities of citizenship.
7. Every school in America will be free of drugs and violence and will offer a disciplined environment conducive to learning.
8. Every school and home will engage in partnerships that will increase parental involvement and participation in promoting the social, emotional, and academic growth of children.

At first glance, these goals might sound reasonable. And, if pursued by private means and voluntary programs, some of them might even be praiseworthy. However, Goals 2000, backed by related legislation, aims to expand government-as-nanny programs much more, and all attempts at subtlety are likely to disappear. The "partnership" is shaping up to be an invasion.

Goal 1

Obviously, all of these goals don't apply to Joe and Nancy's situation as parents of a newborn, but eventually this young family will encounter the government nanny behind each goal in the plan. We will tackle our analysis of the goals in sort of a cradle-to-grave order; thus we start with the first.

The first national goal sets the stage, providing the excuse for government nanny programs, but it might not be obvious to the casual reader. All children starting school ready to learn sounds sensible. After all, why send children to school if they are not ready to benefit from the experience? Too many children from disadvantaged backgrounds have little or no exposure to learning readiness activities. They might not be able to tell the difference between a circle and a square. They might confuse red with blue. They usually know their own names, but parents are referred to only as mommy and daddy. Numbers and letters might as well be calculus symbols for all the recognition they evoke.

Frustrated with the difficulties involved with teaching such unprepared children, educators have decided that the best strategy is to intervene long before children reach kindergarten age. To make sure children are "ready to learn," sociologists, educators, bureaucrats, and legislators have determined that they must monitor and even participate in the raising of children from the very beginning. A National Education Goals Panel report says, "Readiness to learn necessarily begins long before school, even before birth itself, and we conclude that 'school readiness' relates to the child's health, to the home environment, and to preschool education."[1]

Most of us agree that before-school experiences and environment can mean the difference between a child who is ready to learn to read and do arithmetic and a child who is not. Yet, the lack of prior preparation does not make it impossible for a child to learn. Many children simply need to spend the first year of school covering some readiness activities. There certainly can be long term handicaps for children who grow up in homes where books are neither available nor valued, where a luminous television is as crucial as a refrigerator, and where the most stimulating conversation consists of arguments over which sitcom to watch and which to tape. However, these problems cannot be easily solved. They reflect much deeper societal problems that are not likely to be cured by the government's takeover of parental responsibilities. In fact, that strategy is likely to make the situation worse.

History and common sense tell us that people are more likely to assume responsibility when they know that no one else will. If I knew that no one else was going to watch my car's gas gauge and remind me to fill the tank before it hits empty, I would do it myself. But, my husband watches it closely and puts gas in the car for me. As a result of his kindness, I rarely even look at the gas gauge.

When government agencies take over responsibilities that properly belong to parents, parents tend to become lazy about their end of the job. If they know that a social worker will remind them that a child should be getting vaccinations, they won't think about vaccination schedules. If the school provides free breakfast and lunch for children, families tend to stop worrying about providing nutritious meals.

As societal ills have increased, legislators have increased their attempts to fix family problems. Lack of coordination between family assistance programs, along with poor results, have caused those in government to look for a better solution. They saw that the public schools were the one constant in the lives of most children. So they decided to reorganize assistance programs around the hub of the local school.[2]

Naturally, this strategy affects the mission of the public schools. Fixing families is beginning to dominate the school agenda. On top of that, too many "uncivilized" children are coming to schools from families who have abdicated their responsibility to teach even basic manners and courtesy. Teaching children social interaction and group behavior then becomes another important part of the school's mission. Of course, academics have to be de-emphasized to make room for these more important goals. Unfortunately, the emphasis on "fixing" people rather than teaching academic skills carries over beyond kindergarten readiness as we will see when we discuss educational restructuring.

The African proverb popular in education circles and making the rounds at problem-solving education and social issue summits says, "It takes a whole village to raise a child." As it is being applied here in the United States, the result is pure collectivism– the idea that the community, government, businesses, and parents all share the task of raising children. It is no longer the exclusive role of parents. Popularizing this proverb is one thing, but when government decides to build their legislative agenda around it, as they have done with Goals 2000, what it ultimately means needs to be seriously addressed.

The Whole Child

Even though education has never been limited strictly to academics, parents have never felt their roles were being usurped by home economics or wood shop classes. Successfully compelling parents to accept the expansion of the school's responsibility into health, home environment, preschool, and prenatal care on the proposed scale, however, enlarges the school's control over the whole life of the child. We get a better sense of the scope of this takeover of family rights by looking at the objectives of the first national goal that spell it out in more detail.

1. All disadvantaged and disabled children will have access to high quality and developmentally appropriate preschool programs that help prepare children for school.

2. Every parent in America will be a child's first teacher and devote time each day to helping his or her preschool child learn; parents will have access to the training and support they need.

3. Children will receive the nutrition and health care needed to arrive at school with healthy minds and bodies; and the number of low-birthweight babies will be significantly reduced through enhanced prenatal health systems.

Notice the language: "all children" and "every parent." We're not just talking about problem kids. No one is to be left out. And since not all parents will have the resources or the inclination to do all of the above on their own, government assumes the implicit authority to see that the objectives are met. Some families might not mind, but there are many of us who are strongly opposed to government interference. How will government nannies respond to a firm, "No, thank you."?

At-Risk

Definitions are crucial because they often mean far more than the outsider might assume. For example, the term "disabled and disadvantaged children" used in the first objective opens a Pandora's box. Most people think of severe problems when they hear these terms, but in Goals 2000, they mean much more. Disabled can mean blind or crippled, but it can also mean a child who has a minor learning disability. Disadvantaged can mean a child from a single parent household or a child from a family that has purposely chosen a simple, non-materialistic lifestyle. Disabled and disadvantaged labels are applied as freely as the more general "at risk" label. The term "at risk" is broadly defined in numerous states, almost as a catch-all method for bringing children into government programs, and often so vague as to include almost all children. For example, "Risk Factor Definitions," published by the Missouri Department of Education, lists the following situations (with explanations for social workers) that they claim put a child "at risk":

1. Illness or handicapping condition at birth
   This category includes conditions present within three days of the birth—prematurity, birth weight under five pounds, emergency delivery, birth trauma, prolonged hospital stay for baby, etc.
2. Signs of failure to thrive
   This can include such signs as low weight gain, slow

growth in length or head circumference, poor appetite, frequent illness.

3. Delay in any area of development detected through observation and screening

    This title should read "Delay in any area of development detected through observation and/or screening." Include information gained through the informal screening the parent educator does on every visit. We are not requiring the formal screening tools to be the sole backup for this category. The parent educator should use her expertise in child development to determine if a child should be watched more closely.

4. Inability of parent to cope with inappropriate child behavior (e.g., severe biting, destructive behavior, apathy)

    This is really a discipline issue, and will become apparent more after the child enters Phase VI. Does the parent seem to have to "punish" the child, rather than "teach" the child. Is spanking the only method used? Is the parent unable to set consistent limits? This issue can go to either extreme.

5. Low functioning parent (due to limited ability or illness)

    Is the parent too ill, too heavy, too tired, or too depressed to get up and regularly deal effectively with the child? Does the parent seem to have low-level intelligence or be mentally retarded? Does the parent appear to abuse alcohol or drugs? Is the parent handicapped? Is the parent injured?

6. Inability of parent to relate to or connect with child

    Does the parent usually ignore the child? Does the parent fail to give the child affection and exhibit a caring attitude? This also includes the parent who is not able to understand baby's cues and/or have an effective parent-child relationship.

7. Overindulgence, undue spoiling on part of parent

Has the child learned to expect immediate gratification? Does the parent give in to temper tantrums? Does the child always get his way? Does the child "rule the roost" (in control of the household)?

8. Low level of verbal response or communication with child

This is the situation where the parent rarely talks to the baby, rarely answers the baby's sounds or words or rarely returns the baby's smiles.

9. Negative or hostile behavior toward child

Does the parent indicate that he does not like his child? Is he often derogatory about the child or does he call him bad names? Does the parent seem to have trouble controlling his own temper? Does he get unreasonably angry about things the child does?

10. Undue stress that adversely affects family functioning

There are numerous stress factors that can affect family functioning. These can include such things as a death in the family, divorce, separation, a parent that travels frequently, moving to a new home, birth of a sibling, three children under the age of three living in the home, prolonged illness in the family, loss of a job, low level of income, over crowded conditions in the home, frequent arguing or conflict in the home, etc.

11. Indication of child abuse

Are there indications on the child's body, in his behavior or in the parent's statements that abuse may be happening?

12. Other (that wonderful catch-all!)[sic]

This can include a wide variety of conditions that can potentially impact a child's development. Consider such things as allergies, heavy cigarette smoking in the house, family history of hearing loss as indicated by the Semel Questionnaire, lack of stimulation or over-stimulation predominately inappropriate or very few toys and total lack of routine in the home. Other individual concerns should be included here.[3]

Under this definition, practically every child could be considered at-risk. Children whose pets have just died, children whose parents don't buy them enough toys according to the social worker's opinion, children in large families, and children whose fathers travel frequently for their jobs are all in danger.

Some schools have been bold enough to classify all students as being "at-risk." The restructuring proposal for La Paz Middle School in Mission Viejo, California, says "all students should be considered 'at-risk' during this time..."[4]

The Gerrymander Bonus

Almost all school personnel are deeply concerned about the needs of children, but we still must recognize that there is an additional incentive for schools to label their children under special "at-risk" categories: money. Minority status, learning disabilities, children suffering from neglect or abuse, delinquents, and other labels all bring in extra funding to address those special needs.

A companion bill to Goals 2000 is the Reauthorization of the Elementary and Secondary Education Act. This $11 billion act aims to expand the number of children receiving government largess for special needs by allowing more school-wide programs. Instead of targeting individual children, schools having 50 percent[5] of their students at or below poverty level receive funding for the entire school. We can well imagine the inter-school shuffling of students that will take place so that schools have just 50 percent "poor" students.[6]

Consider a hypothetical school district with an enrollment of 10,000 students, with those students conveniently divided into 1,000 in each of ten schools. The district as a whole has 40 percent of its students at or below the poverty level. Unfortunately for the district, those "poor" students are evenly distributed so that each school also has 40 percent of its student body meeting the poverty guideline. Since none of them reach the 50 percent mark, none of the schools qualify for the $200 (hypothetical but realistic figure) per student bonus from the federal government. (See Chart 1.) The shuffle begins. The district decides to concentrate "wealthy" students in two schools. So they take 100 "wealthy" students from each of the other schools and place 400 each in the two designated schools. Then they take the 400 "poor" students from each of the "wealthy" schools and assign 100 each to the remaining eight schools. Now they have eight schools meeting the 50 percent guideline, and the district qualifies for $1,600,000! (See Chart 2.)

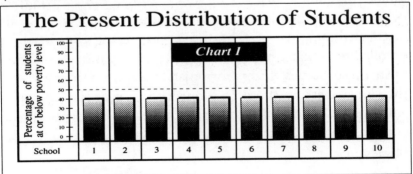

The Present Distribution of Students

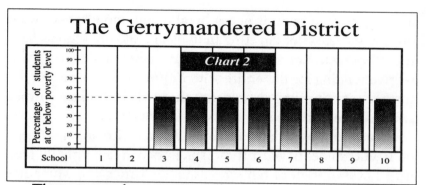

The Gerrymandered District

Chart 2

Percentage of students at or below poverty level

School | 1 | 2 | 3 | 4 | 5 | 6 | 7 | 8 | 9 | 10

There is another reason to be wary of "at-risk" labeling. Too often, well-intentioned educators and social workers, in their quests to take care of at-risk children, trample on parental and family rights. When they try to control or solve "risk-causing" parenting and family-life problems, they invade the privacy and autonomy of families. Parents As Teachers, Family and Children First, and similar programs are good examples as we will see shortly.

Preschool Services

Imagine the level of panic the architects of these programs experience when they suspect a child exists outside of their microscopes and charts. Who knows what might be happening to those young children who do not attend preschool but are under the care of parents or relatives all the time? If they never go to preschool, the government might have to wait until children are of school age (assuming they will be enrolled in public schools) before they can monitor the activity in those homes. Interventionists are not content to wait that long. Getting those children into preschools, especially government-funded preschools, provides a window to check out those home situations, watch for abuse, and look for at-risk factors.

The push to expand preschool programs to include all, even those not needing "readiness" training, was in place long before Goals 2000. In 1970, the White House Conference on Children claimed, "Society has the ultimate responsibility for the well-being and optimum development of all children." Day care was viewed by the conferees as a tool for teaching young children "values, fears, beliefs, and behaviors." They recommended "that the federal government establish a network of 'comprehensive developmental child-care centers' to accommodate 5.6 million children by 1980, and to fund and train an additional 500,000 child-care workers."[7]

The percentage of three-to five-year-olds enrolled in preschool nearly doubled between 1973 and 1992. Even more telling is the money that the federal government has poured into the expansion of preschool programs: it has nearly doubled in the past four years (1989-1993) growing from $10.3 billion to $21 billion. But all of that "preschool money" does not go to what most of us think of as educational preschool programs like Head Start. Educational need is used as the excuse to get the legislature to authorize funding, which is then used for a whole range of other services to families with preschoolers.[8]

In January, 1993, the Advisory Committee on Head Start Quality and Expansion, reporting on Head Start programs, made a number of recommendations. Among those recommendations was the expansion of services to the zero-to three-year-old group. Donna Shalala, Secretary of Health and Human Services, said that "serving younger children ties in with the Administration's goal of creating a 'seamless' system of interventions from prenatal care through the early grades."[9]

How far away can we be from Aldous Huxley's *Brave New World* where all prenatal development occurred in test tubes, and babies were conditioned in "Neo-Pavlovian Conditioning Rooms" with the correct attitudes and behaviors?

Many states already have preschool programs in place, but Goals 2000 wants more. How can the federal government seduce states into expanding their preschool services? Funding under the Reauthorization of the Elementary and Secondary Education Act will be the carrot that enlists their cooperation. In summarizing their proposal, the Department of Education says, "...requiring coordination of educational services [those funded by ESEA] with Head Start and other preschool services, coupled with new emphasis on ensuring intensive and sustained high-quality professional development, expanding the schoolwide program approach, increasing parent involvement, encouraging coordination with health and social services, and requiring health screenings for students in high-poverty elementary schools will support continuity and increased attention to transition as children move from preschool to school."[10]

Thus, the funding will be conditional upon expanded preschool programs, teacher training (the type that trains teachers to go along with the agenda), parent involvement (usually through programs such as Parents as Teachers), and the extremely important tie to health and social services, so that social workers can decide if children are receiving proper parenting.[11] Often, the funding available to a school district is dispensed only when every school in that district complies. Even if a school should desire to be more responsible to its community, the likelihood of such a stand-off against intervention lasting very long is negligible. In addition, "schools that effectively link education and other one-stop shopping services for low-income children could be tangibly rewarded with more money, more flexibility, or waivers from troublesome regulations."[12]

One-Stop Shopping for Services

Mrs. Miller walks her third-grade daughter to school some mornings. She's not worried about her daughter's safety. Mrs. Miller just happens to be going the same direction. When her daughter heads for the classroom, mom heads for the Office of Coordinated Services over behind the school cafeteria. She needs to see about a problem with their welfare checks, and the social worker can help with that. Next week, she will be bringing her three-year-old son for his check up with the health nurse. Wednesday evenings Mrs. Miller, her husband, and their sixteen-year-old son meet with the family counselor who helps them work through some of the problems that prompted the boy to run away from home last month.

In the not-too-distant future, the Millers and millions of other families will frequently visit their local schools. Expanding preschool services is only the tip of the iceberg. Preschool services are often tied together as a package deal with coordinated one-stop-shopping health services, social services, parent education, welfare assistance, education, family counseling, and outcomes assessments.

The Reauthorization of the ESEA encourages these package deals. So does the Comprehensive Services For Children and Youth Act of 1991, which directs the Secretary of Education to encourage schools to set up "one-stop shopping centers" by awarding federal grant money to those that comply.[13]

To become a recipient of one of these grants, your local school district must offer their student population and their families on-site access to "public health, child welfare, social services, job training, public housing agencies or other public agencies providing services to such at-risk youth and their families."[14]

Many people view the one-stop shopping for government services as a progressive move that promotes efficiency. They denounce critics as being selfish and uncaring and point out that linking "service" agencies can more effectively deliver those services to "customers." An *Education Week* "Commentary" (March 3, 1993) explains that, "Schools are often the only stable institution that reaches almost all children. Even when school-linked services are cumbersome, they are often the best, and sometimes the only, option." Additionally, schools are usually located reasonably close to home, so parents who can get their children's vaccinations and deal with the welfare office at the school site save bus fare and the inconvenience of traipsing downtown to various agency offices.

Remember that the point of one-stop shopping is supposedly to improve government delivery of services for family well-being. The theory is that once social needs are provided for, academic performance should improve. The New York State Community Schools Program has been the testing ground for the theory. Following the well-trodden path of other government solutions, this one, too, has failed to deliver the promised benefit thus far. A study of the New York State Community Schools Program by the Bruner Foundation found "no evidence of improved academic outcomes." This project was "notable for its explicit inclusion of academics," unlike many other such projects. Yet the only significant success they could point to was that the schools now offer recreational programs for students.[15]

Meanwhile, other states are going ahead with one-stop shopping. Missouri announced plans to "set up centers for learning and neighborhood services at four pilot school sites..." Although the centers will be based at city schools, they will be open to neighborhood residents and will offer health, counseling, and referral services. Rhode Island plans to spend "more than $435,000 to launch family centers providing an array of health and social services in 20 of the state's 36 school districts."[16]

It is bad enough that such programs never seem to fulfill their stated purposes, but too often criticisms get bogged down in arguments about design and implementation rather than challenging the purposes themselves. If the true goal is convenience and efficiency in delivering government services, it should be possible to improve the situation by consolidation. But the real issue is the proper role of government. Should the government even be involved in providing all of these services? And, what does it mean to families when it does?

Developmental Delays, Excuse for Family Intervention

Mounting evidence shows government sitting in the driver's seat, invading family privacy to obtain the information they want, then directing parents how to raise their children. The push begins as early as possible.

Two years in a row, almost identical bills have been introduced in California pushing for family screening at the time each child is born. The latest bill, AB 3345 [Sec. 1 (b)], says, "Years of experience, in California and elsewhere, have taught that the most effective strategies to combat child abuse are those that are family focused and begin very early in a child's life, preferably when a child is a newborn."

Screening involves looking for risk factors, including those listed at length earlier, as well as potential developmental delays. "The five major developmental delays are cognitive development, physical development, language and speech

development, psychosocial development, and self-help skills."
States are left to define what each of these terms means.[17]

Tests are commonly used to show development delays, but
sometimes social workers label children "developmentally-
delayed" based on the mere possibility that such a delay might
occur. Thus, any child with a less than ideal background, a
late bloomer, or even a small child whose size reflects his
genetic inheritance of his parents' small frames can be labeled
at-risk. Considering how few children actually meet the "statistical norm," almost all children could be categorized under
one of these five criteria at one point or another in their lives.

The range of what is considered normal for children is
growing smaller and smaller. It begins to sound all too much
like the story from Greek mythology about innkeeper
Procrustes who desired that all his clientele fit into his beds
properly. The overly tall, he cut down to standard-bed length,
and those with height deficiency he stretched on the rack.

And What Do You Do in Your Home?

The idea of ensuring that all children are ready to learn is
being stretched to the extremes in other ways. In a report from
the Goal 1 Panel, discussing how to assess readiness, they say
that "the number of low birthweight babies [a factor that puts a
child in the "at-risk" category] will be significantly reduced
through enhanced prenatal health systems." To check on nutrition, the government will need mothers to "report on their children's diets." In addition they will use the National Health and
Nutrition Examination Survey which "involves an actual health
examination of those in the sample." They want access to vital
information on parents, particularly mothers, so they say, "we
recommend that vital statistics...be used to locate information
regarding the age and educational status of the mother."

The National Household Education Survey is recommended to "provide information regarding attitudes and activities in the home. Developed by the Department of Education, this survey asks parents about such activities as reading, television viewing, museum visiting, games or sports, and arts and crafts activities. It also asks about child care and preschool programs... We recommend that this important survey be expanded to include other parenting questions."[18]

Home visits are an important means of determining what goes on within families, so they say, "We recommend that the National Household Education Survey be supplemented periodically through a national subsample for home visits... This screening procedure, used by home observers...is useful for studying the developmental environments of 3 to 6-year-olds."[19]

Home observers use checklists that record very personal family interaction. The following are examples of questions that appear on some of the surveys or checklists:

> Mother neither slaps nor spanks child during visit
> At least ten books are present and visible
> Father provides some caretaking every day
> Parent does not offer food when the child looks away, looks
>   down, turns away or turns around
> Parent does not compress lips, grimace, or frown when mak-
>   ing eye contact with child
> Parent does not make negative or uncomplimentary remarks
>   to the child or home visitor about the child or child's
>   behavior[20]

All of this exhibits a massive mistrust of parents. Government would have absolutely no need to know what goes on within our families unless they intended to do something about it. Because they have assumed the right and the authority to fix our families, they see nothing wrong with these invasive practices. The first goal provided a broad justification for intervention. In a later chapter, it will be seen how the eighth goal reinforces the government's role as a partner in parenting.

End Notes

[1] National Education Goals Panel, *Measuring Progress Toward the National Education Goals: Potential Indicators and Measurement Strategies, Compendium of Interim Resource Group Reports*, Goal 1, p. 6.

[2] *The National Education Goals Report, Vol. 1*, Washington D.C.: US Government Printing Office, 1993, p. xiii-6.

[3] "Risk Factor Definitions," Missouri Department of Elementary and Secondary Education, PAT National Center, revised edition, 1990.

[4] James Fenwick, *The Middle School Years*, quoted in "La Paz Context and Future Needs" paper.

[5] An early version of the legislation used the 50 percent figure. The Senate passed S 1513 requiring only 30 percent, while the House passed HR 6 requiring 60 percent. A conference committee is working on the compromise version as we go to print. The final figure might well be 50 percent but the figure is not set at this time.

[6] *Improving America's Schools Act of 1993: Reauthorization of the Elementary and Secondary Education Act*, U.S. Department of Education, Sept. 13, 1993, Title I, p. 9.

[7] "Report to the President, White House Conference on Children," Washington, D.C.: U.S. Government Printing Office, 1970; and Allan C. Carlson, *Family Questions*, Transaction Books, New Brunswick, 1990, p. 9.

8 We generally think of Head Start programs when we think of government-funded preschool. However, Head Start, in 1992, received only $2,779,000,000 or 13 percent of the funding. Among other major funding recipients are Medicaid for Children, Family Support Payments for Child Care, Payments to States for day care, and Childhood Immunization under the Department of Health and Human Services. Medicaid for Children alone received $7,476,000,000 – far more than Head Start. [*The National Education Goals Report 1993*, *Vol. 1*, Washington, D.C.: U.S. Government Printing Office, pp. 28,188.]

9 Deborah L. Cohen, "Coordination Between Head Start, Schools Urged," *Education Week*, Jan. 19, 1994, p. 16.

10 Improving America's Schools Act of 1993: Reauthorization of the Elementary and Secondary Education Act," U.S. Department of Education, Sept. 13, 1993, Title I, pp. 11-12.

11 Ibid.

12 Margaret Dunkle and Michael D. Usdan, "Putting People First Means Connecting Education to Other Services," *Education Week*, Mar. 3, 1993.

13 The Comprehensive Services For Children and Youth Act of 1991 (S.1133), "[a]mends the Augustus F. Hawkins Human Resources Reauthorization Act of 1990 to direct the Federal Council on Children, Youth, and Services to make recommendations to facilitate coordination of educational and social services." It also directs the Secretary of Education to award federal grants to LEA's (Local Education Agencies: school districts, community-based service centers) to encourage the transformation of their sites into "one-stop shopping agencies."

14 Comprehensive Services For Children and Youth Act of 1991, Section 5(a)(1).

15 Ann Bradley, "Mixed Bag Found at N.Y.C. Schools Striving To Link Services," *Education Week*, Mar. 9, 1994, p.7.

[16] Deborah L. Cohen, "N.G.A. Documents Integrated Services for Children," *Education Week*, April 6, 1994, p. 12.

[17] Ann Herzer, "School Restructuring" (Tape 1), Indianapolis, IN, [video] Nov. 18, 1993.

[18] National Education Goals Panel, *Measuring Progress Toward the National Education Goals: Potential Indicators and Measurement Strategies, Compendium of Interim Resource Group Reports*, p.7-8.

[19] Ibid.

[20] Ann Frazier, "Part III: Parents as Teachers," article published in *America 2000/Goals 2000-Moving the Nation Educationally to a "New World Order,"* James R. Patrick, ed., Citizens for Academic Excellence, Moline, IL, 1994, p. 549.

Chapter Two

Need Some-Force All

Typically, bad laws are written and personal freedoms are violated in attempts to fix problems affecting "some people." When bureaucrats say that "children will receive the nutrition and health care needed to arrive at school with healthy minds and bodies; and the number of low-birthweight babies will be significantly reduced through enhanced prenatal health systems," they are using the excuse that since some children do not receive proper care prenatally or during early childhood, the government must oversee all children. This principle is called "Need Some-Force All" (NS-FA). It is applied to numerous government programs with wording to the effect, "Since some people need _____, we will require all people to _____." The NS-FA assumption in this case is that some irresponsible families need help to do what is right for their children, so we will require all families to raise their children according to our guidelines.[1]

Healthy Tomorrows

Across the country, a number of programs that allow the government to take over parental rights and parental responsibility are in proposal stages or are already operating.

Healthy Tomorrows is an elementary school-based health services program in Santa Ana, California. Healthy Tomorrows is about more than medical health, as you can imagine. It's a comprehensive health care approach that purports to treat the "whole child" (i.e., physical, behavioral, emotional, psychological, and educational). Like many other such programs, it was introduced in a poor district where most families speak English as a second language. It makes one wonder if these districts are not chosen on purpose because most of the parents are reluctant or fearful to complain—if they even understand what is happening. Quite often, many parents are illegal immigrants, afraid of deportation if they rock the boat. For poor children and their families, Healthy Tomorrows is an invasive program that allows social workers and other government agents a direct line into their homes through their children.

A mobile medical van, carrying a bilingual pediatrician, a registered nurse, and a secretary/driver/health insurance counselor, travels among a group of schools. Among the tasks performed by the van staff are referrals to outside agencies, providing one-on-one parent/student health education, assistance to parents applying for Medi-Cal, and procurement of consent for the release of confidential information from outside referrals to Healthy Tomorrows and the school. The referrals mentioned are to government programs/agencies for funding and further oversight of children and families. Child Protective Services and the Department of Social Services are the primary recipients of those referrals. This is facilitated by the fact that Healthy Tomorrows is run by a School Site Interagency Services Team (stationed on school property) that consists of five Family Services Social Workers, a Home-Based Intervention Specialist, parent education staff, graduate student social worker interns, Social Services Agency clerical staff, a Medi-Cal technician and "outstationed staff" (i.e., staff from other agencies such as Drug and Alcohol Abuse, Orange County Probation, and Community Service Programs).

The folks on the Interagency Team are all non-school personnel. They are from outside agencies governed by regulations other than those regulating the schools, hence, they are not answerable to principals, school personnel, school site committees, or school boards. Only their agencies can control their actions. Although "health" is the excuse for this massive invasion of the schools, the medical role of this program appears to be of secondary importance to expanding the State's control over children and families.[2]

The Ohio Plan

Ohio's Family and Children First program is another method of implementing the National Goals plan. "Ohio is one of many states participating in an effort to merge, under one authority, all child and family service systems including education. This has resulted in the teaming-up of the Ohio Department of Education and the Department of Human Services."[3]

In August of 1992, Governor Voinovich created the *Ohio Family & Children First* Cabinet Council which oversees the superintendent of public instruction, the head of the department of health, the head of the department of human services, and other state agencies that provide services for families and children.[4]

Researcher Diana Fessler tells us:

> *Family and Children First* (FCF) requires all state
> agencies and departments serving children to adopt
> certain policies. One policy is designed to "protect the
> integrity of the family." On the surface this is a posi-
> tive statement, but the FCF *Briefing Book* defines a
> family as "a group of people, related by blood or cir-
> cumstances, who may rely upon one another for suste-
> nance, support, security, socialization and/or stimula-
> tion."

Some would attempt to defend this definition of
family by saying that it is intended for those individuals who, because of mental retardation or developmental delay, live in a "group home," or that it is for individuals with no living relatives. Nonetheless, this definition establishes government-approved non-family
"families." Such a definition would include: three people in an elevator, two people sharing a bag of chips,
cell-mates, school-mates, room-mates and just "mates,"
all of which are a far cry from people related by blood,
heterosexual marriage, birth, or adoption, a definition
that includes single-parent families as well as grandparents functioning as parents since, in both cases,
there is a blood relationship.

Based on the *Initiative's* definition of family, it is the
mission of the Ohio Family & Children First Cabinet
Council to develop a state family policy in order to
meet Goal #1 of *America 2000*: All children will start
school ready to learn. According to the *Briefing Book*,
the focus will be "to create partnerships between families and their communities...draw(ing) upon the moral

authority of each Ohio community." We are to understand that "building a better service delivery system
begins with setting goals for Ohio's families and children." To implement *FCF*, six goals have been set,
three of which are the initial targets.

Families and children will have the nutrition and
health care needed to have healthy minds and bodies.

Families will understand and address the developmental needs of their children.

Family members will be literate and possess the
knowledge and skills necessary to be productive and
responsible citizens.

Families will have the opportunity to earn adequate
incomes to meet basic needs.

Families and communities will be free of violence
and crime.

Families and communities will be free of the abuses
of alcohol or other drugs.[5]

Notice the firmness and assurance with which these goals
are stated. It is intended that no one will fail to comply or be
permitted to disagree. But has anyone taken the time to consider whether such goals are even achievable? Or do they represent a utopian vision that requires man, society and the
earth to all reach impossible levels of perfection?

Initial Targets

Because of limited resources, *FCF* will focus only on the
first three goals listed above and establish "measurable outcome indicators" to ensure that goals are met. Those indicators, according to the *Briefing Book*, "mirror those chosen by
Ohio's education community." For example, early education

program services (such as Head Start) are to be provided for all three, four, and five-year-old children deemed economically disadvantaged.[6]

Any child whose family earns below 185 percent of the poverty level is economically disadvantaged. Incredibly this means that families whose income is almost double the national poverty level are considered "disadvantaged." Fessler tells us, "A two-parent family with three children living on an income not greater than $31,099 is an example of such 'eligibility.'" Obviously we are not talking only of reaching the poor, but of extending state aid to what many consider the middle class. "The assumption that so-called 'economically disadvantaged' families are unable to provide an education for their children is demeaning, patronizing, dangerous, and in no way 'protects the integrity of the family.' Many families fall into this category because they choose to live on a single income because their commitment to care for their children supersedes their desire to attain material wealth."[7]

Families who choose a simpler or less materialistic life style will be penalized by having their children placed in a government-approved preschool program, an outcome that supposes to "protect the integrity of the family." Other means to achieve this goal of family integrity are increasing the number of children enrolled in subsidized day care and increasing the percentage of "eligible" women and infants on WIC (Women, Infants, and Children) to 100 percent.[8]

Screening and Assessment

As discussed in chapter 1, screening for "at-risk" characteristics is used to initiate families into these programs. According to the *Ohio Family & Children First Briefing Book*, programs and service systems "at the core should...seek to intervene early, and be preventive." Thus, a statewide screening/assessment tool is being developed. The "initial target group for screening, assessment and 'service' is children 0-8, pregnant women, and their families," thereby empowering the state to intervene in the rearing of children even before birth.[9]

It is yet to be determined what will happen to parents who choose not to submit to the screening/assessment process. What will be the consequences for families who refuse to accept services which the government has determined they need is another guess. It might not be long before we find out who really gets to call the shots in our families.

New Districts

Ohio is also on top of things by reorganizing its districts along the one-stop shopping lines decreed by the federal government. They plan a major reorganization of service delivery regions. Counties and school districts will become "education and human service delivery districts," and schools will become "delivery sites."

> These new entities would assume responsibilities that now rest with school districts, counties, cities, library boards, mental health districts, MR/DD districts, and other local jurisdictions now administering human services. All publicly funded human services programs that concentrate on families and children, including educational programs now provided by schools, are to be governed by and funded through the governing boards of the delivery districts. Such governing boards would develop family and children's delivery district goals and policy consistent with state law and federal guidelines for human services, including education.

Researcher Diana Fessler summarizes: "*FCF* advances the idea that the state is the ultimate guardian of children, and parents are little more than state-approved guardians of their own children."[10]

Goals 2000 Across America

The orchestration of the goals and their implementation from the federal level down through state and local levels has been well developed as we can see through the examples of California and Ohio. In 1992, the government published *America 2000 Community Notebook*, which spells out exactly what they want to bring about on the local level. A host of "community projects" already in place will provide the foundation for the implementation of Goal 1. The following are those projects and their states of origination and operation:

- Abbeville-Greenwood Library Project, Greenwood, South Carolina—a literacy program that links families with social service agencies.
- Infants and Toddlers Program, Anne Arundel County, Maryland—multi-agency service delivery.
- Early Childhood Family Education, Moorhead, Minnesota—parent education, home visitation.
- Family Connection Project, Decatur, Georgia—families are connected with programs such as Parents as Teachers, public school child development centers, Head Start, and Project Rebound.
- HIPPY/Miami, Dade County, Florida—parent education, home visitation, referrals to social services and health agencies.
- Parents as Teachers (PAT), Ferguson-Florissant School

District, Missouri—program to meet state-mandated parent education and family support services, including home visitation, screening, referrals to other government agencies. [Note: Even *America 2000 Community Notebook* mentions on page 29 that, "critics of PAT complain that the program may undermine parental confidence in raising children and facilitate government intrusion into family life."]

- Poudre County Even Start, Fort Collins, Colorado—parent education, home visitation, referrals to social services and health agencies.
- Success By Six, Charlotte, North Carolina—community service integration, referrals to agencies, parent education, day care.
- Syracuse Pre-kindergarten Program, Syracuse, New York—parent education, social worker involvement.[11]

Parents as Teachers Programs

States are not waiting for federal legislation to implement programs which accomplish the objectives of the National Goals. The Parents As Teachers (PAT) program laid the groundwork, and in the process it has gained a great deal of notoriety.

One of the most insidious invasions of the family ever launched in the United States, PAT began as an experimental program in Missouri in 1981. In 1985, only four years later, PAT researcher, Laura Rogers tells us the Missouri legislature "mandated that the PAT program be offered to all schools and children in Missouri." PAT has since spread to at least forty other states and eight foreign countries. In 1987, "the Education Commission of the States announced eight spin-off programs with different names and similar goals."

Rogers tells us that,

> ...the program pivots on assigning to all parents and children a "certified parent educator." This state employee evaluates the child (under the guise of educational screening), assigns the child a computer code classification and initiates a computer file that the state will use to track the child for the rest of his or her life. All of the computer code designations label the child to some degree "at-risk," and there is no classification for "normal."[12] The state agent conducts periodic home and school visits to check on the child and the family, dispersing gratis such things as nutritional counseling, mental-health services, and even food. Schools under the PAT program provide free day-and-overnight care. The "certified parent" might forbid the biological parents to spank their child and might prescribe, if the child is deemed "unhappy," psychological counseling or a drug such as Ritalin. If the parents refuse the recommended services or drugs, the state may remove the child from the home, place him in a residential treatment center, and force the parents to enroll in family counseling for an indefinite period.[13]

The PAT program also bills itself as a child abuse prevention program, and the parent educators serve as child abuse investigators. Laura Rogers visited seventeen Department of Family Services offices around Missouri, attempting to pin down what these investigators considered "abuse." "One man listed as a risk factor families who are part of a subculture, but he couldn't define a subculture... 'Having a dirty house or diaper rash is neglect,' chimed another. And one investigator openly admitted, 'We don't have checklists (to determine risk or abuse) or anything like that.'"[14]

One family found out the hard way how arbitrary PAT parent educators can be. George and Gabrielle Copp relate their experience with a parent educator: "She'd come in and she'd tell us, 'You have to do this and you should be doing this.'" George describes his reaction to the domineering attitude assumed by this expert: "Who died and put you in charge?...I don't like the way you're telling me how to raise my children." The parent educator also objected to the Copps spanking their children. Gabrielle recounts, "She was undermining our authority as parents." The Copps were not beating or abusing their children but were following what they believe to be biblical guidelines. The Copps quickly dropped out of the PAT program.[15]

Unsubstantiated Child Abuse and Social Services

Perhaps all of these coordinated services sound like good solutions to some readers. At least someone is coming up with solutions. Many think, "Who better to go to than those who are experienced in aiding others, like social services?" Many struggling families find the going tough, and all the assistance one could hope for at one's fingertips is hard to turn down, at least at first. The objections to one-stop shopping do not arise on the grounds that families should not get outside help. Instead, the concern seems to focus on the track record of social services agencies. The term "social services" itself is a catch-all, hiding the growing agenda of government agencies to take over the responsibilities and rights of parents. Most of us have no idea how extensive the tentacles of social services have grown. The Comprehensive Services for Children and Youth Act of 1991 says:

The term 'social services' means case management, child nutrition, preventive and primary health and mental health services, developmental screening and referrals, individual, group and family counseling, substance abuse prevention and treatment, infant and toddler health and child care for children of school age parents, before and after school child care, child welfare services, recreation, juvenile delinquency prevention and court intervention, job counseling, training, and placement, and alternative independent living arrangements for at-risk youth from dysfunctional families, crisis intervention, gang and community violence counseling, and information and referral.

Very few families can go through life without being touched, or at least knowing someone who has been touched, by one or more circumstances that could be addressed by one of these services. It is absolutely pervasive.

Too often, social services agents operate like those of the IRS, showing little regard for constitutional rights, privacy, and parental prerogatives. Child abuse accusations are an important piece of the puzzle because they are often used as justification for social service intrusion into families and, many times, a vehicle to achieve family separation.

Christopher J. Klicka, attorney with the Home School Legal Defense Association, recounts a conversation with a social worker in Chicago who told him that "well over 50 percent of all referrals to her child welfare agency are 'unfounded.' Unfortunately, she complained, many of the cases are deemed unfounded after families are broken apart and children are put in foster homes... In the old days, social workers tried to prove a reported family was innocent and considered the family innocent until proven guilty. Now the 'system' operates on the principle that a family is 'guilty'...period."

Klicka also tells of two former social workers who both "admitted intimidation was a routine procedure they were taught and always used to get their way... Both of these social workers admitted 60 percent to 70 percent of their cases were 'unfounded.'"[16]

California's Little Hoover Commission chairman, Nathan Shapell, said that "...anywhere from 35 percent to 70 percent of foster children were taken from their parents unnecessarily, suffering more psychological damage than if they stayed home."[17]

The cases of abuse among the practices of social service agencies are alarming, increasing in number, and heart-rending even to the casual observer. All too common are stories such as Jaime and Paul Lonthair's. Jaime's three-year-old son C.J. was taken to the hospital emergency room with inexplicably swollen and tender feet. Since the parents were unable to provide a satisfactory explanation, a doctor decided that the case should be referred to Child Protective Services. (In most states, doctors, teachers, child care workers, volunteers, and others are legally required to report any cases where there is the possibility of abuse.) Child Protective Services then decided that C.J.'s problem might be the result of parental abuse. C.J. along with his brother and sisters, including ten-month-old Katie, who was still nursing, were taken from their parents by social workers and placed in the county home for children.

In one way, the Lonthairs might be considered fortunate. While C.J. was at the county home, his elbows, wrists, and back swelled up and turned yellow, forcing the caretakers to again rush him to emergency. This time a doctor figured out that the culprit was an infection rather than parental abuse.

The children were allowed to return home. One can only wonder what would have been the outcome if C.J. had not taken a turn for the worse.

Gene Howard, head of Children's Protective Services in Orange County, California, where this incident occurred, admitted that the Lonthairs and other parents might be traumatized by such experiences. Yet he claims that in this situation, the system worked just as it should. "We have a system that errs on the side of protecting the child and that's going to bring some family trauma," Howard was quoted as saying. His agency takes custody of 150 children every month.[18]

In Florida, a meddlesome grandmother wanted custody of her grandson. She made a false accusation against her son and was awarded custody. After six years, she returned the child to his parents because she could no longer handle him. When the wife attempted to clear her husband's name, grandma threatened to make another phone call and have all of the children taken away. Two months later, that is exactly what happened. The children were removed from school, and the parents were not even notified. Friends, teachers, and the family doctor all defended the parents to the HRS (Health and Rehabilitation Services), but to no avail. The fact that the father's name was listed on the Child Abuse Registry (from the false accusation years ago) allowed HRS to label these children "at-risk." The family lost their home, their possessions, and a small business, and in addition, had to pay for court-ordered counseling for themselves. They illegally took their children back and left the state. Tracked down eight months later, the parents were jailed, and the children were put into two different homes.

Another parent described their family's experience with HRS and the foster care system:

"My twins were born with a urinary tract infection. Since they were infants, HRS was called in. HRS brought in their own doctors and changed the medical doctor's diagnosis from urinary tract infection to 'failure to thrive.' Since then HRS has tried six times to charge us with child abuse. All six times HRS had to give our children back. When our children came home from the shelter, they had many bruises, black eyes, and once they needed to be hospitalized. I have papers from a police report and hospital records to prove what I say. (The last time) HRS took our twins, within seven days one was in the hospital with bruised legs, arms, and toes. At court HRS said when it happens at home it is abuse. In HRS shelter it is an accident."[19]

A child's aunt says, "My niece fell off her swing set, and HRS was called. They said my brother was the one who hurt her arm. She was taken away and put in a foster home where she was mistreated. I don't think she will ever recover. She wakes up at night and screams and cries. HRS did this to her."[20]

In Bothell, Washington, Bill and Kathy Swan were charged with sexually abusing their three-year-old daughter. She was taken into custody by the Washington Department of Social and Health Services (DSHS), and her parents were taken to jail. The State's case was based on the hearsay evidence of the day care teacher, a woman with a history of either horrible sexual abuse or a tremendous disregard for truth. This teacher admitted that she hated men, and she told of at least twenty other occasions when she had attempted to turn in sex offenders to authorities. An inconclusive physical examination of the child by a nurse practitioner (who claimed no expertise in recognizing sexual abuse) was offered as corroborating evidence. In spite of the lack of evidence and community support for the innocence of the parents, they were convicted, and their daughter was put into foster care.

The Swans were offered the opportunity to plea bargain. "Plead guilty and you will serve only nine months in prison, and we might let you see your daughter again." They chose to stand on principle, so they went to prison. After a few years, they were finally released from prison; but, at this time, they still do not have their daughter back. They are registered as sex offenders. In 1991, a great aunt was able to get a physical examination of the Swans' daughter (in spite of DSHS disapproval), and the doctor stated that she showed no evidence of the abuse for which her parents were convicted. With this new evidence in hand, they tackled the court system again and are still fighting to prove their innocence and reclaim their daughter.[21]

Tales of false accusations of child abuse and parental neglect abound. In fact, there are so many cases founded on lies and assumed guilt that, if the Lonthair incident in California is used as an example and there truly are 150 children taken into custody per month, it is not irresponsible to question whether the greater number of those are based on false accusations. The problem has become so widespread that at least two books, *The Child Abuse Industry* and *Out of Control: Who's Watching Over the Child Protection Agencies?*[22] have been written to alert parents and others concerned about a child welfare system that has run amuck.

Interestingly, the agenda of those overzealous social service agencies might have been revealed at the first Governor's Conference on Children and Youth. A "keynote speaker told the conferees how wonderful things were in China, where children go to school all week long and only go home on weekends." Conferees were also advised that, "[T]he way unwilling parents would be forced to participate in the state's child/family management system was through referral of a professional or a charge of child abuse or neglect."[23]

State Family Policy

The massive, growing organism of social services programs and bureaucratic policies has aroused public outcries over governmental intrusion into the family. But now, through federal legislation, the government wishes to expand one of these, Parents As Teachers (PAT), to cover "all parents of children from birth through age 5..." PAT programs, under this legislation, must provide each participating family with regularly scheduled personal home visits...by certified "parent educators" and "regularly scheduled developmental screenings..."[24] Parents As Teachers programs are such an integral part of Goals 2000 that the legislation authorizing federal funding for PAT programs in all states was integrated into the final Goals 2000 bill itself.

Should We Have a "State Family Policy"?

We can legitimately attack these programs based solely on concerns about social services, but the more important issue is the very idea of a state family policy. As a society we are desperate for solutions to education, child care, health, and other social problems. In our search, we have recognized how difficult it is for families and individuals to always solve their own problems. We do not trust the truly local community of friends, family, church, and neighborhood to help meet their needs, and truthfully, some of us have tired of all the demands our community makes on us. To satisfy our need to consider ourselves compassionate, we have transferred what formerly were considered to be individual or local problems to the larger community of the state and federal government, labeling the problems as our collective responsibility.

While compassion was and remains a major motivation for society shouldering the problems of families and individuals, we must admit that "maintaining the common good" is another motivation. Whether we are fearful of the acts of desperate people, desire a more uniform level of safety, or are concerned about our property values, there is an undeniable element of self-interest to these programs.

Unfortunately, any collective attempt to fix such problems means that the collective entity must impose its beliefs, values, and methods upon the individuals and families designated for assistance. Those who resist assistance are perceived as harming the common good. With this mindset, it is easy for state agencies to slip into intimidation and coercion to enforce their will, which is, of course, for the common good.

Author Don Feder asks, "Where might all of this lead?" His answer: "In a 1988 issue of *Family Law Quarterly*, Claudia Pap Mangel proposes licensing parents as the most efficient way to check violence against children. Prospective parents would need state certification before they're allowed to procreate. Winston Smith, your sizable sibling is calling."[25]

End Notes:

---

[1] Marshall Fritz, "Why OBE and the Traditionalists are Both Wrong," *Educational Leadership*, March 1994, p. 81.

[2] *Orange County Chapter of the American Academy of Pediatrics and The Santa Ana Unified School District Healthy Tomorrows Partnership for Children Proposal*, PHS-5161-1, Submitted June 19, 1992, Santa Ana, CA.

[3] Diana M. Fessler, "Family and Children First," Legislative Update, May/June 1993, Huber Heights, OH, pp.1-4

[4] Ibid.

[5] Ibid.

[6] Ibid.

[7] Ibid.

[8] Ibid.

[9] *Ohio Family & Children First Briefing Book*, Governor's Office, Columbus, OH, 1992, p.8.

[10] Diana M. Fessler, "Family and Children First," Legislative Update, May/June 1993, Huber Heights, OH, pp.1-4.

[11] *America 2000 Community Notebook*, U.S. Government Printing Office, Washington, D.C., 1992, pp17-34.

[12] There are twelve possible codes for "at risk" categories to "define" each child. If the child does not fit into the first eleven, he fits in number 12 which says, "Other."

[13] Laura Rogers, "In Loco Parentis I and II," St. Charles, MO, 1993.

[14] Ibid.

[15] The 700 Club, video of television broadcast on Dec. 2, 1993, Christian Broadcasting Network, Virginia Beach, VA.

[16] Christopher J. Klicka, *The Right Choice: The Incredible Failure of Public Education and the Rising Hope of Home Schooling*, Noble Publishing Associates, Gresham, OR, 1992, pp. 267-270.

[17] "California Foster Care in Trouble," *The Sacramento Union*, Sacramento, CA, Apr. 10, 1992.

[18] Bonnie Weston, "Mother Shaken By Abuse Suspicion," *Orange County Register*, April 1, 1994.

[19] *Family Rights* newsletter, Family Rights Committee, Inc., Orlando, FL, Nov. 1993.

[20] Ibid.

[21] Trevor Armbruster, "When Parents Become Victims," *Reader's Digest*, April, 1993; and information from the Swan Defense Fund, Seattle, WA.

[22] Mary Pride, *The Child Abuse Industry*, Crossway Books, Westchester, IL, 1990, and Brenda Scott, *Out of Control: Who's Watching Over the Child Protection Agencies?* Huntington House, Lafayette, LA, 1994.

[23] Laura Rogers, "In Loco Parentis I and II," St. Charles, MO, 1993.

[24] H.R. 1804, Title IV, Sec. 405, (2)(C)(i) and (ii).

[25] Don Feder, *A Jewish Conservative Looks at Pagan America*, Huntington House Publishers, Lafayette, LA, 1993, p.31.

GOALS 2000-HOW LARGE IS YOUR VILLAGE?

Remember our aphorism, "It takes a whole village to raise a child"? Let's revisit our village which is already claiming partnership with parents in raising children through all of the "getting children ready to learn" programs. As a result of these programs, this issue of who has responsibility and authority over children has become quite muddled. During the school years, when the issue becomes even more crucial, a muddle can turn into a disaster.

Since public schooling has been around for so long, most people accept "the public's" interest in providing education for everyone. Until recently, that interest has been fairly narrowly defined. Most people assumed that schools would take care of academics while families would retain responsibility for character education, values, and beliefs. But the numbers of students coming to school without any evidence of character training and without any apparent value system directing their lives grew. Too many have rejected the value of work, responsibility, and preparation for life. They drop out of school or go through the motions of serving time in school without learning anything. Concern for the future has aroused even the most self-absorbed, who fear that society will crumble under the weight of ignorance.

Many citizens reason that the "village" needs to step in and assume responsibility, not just for academics, but for the affective areas of beliefs, values, and attitudes. In other words, business, community organizations, government, and parents should all become partners in training the whole child. But, as controversies over the meanings of values and beliefs and the purpose of schooling strain the village seams, we have to ask, is education truly everyone's responsibility? Do parents have the right to pass on their beliefs to their children, or does the village have the right to override parental convictions? Who determines the school agenda? Should parents have the right to reject all or part of an agenda determined by the village?

I realize that these questions suggest far more than a challenge to a few programs. They cut to the heart of educational philosophy in the United States. They even question the right of government to be involved in education at all. It is time that such challenges be addressed. Having shied away from them because the educational system seemed to be working fairly well has served little purpose other than to surrender the argument to the ever-growing educational bureaucracy.

For over a hundred years after compulsory schooling laws were passed, most families experienced minimal problems with government control of education. The families who suffered under the system were few, and they usually belonged to unpopular minorities. But now many "mainstream families" are unhappy with the system, and their complaints are demanding more attention. The situation has gotten so bad that most people acknowledge that our educational system is in serious trouble. But unless we figure out why that is so, we are unlikely to choose the right solution.

Let's consider an analogy; substitute nutrition for education. Most families do not produce all their own food. Few have any idea how to cultivate a garden, run a farm, or process food, and even fewer have the inclination to learn how to do so. Few parents have degrees in nutrition, and few are professional cooks. As a result, very few parents are formally certified to feed their children properly. Some children might grow up with nutritional deficiencies that can limit their capacity to work and function within society. This impacts everyone, so we must conclude that the entire community must assume responsibility for ensuring that the nutritional needs of all children are met. Children will be assigned to nutrition districts according to where they live. Compulsory nutrition laws will ensure that all children show up for their meals. They must eat everything on their plate whether or not they are hungry and whether or not they like the food because professional nutritionists have determined the appropriate diet— serving size and content—for children at each age level.

Proper nutrition is more essential to survival than education, but we have not yet passed compulsory nutrition laws. In spite of steps in that direction (school breakfasts and lunch), we, as social communities, are still reluctant to assume nutritional responsibility for all children. We allow parents to purchase some of their food at the supermarket, some at the wholesale warehouse, and some at McDonald's. We allow children to eat grandma's cookies and the after school snack offered by their friends' mothers. We even allow some people to grow and eat their own food without government inspection. In spite of allowing such freedom in this area, the vast majority of children grow up without serious nutritional handicaps.

Somehow, we came to view education differently than nutrition. We could not trust parents to find the resources to meet their children's educational needs as they are able to do with food. We overlooked, or tallied as a negligible minority, parents who demonstrate resourcefulness and responsibility and utilize all sorts of learning opportunities for their children. We forget about Little League, soccer, trips to parks, museums, and aquariums. Some parents even approach trips to the grocery store and the post office as if they were school field trips, and the grocery clerk and post office clerk, sometimes unwittingly, often deliberately, aid in the child's training. Most parents take advantage of resources available throughout the community for their children's educational growth. Most parents do these things as a matter of course.

There are certainly exceptions. Some parents do not adequately provide for their children, and some feel that electronic entertainment satisfies a child's need for educational enrichment. However, before we use less-than-admirable parenting examples to justify control over all parents, we should consider the circumstances.

We have had compulsory schooling for generations. On top of that we have provided welfare, food stamps, subsidized housing, government-funded preschool programs, etc. The unintentional message sent to parents by the multitude of government programs is that parents need not endeavor to fulfill their responsibilities in regard to their children because government will take over and do it for them. Essentially, why start now? What was intended as a safety net has turned into a release from responsibility. Consider: if all such programs were removed at once, would parents continue to ignore their responsibility?

Compulsory schooling laws can serve as an example. Before we had compulsory schooling, was education neglected in our country? Evidence to the contrary is overwhelming. The literacy rate in the early 1800s far surpasses today's; Pierre DuPont de Nemours found that nearly 99 percent of the population (excluding slaves) was literate. He said: "Most young Americans...can read, write, and cipher. Not more than four in a thousand are unable to write legibly—even neatly—while in Spain, Portugal, and Italy, only a sixth of the population can read; in Germany, even in France, not more than a third; in Poland, about two men in a hundred; and in Russia not one in two hundred."[1]

After researching early American literacy, Christopher Klicka related, "John Adams discovered in 1765 that a 'native of America, especially of New England, who cannot read and write is as rare a Phenomenon as a Comet.' Jacob Duche, the Chaplain of Congress in 1772, said of his countrymen, 'almost every man is a reader.' Similarly, Daniel Webster confirmed that the product of home education was near-universal literacy, when he stated 'a youth of fifteen, of either sex, who cannot read and write, is very seldom to be found.'"[2]

The widely touted justification that public schooling is a key element of our democratic form of government has no basis in fact. Economic necessity also proves baseless from the historical perspective. Myron Lieberman tells us:

> Contemporary rhetoric asserts that public education is essential to democratic representative government and economic growth. The reality, however, is that public education was the result, not a cause, of these things. In both Great Britain and the United States, a democratic system of government was firmly established long before

public education was widely adopted. In both countries, massive economic growth preceded public education. Great Britain experienced its most impressive economic growth in the late eighteenth and early nineteenth centuries despite the absence of government-supported education... Similarly, in the United States, public schools did not emerge on a large scale until the mid-1800s, and then only at lower grade levels. The United States experienced huge economic growth while public education was nonexistent or very limited.[3]

Since improving literacy, maintaining a democracy, and developing economic strength are invalid excuses for the imposition of compulsory schooling laws, what then was the real reason? It appears that at least three motivations were at work, coming from religious conservatives, Unitarians, and Socialists.

Lieberman describes the motivations of religious conservatives:

During the early 1800s every state provided assistance to private schools, including denominational schools. By the mid-1800s most white children, including those from the lower and middle classes, received an elementary education. This was true even though parents were expected to share some of the costs from their own pockets... What changed this situation was the influx of Catholic immigrants in the 1840s... More than 700,000 Catholic immigrants entered the country during this decade. States that had provided aid to Protestant denominational schools on a non preferential basis balked at providing such aid to Catholic schools. Their solution was to discontinue non preferential aid to private schools and to establish public schools with a pronounced Protestant bias... Its [public education's] raison d'être was religious prejudice, not the need to educate all children.[4]

The second motivation came from a different direction. It too was philosophical in nature. Unitarians believed that both man and society were perfectible, and that schools were the best vehicle for raising man to his highest potential. "As an intellectual elite, they also viewed public education as the means of exerting social and cultural control over a changing society."[5]

The Socialist movement was the third force at work. Socialists believed that before all people could be truly equal, they must all have equal education. According to their dogma, education would be the force that would break down the "class" barriers of inequality and servitude in preparation for the ushering in of a classless socialist society.

Paradoxically, part of the Socialist agenda for public schools was to rid society of Christianity. Robert Owen and his followers were immensely influential as spokesmen for the Socialist movement in education. A former Unitarian minister and follower of Owens, Orestes A. Brownson, wrote of the Owenites, "The great object was to get rid of Christianity, and to convert our churches into halls of science. The plan was not to make open attacks on religion...but to establish a system of state—we said national—schools, from which all religion was to be excluded...and to which all parents were to be compelled by law to send their children."[6]

All of these seemingly contradictory influences worked within the system, gradually shaping and influencing it.

Protestantism seemed to be dominant, but from the beginning, and not solely in the educational arena, Unitarian influences were corroding the theological underpinnings. Socialism maintained a more invisible presence until recent years, although the Socialists claimed a major victory early on when the state claimed authority to require parents to send their children to school and used taxation as the means to pay for it.

The public school curriculum maintained a Protestant bias up through the 1960s, even though the theology was watered down to a nominal level in most schools. Over the past thirty years, what little Protestant bias remained has been replaced by a different bias—called secular humanism. The public school curriculum of recent history rejected Protestant presuppositions and the accompanying worldview. Suddenly, the former majority who seemingly dominated the education system found themselves in the role of the disregarded minority. Protestants have realized what the Catholics realized in the 1800s—it does make a difference who controls education. And it make a huge difference to minorities and to those who disagree with the majoritarian worldview.

Modern educators are unlikely to describe the purpose of compulsory schooling as one of controlling religious ideas or worldviews. Rather, they justify it by claiming the need for literate, functioning citizens, just as did the original proponents of government-sponsored common schools. Still, many observers feel that public schools have been more successful in shaping religious or philosophical ideas than they have been in turning out well-educated citizens. And few of those who support public schools for universal literacy realize that we were far closer to achieving that goal before we had compulsory schooling laws.

There are many good things happening in publics schools, yet the overall results are on a downward slide that only seems to get steeper and steeper. No matter how much we prefer to cling to idealized notions of public schools, the evidence cannot support that confidence. Numerous authors such as Blumenfeld,[7] Leiberman,[8] Klicka,[9] Gatto,[10] and Sowell[11] have exposed incontrovertible evidence of public schooling's dismal descent, which those who have any doubts can investigate.

Who's To Blame?

Why are things so bad? Parents, teachers, administrators, and students all point the finger of blame at each other. "Teachers don't know how to teach." "We have too many administrators who don't do anything." "Parents don't support the schools." "Students are rebellious and disinterested." While all of these accusations might have some degree of truth, it is more productive to ask why the concerned parties are not performing according to our expectations. I believe that the major part of the blame for failure in that area can be laid at the feet of government.

Teachers receive little respect from parents, administrators, or students. Government education codes restrict their efforts, and they are asked by legislators to assume the impossible burden of meeting all of the physical, emotional, and academic needs of thirty students (or more in the case of an upper grade teacher) every day. And most of those students would rather be anywhere else but in that classroom. Administrators are busy with government regulatory paperwork, and parents have relinquished responsibility to the school, so teacher support is not likely to emerge from either of those quarters.

Too many teachers get overwhelmed and discouraged. Some reach a point where they simply go through the motions; they don't quit because it is a secure job no matter how badly they perform.

Administrators are so swamped with reports and forms that they rarely accomplish anything significant. But they need to keep that government money coming in to pay the bills.

We can understand what happened to parents by looking at the evidence assembled by Charles Murray[12] regarding what happened when government began providing for other family needs—personal responsibility decreased and, in some cases, disappeared. Isn't it likely that we have suffered the same result with public education? Since government requires it, government supplies it, and government decides when it is properly accomplished, what role do parents have other than assisting with homework and supplying store-bought goodies for birthday parties?

Even when schools ask for parental input on important issues, too often it is a smoke screen used to validate what the school authorities have already decided to do. A classic example comes from Euclid Avenue Elementary School in Los Angeles. The school had an election to determine whether they would continue with year-round schooling or switch back to a traditional school calendar. Three hundred eighty-six parents and sixty-five school staff members voted. A simple majority would mean a return to the traditional calendar. School personnel, who preferred year-round schooling, felt that their votes should each carry more weight since there were fewer of them. A vote-counting formula was hatched that gave the vote of each school staffer the weight of 6.32 parents' votes. Then they announced that year-round schooling won.[13]

A similar phenomenon has been reported by parents who attended school meetings purportedly called to determine educational outcomes. Parents are assigned to small groups, each with a coordinator. Suggestions for educational outcomes are elicited, recorded on large pieces of paper, and posted on the wall. Supposedly, each group arrives at a consensus about those outcomes. At the end of the exercise, the school announces a list of outcomes that bears little resemblance to those offered by parents and great resemblance to those outcomes listed in the books provided to coordinators.

After years of being patronized and ignored, is it any wonder that many parents from all socioeconomic levels have abdicated responsibility for their children's education?

Students are little more than pawns in the educational game, and they know it. Why should they cooperate? A few see their own self-interest tied in with the school's agenda, but most do not. Sadly, none of these four groups have both the power and the incentive to improve the situation.

In medicine, there is a term "iatrogenic disorder." It is used to describe a medical problem which is itself the result of a medical treatment. In simple terms, a cure is the cause of the problem. Most of the problems of public schooling are iatrogenic, resulting from the system itself rather than outside events or influences. The system depends upon government entities for both funding and marching orders, essentially a socialist structure. As we have seen in the former Soviet Union, the concept of socialism is fundamentally flawed. The Soviets kept creating five-year plans for increasing farm production with increasing government controls, but the results were always a decrease in the amount of food available to the people.

We might also liken the education system to Congress. Unable to master its wanton spending habits, it increases the burden on taxpayers, those they are supposed to be serving. Public education can do little to change administrators and teachers, but it can demand more from parents and students, those they are supposed to be serving. With this strategy, they are unlikely to get the positive response or results they expect.

If schools want parents to be more supportive, there are only two ways to accomplish it. The first solution they refuse to entertain—returning to parents control over their children's schooling; so they are left with the second—extending their own control over parents to require support and cooperation. Since the first alternative is self-destructive to the system, the second is the chosen route. Thus we see the plan for expanded control appear most obviously in the eighth goal, which says, "By the year 2000, every school will promote partnerships that will increase parental involvement and participation in promoting the social, emotional, and academic growth of children."

Unable and unwilling to repair itself, the educational monopoly actually has used its own failures to justify a plethora of new and expanded government programs. But this admission to failure does not come from humble and contrite hearts. There is no apology involved; instead they are blaming lack of sufficient funding and too many restraints on their freedom to control. Essentially, society should be ashamed of itself for not giving the educational system what it wants (again) so that this time it can be successful. For those who might still have faith in the education system's ability to fix itself, we should review their track record in applying solutions.

Would You Buy a Used Car from the Education Department?

If the car dealer down the street sold you a lemon a few years back, would you be likely to head for his car lot next time you need a car? We've bought an awful lot of lemons from the educational establishment, but for some reason, we keep going back for more.

The most expensive educational reform is the Chapter 1 program, cornerstone of the Elementary and Secondary Education Act. The program has operated since 1965, but not until recently did federal lawmakers get around to gathering information and analyzing the results, authorizing a study since none had been done. As studies often do, this one will take a number of years to complete. But, since the Elementary and Secondary Education Act was up for reauthorization in 1994, lawmakers asked for an interim report so that they could get some idea of how well it was working. The results so far are disconcerting. After pouring in more than $70 billion over almost thirty years (now funded at close to $6,000,000,000 per year), the data thus far shows that the federal compensatory-education program has failed to improve the achievement test scores of the educationally deprived children it is intended to serve.[14] There has been no significant difference in achievement between Chapter 1 students and similar students who did not participate in the program.[15] These results resemble too much the dismaying results of studies of government social welfare programs revealed by Charles Murray's research. (Murray's landmark book, Losing Ground,[16] is must reading for those who are concerned about the effectiveness of government social programs.)

Government programs and reform efforts are not limited to the underprivileged, and this is particularly so in education, where reform efforts are often aimed at all students. Douglas Carnine, a professor of education at the University of Oregon and director of the National Center for Improving the Tools of Educators (NCITE),[17] knowledgeably offers a professional evaluation of those efforts. What he found is not encouraging. He says, "Educators at all levels, from classroom teachers to national policymakers, routinely use and approve materials and techniques without testing or evaluating them. This costs schools millions of dollars and does not yield the results educators and the public are clamoring for." Carnine relates examples from various levels of school governance: "A state government imposes new requirements without studying whether the requirements will result in any improvement in learning. A school district announces a new curriculum for September that has not even been written, let alone tested, by August. A district, working with a college of education, creates an elaborate teacher training program to teach methods that have never been proven to work." He goes on to say, "In education, untested fads sweep through the profession, gathering authority by the number of schools using them, not by proven gains in learning."[18]

Those paying attention when schools implemented open classrooms or the teaching of new math saw prime examples of what Carnine describes. Unfortunately, the wasted time, energy, and resources do not faze the educational bureaucracy when it finds something new to try.

Myron Lieberman relates educational reform efforts to the breakup of the Soviet Union:

> Just as changes required to restructure the Soviet economy upset the distribution of political power, so will the changes required to reform education in the United States: the changes that are needed threaten powerful political and educational interest groups. These groups block fundamental changes, but realize that they must be perceived as supporting it. Consequently, educational

nostrums are a growth industry; attention is focused upon cosmetic changes that pose no threat to the status quo. Choice within public schools, cooperative learning, teacher empowerment, school-based management, parental involvement, peer review, open education, non-graded classrooms, differentiated staffing, higher graduation requirements, textbook reform, career ladders, merit pay, charter schools, and accelerated learning are examples... None will make a significant difference in the power structure of education, the way education is carried on, or student achievement.[19]

If Schools Were Businesses...

If businesses operated like the educational system, they would be defunct. If CEOs or small business owners continually wasted money on unproven innovations, and product quality was on a perpetual downward slide, the business—large or small—would not survive. And going to the board of directors to ask for expansion money would certainly be out of the question.

Despite a track record that rivals those of the most poorly managed businesses, the educational establishment has the gall to ask for more power and money. The request isn't new; it happens every year. What is new is the scope of their requests. The cost and extent of the Goals 2000 restructuring far surpasses anything else previously attempted. Perhaps the psychology behind it is to overwhelm legislators with the sheer audacity of the plans. On the other hand, the education system shares with legislators a desire for control, and both groups are rewarded under Goals 2000.

Centralization—a Plan or a Cop-Out?

The fix-it plan depends upon the continuance of centralization, but not for the purposes of economies of scale or efficiency as one might expect. A centralized education system has resulted from "passing the buck" more than anything else. When local entities could not resolve problems, they sought help from the state, which was perceived as having more resources (money). When states also were unsuccessful, they looked to the federal government for solutions and financing. Assigning educational responsibility to increasingly distant levels of government has meant sacrificing local control.

Parents opposed to restructuring reforms now discover how little control they can exert on their local schools. If they do not like what is happening, they are unlikely to get it fixed through their school or school board. There are two dynamics involved.

When parental complaints address any part of the restructuring plan, too often school boards and administrators are unreceptive. Many take the attitude that this is *the reform* that has been chosen, and though discussion is invited, their minds are made up.

In Adrian, Michigan, Superintendent Al Meloy was put on the defensive when their school system chose to participate in the Communities for Developing Minds (CDM) project, a long-term systemic reform initiative. Concerned parents collected 2,446 signatures on petitions complaining about the program. Meloy was ready in advance with a three-pronged strategy to diffuse criticism. First, he and his staff calculated that these signatures amounted to only 8 percent of the district residents, then dismissed their input as coming from an insignificant minority. In most districts, a large percentage of residents do not even have children in school, some are unable to be involved, and some choose not to. That means that there is a small percentage of people who will have an opinion on the issue in the first place. Getting 8 percent of a total that includes all of these groups to sign petitions actually shows very significant opposition in spite of Meloy's assertions. The second part of the strategy was a series of newspaper articles labeling the opposition as radical right fundamentalists being manipulated by outsiders. Third, there was a concerted sales pitch of the curriculum. Notice that the strategy nowhere included addressing the parents' concerns to determine if they were legitimate.[20] Classic fallacies in logical debate were employed: First, dismiss the opposition because of their minority status; second, launch an *ad hominem* attack; and third, squirm out of presenting a legitimate response to the argument —otherwise known as *petitio principii*. What hope do the parents of Adrian, Michigan, have if the leaders of the school system succumb to typically sophomoric fallacies in argumentation?

In California, numerous lawsuits have been filed against school districts over the CLAS (California Learning Assessment System). Alarmed parents and activists managed to obtain questions from some of these tests, circulated them, and created a firestorm of protests. Parents are concerned about questions that touch on private family or personal issues, not to mention the validity of the tests themselves, and focus their research and questions on those issues. No one seems to be motivated by an attempt to destroy the "integrity" of the tests. However, instead of addressing the legitimate parental concerns, the educational bureaucracy responded in their typical manner—two pieces of legislation have been introduced that make it a serious crime for any unauthorized person to view, copy, or possess the tests.

Some school districts decided not to administer the tests to their students rather than use a possibly flawed test that might create legal problems for the district. The state cannot abide district independence, so the new legislation imposes a $100 per pupil fine on districts that refuse to administer the tests. In this way, the system that proposes to promote topic exploration and open discussion in the classroom advocates silencing alternative opinions. Issues about test quality and invasion of privacy will not be addressed by the schools unless the courts force them to do so.[21]

School boards and administrators too often are reluctant to address the issues rather than defend their programs. It does not seem to matter if the concerns address a program's lack of research and evidence of success, high price tag, or unspecified goals.

The other reason parents fail to influence local school boards is that the authority to make decisions has been usurped by state and federal agencies. If parents complain to their school principal, the principal might respond, "We can't do anything about it. It's a state requirement." State curriculum-framework requirements, bussing, mainstreaming handicapped students, and other such issues often fall into this category.

Big Brother Can Do It Better

We have been moving toward federal control for at least four decades. In 1961, Congressman John Ashbrook of Ohio warned:

> A great number of citizens in this country are honestly in favor of Federal aid to education...Most of those who favor Federal aid in the new, direct general aid sense believe this can be done without control of local school

districts from Washington. I feel that a majority of those who honestly favor aid to education in the manner provided in the administration proposals also believe that there should not be control.

It is my opinion that it has been folly to argue that we could have a comprehensive aid to education program without controls. The current bills which are stalled in Congress do have controls. Of course, they are given other names by the sponsors and supporters of these bills. When asked how they reconcile these obvious controls in the aid to education bill with their protestations that no controls exist, the sponsors merely say, "These aren't controls, they are merely 'criteria' by which you determine the aid." It matters not whether you refer to controls as criteria, standards, or any other words if they basically designate and set out controls.

That there was any doubt of the Federal bureaucrats' intentions in this matter was laid to rest with the discovery of a Health, Education, and Welfare publication, "A Federal Education Agency for the Future," which is a report of the Office of Education, dated April 1961....[I]ts pronouncements are a blueprint for complete domination and direction of our schools from Washington.

Congressman Ashbrook elaborated on the details, including the mixed motives of the social engineers advancing these proposals. He said:

During recent decades there has been an increasing directness of relationship between education and national security, the general economy, and other areas in which the Federal Government has a major concern.

Historically, there has been only limited consideration
of the implications of these activities for education itself.
Consequently, while the educational community has
been instrumental in the achievement of the diverse
ends of a large number of governmental programs, these
programs have not had in all cases a fortunate effect on
the ends of education.[22]

What we now see are experimental programs being used to
implement an agenda at the national level that encompasses
far more than traditional education. Ashbrook saw what was
coming, but his protests were obviously ineffective. The passage of Goals 2000 marks a huge transfer of power to the federal education department. Instead of accurately identifying
problems as arising from the system itself, the education
monopoly has followed the only course open to it that will
allow for its survival—expansion of power and control.

End Notes:

[1] Pierre DuPont de Nemours, *National Education in the United States of
America*, University of Delaware Press, DE, 1923, pp. 3-5.

[2] Christopher J. Klicka, *The Right Choice: The Incredible Failure of Public
Education and the Rising Hope of Home Schooling*, Noble Publishing
Associates, Gresham, OR, 1992, pp. 115-116.

[3] Myron Lieberman, *Public Education: An Autopsy*, Harvard University
Press, Cambridge, MA, 1993, p. 14.

[4] Ibid., p. 15.

[5] Samuel L. Blumenfeld, *Is Public Education Necessary?*, The Paradigm Company, Boise, ID, 1989, p. 132.

[6] Ibid., pp. 79-96.

[7] Ibid.

[8] Myron Lieberman, *Public Education: An Autopsy*, Harvard University Press, Cambridge, MA, 1993.

[9] Christopher J. Klicka, *The Right Choice: The Incredible Failure of Public Education and the Rising Hope of Home Schooling*, Noble Publishing Associates, Gresham, OR, 1992.

[10] John Taylor Gatto, *Dumbing Us Down*, New Society Publishers, Philadelphia, PA, 1992.

[11] Thomas Sowell, *Inside American Education: The Decline, The Deception, The Dogmas*, The Free Press, NY, 1993.

[12] Charles Murray, *Losing Ground: American Social Policy 1950-1980*, Basic Books, 1984.

[13] Joanna Richardson, "Vote at School in L.A. Stirs Up Local Debate Over Balance of Power," *Education Week*, May 4, 1994, p. 9.

[14] U.S. Department of Education, "Prospects: The Congressionally Mandated Study of Educational Growth and Opportunity (The Interim Report)," July, 1993.

[15] Mark Pitsch, "Chapter 1 Fails to Spur Gains, Data Indicate," *Education Week*, Nov. 24, 1993, pp. 1,15.

[16] Charles Murray, *Losing Ground: American Social Policy 1950-1980*, Basic Books, 1984.

[17] NCITE is funded by the U.S. Department of Education.

[18] Douglas Carnine, "Facts Over Fads," *Education Week*, Dec. 8, 1993, p. 40.

[19] Myron Lieberman, *Public Education: An Autopsy*, Harvard University Press, Cambridge, MA, 1993, p. 2.

[20] Fritz Detwiler, "A Tale of Two Districts," *Education Leadership*, Dec. 1993/Jan. 1994, pp. 24-27.

[21] California bills AB 3506 and SB 1273 (1993-94 session).

[22] John Ashbrook, speech entered into the *Congressional Record*, July 18, 1961, pp. 11868-11880. Full text reprinted in *The Wisconsin Report*, Volume XVII, Nos. 38-41.

CHAPTER FOUR

OUTCOME-BASED EDUCATION

When we potty train one-year-old Johnny, we are looking for a particular outcome or performance. He will not simply be taught the skill, given an A, B, or C grade and left to function at what might be less than a satisfactory level. This is an example of an outcome-based education performance.

Any education program that mandates results in terms of a performance is outcome-based education. The fundamental idea of education oriented toward outcomes is not the problem, but the nature and origin of those outcomes is.

"Stop OBE!" is becoming the new battle cry at school board meetings. Many people have heard or read about outcome-based education (better known as OBE), but have fuzzy ideas about what it is. Some anti-OBE activists successfully stir up parents by revealing how schools are throwing out all the traditional accoutrements of education that they experienced—no more age-segregated classrooms, no more letter-grade report cards, subject areas mushed together under thematic learning topics, projects instead of memorization and drill, and no Carnegie units for graduation. Parents have a hard time imagining how school can still be school without all of these elements.

They have cause for concern, but by dwelling on classroom organization and teaching techniques, they miss the bigger issue of the school's mission. Their error is in assuming that it is still basic academic education. Few realize that the mission has been redefined to encompass much broader goals. The National Education Goals Panel sums up the mission as, "...meeting the competition of this global economy, assuring a high quality of life, and preserving our democratic system and ideals."[1]

Education reformers claim that because the mission is so ambitious, it needs to be coordinated at the federal level. Uniform standards are also necessary, they claim, and all students in our country must achieve them. The educational model for this ambitious agenda is outcome-based education.

Will the Real OBE Please Stand Up?

Outcome-based education has different definitions depending upon whom we ask. To make things worse, even those who supposedly invented it don't agree on what it is.

Dr. William Spady, often called the father of OBE, has been the most visible proponent. His organization, the High Success Network, puts on training seminars and offers assistance to schools interested in switching to OBE. Spady believes in locally determined outcomes that are very specifically defined. He claims that in his OBE model, schools are not involved with inappropriate emotional and attitudinal goals. When he refers to attitudes and orientations, he says that he is talking about attitudes towards schoolwork and learning rather than politically correct issues. However, Spady does believe that local school districts have the authority to establish whatever outcomes they choose, and those outcomes might incorporate what he calls public (or broadly civic) values. He tries to differentiate between personal values and public values, claiming that there are universally accepted public values to which no one objects. If it should come down to the question of who has the final say about what a child learns in school, Spady would side with the school district rather than with the family.[2]

John Champlin, who works with an OBE model called Outcomes Driven Developmental Model, says that the government has no business getting involved with outcomes that have to do with beliefs, attitudes, and feelings.[3] But Champlin and Spady disagree with each other on the details of OBE. Other OBE groups, wary of attacks by OBE opponents, try to distance themselves from Spady, the lightning rod for most of the criticism.[4]

What we glean from all of the information is that OBE operates on two levels: theory and implementation. OBE in theory has much to commend it. Recognizing that too many students merely serve time in school without learning, OBE says that serving time should not earn a student a diploma. Students should instead be able to demonstrate that they have actually learned something and can apply what they have learned. OBE condemns the cookie-cutter, factory model of schooling that expects all children of a certain age to learn the same things at the same rate. It allows for much greater individualizing of the curriculum.

Many OBE ideas deserve careful consideration. Some of them are being implemented with varying success in schools around the country. Spady claims that anything less than full implementation of transformational OBE will fall short, yet there are no schools in the country which are fully implementing Spady's OBE.

Johnson City Schools in New York use the ODDM (Outcomes Driven Developmental Model) and are touted as one of the most successful models of OBE. However, 1989 census data for Johnson City Village shows that the demographics of the population are far from typical. Ninety-six percent of the residents are white; .02 percent speak English "not well" or "not at all" (this figure includes citizens of all ages.) Thirty-six percent of the population (all ages) have attended college; and average family income is $34,218. With a highly educated, generally well-to-do population, Johnson City has all the trappings for success no matter what educational model is used.

Another "successful" OBE model is Jenkintown School District in Pennsylvania. But Jenkintown has a teacher-to-student ratio of 1:14 (about half as many students per teacher as schools across the country). They also spend $9,500 per student, quite a bit more than the average. The district superintendent, Dr. David Barrett, says that "The district is still evolving. We are in a state of becoming. By 1996, all of the pieces should be in place." I find it difficult to understand how the district can be praised as an OBE model when the superintendent tells us that they are still putting it together. And, even if they produce positive results in the future, the cost of duplicating the model elsewhere is prohibitive for most schools.[5]

OBE is still at the theoretical level, not yet succumbing to any kind of thorough testing to evaluate how practical it is. If OBE were presented as the experiment it is and introduced in a few schools where parents could choose to have their children participate or not, there would be far less cause for objections. That's not what's happening though; this is a federally mandated program.

What is being implemented in schools across the country often bears little resemblance to ideal models of OBE as proposed by Spady and other theorists. When schools get enthused about the idea of OBE and decide to implement it in their districts, they have to deal with school boards and parents who do not want their children used as guinea pigs. So they compromise by doing a limited version of OBE. Then the political agenda for education gets thrown into the hopper. The national goals lurk in the background, reminding local school districts that in meeting their states' goals, as required, they will in turn be aligned to the national goals.

We end up with OBE that fits no one's definition of what it should really be. But the situation can never be otherwise within the public schools, because, as government entities, they are very much influenced by political agendas. Most of the theory breaks down at the point of implementation, and OBE is destined to join new math, open classrooms, and other educational experiments in the trash heap.

Meanwhile, since OBE was touted as the central idea of restructuring, there has been a melding together of the two, and now, all of the restructuring ideas get lumped together and labeled under the OBE tag. To be sure, OBE proponents are not innocent in all of this.

At a recent Spady conference, one of the guest speakers was Robert Slavin, director of the Roots and Wings project, one of the New American School Development Corporation's (NASDC) restructuring projects. Eleven such projects were privately funded to experiment with restructuring as an element of President Bush's original America 2000 plan. Bush's version of the legislation never passed, but the NASDC schools were funded privately so that the restructuring experiments could still take place. Slavin, clearly motivated by his concern for children and the social and economic problems that affect their school performance, advocates a cradle-to-grave approach of family intervention as a crucial part of restructuring. As we discussed in the first three chapters, such efforts are a socialist solution, even though Slavin probably does not recognize it. When such presentations are made in conjunction with OBE seminars, those attending cannot help but get the message that the two go hand in hand—OBE and the school as the center for cradle-to-grave government care.[6]

Slavin's Roots and Wings project was only one of eleven original projects funded by NASDC, all of which included some form of OBE and were aligned with the national goals. Services for early education, health care, and parent training were common to all of them. Other restructuring efforts within the public school system include similar ties to government social services in most cases. Because of such linkages, OBE opponents define OBE as including programs such as health care, social services, school-based clinics, and family intervention. Actually, what they are observing is the implementation of Goals 2000, with OBE playing a major role. Before we return to the larger picture of Goals 2000, there are some important elements of OBE that we should examine.

What's a World Class Standard?

Recurrent themes in educational restructuring are "world class performance" and "high standards." The fifth national goal sets the tone by saying, "By the year 2000, U.S. students will be first in the world in science and mathematics achievement." The stated intent is that U.S. students will be the best in the world. This sounds egotistical, but it makes sense if we think about it from the perspective that everyone must meet the same standard. If there can be only one standard, then we want that standard to be very high. Can you imagine anyone accepting the idea that we want everyone to meet the same mediocre standard?

But reality presents a major problem. According to the Goals 3 and 4 Technical Planning Group, "there can logically be only one set of national education standards per subject area." Yet, all students will not be able to work to the highest level, and some will choose not to work to that level. Planners seem double-minded on this issue. They say, "While students should be expected to reach the same world class standards, proposed standards...should provide enough flexibility in implementation to accommodate state and regional differences and local control of education...The standards proposed should support and challenge students achieving at all performance levels. While they should not represent minimum expectations, the standards should be suitable to and within the capabilities of students to learn...Regardless of students' perceived ability, the standards should be achievable with proper supports and sustained effort...Any student who works hard in a good program should be able to meet the standards..."[7]

At some schools implementing outcome-based education, slower students are being allowed the option of coming before or staying after school, to put in extra time so that they can attempt to meet new standards. If a slow student is struggling in all of his or her classes, consider how much extra time this might require. Consider also, that there is only so much a person can absorb in a single day without mental overload. As we will discuss a little farther on, time is supposed to be the flexible element in the new system, but in practical terms, time cannot truly be as flexible as some slow students need it to be.

Despite the rhetoric, the standards thus far developed tend to allow for less than stellar, world-class performance. Reading through the indicators proposed by the National Center on Educational Outcomes that are supposed to tell us whether or not a child is ready to "graduate" from the system, we find a non-specific low level of expectations. Some of NCEO indicators are:

- students who use and comprehend language that effectively accomplishes the purpose of the communication. [A toddler pointing to the faucet and screaming "Wa-wa!" fits this "indicator" or description of competency.]
- students who demonstrate competence in math necessary to function in their current home, school, work, and community environments
- students who demonstrate competence in reading necessary to function in their next environment
[These prior two are settling for mere functional literacy in math and reading!]
- students who demonstrate competence in writing necessary to function in their current home, school, work, and community environments
[Writing becomes something only done out of necessity rather than a form of art.][8]

Even Albert Shanker, president of the American Federation of Teachers, describes OBE standards as "vague and fluffy." He goes on to say, "OBE standards include academic outcomes, but they are very few and so vague that they would be satisfied by almost any level of achievement, from top-notch to minimal."[9]

Educator Gregory Cizek says, "In my home state [Ohio] as in many others we've decided to raise standards so high for 12th graders that we're going to make them pass a 9th-grade test in order to get a diploma...Over four years, students will get about a dozen tries."[10]

Cizek is concerned that the idea of standards has lost any real meaning. In our desire for all students to succeed, we have lowered the measure of success.

> In simple terms, the ethos means that we should accentuate the positive. Conversely, it would be a bad thing to judge that a student is 'not competent,' to deny a diploma, or worst of all—to state that a student has failed... Unfortunately, applying any standard must result in some students meeting the standard and others falling short. Understandably, we don't want anyone to fall short, to fail (ouch!). Hence the predicament: How can we have standards and do violence to no one...? One answer is to set standards that almost everyone can meet.[11]

Many standards proponents remain so while acknowledging the futility of imposing uniformly high standards on everyone. Few seem willing to ask the essential question, "Is it right to have any type of governmentally imposed uniform standards with which all students are required to conform?" Where all this will lead no one can say for sure, but author Kurt Vonnegut took a stab at it in his short story, *Harrison Bergeron*.

The story takes place in the year 2081, and everyone is finally equal due to Constitutional amendments and the vigilant agents of the United States Handicapper General. Poor Harrison Bergeron has the misfortune to be a handsome, athletically talented young man as well as a genius. Such unfair advantages can no longer be tolerated, so Harrison is handicapped with gigantic earphones that send periodic signals that

inhibit his ability to think. Thick, wavy-lensed glasses inter-
fere with his sight and sidetrack him with headaches. He must
always wear a red, rubber ball on his nose, black caps on his
teeth, and shave off his eyebrows to disguise his good looks.
Plus, to offset his tremendous strength, 300 pounds of scrap
metal is strapped to his body.

Harrison and a similarly handicapped ballerina momentar-
ily throw off their handicaps and celebrate in a beautiful
dance. Yet, the enforcers of equality win in the end as the
Handicapper General terminates their rebellion with two
blasts from a shotgun.[12]

Assessments

Enforcement of standards at present is far gentler, with
assessments being key methods.

Assessments (formerly called tests) are crucial for implementation of the national goals and outcome-based education.
A national goals panel report tells us, "The Resource
Group...continues to recommend that a nationwide system
including several examinations in each subject matter, all calibrated to a single national standard...be developed.[13] "The
proposed nationwide assessment system is intended not only
to provide a means of monitoring progress, but to contribute
to the major changes in the nation's education system that are
needed to achieve Goal 3."[14]

Anyone involved in education recognizes that testing drives
the curriculum. Teachers teach what will be tested; otherwise
students score poorly, parents are unhappy, teachers get
blamed, and principals get fired. A saying circulates among
educators: "What you test is what you get." If something
appears on the test, teachers will probably teach it. If it does
not appear on a test, it is a fact that will go ignored.

Tests rewritten to reflect the new educational agenda expressed through the goals, outcomes, and standards force the curriculum to follow suit. This means that the curriculum of your local school will actually be determined by test writers in Washington, D.C., circumventing the constitutional prohibition of federal interference in local curriculum development. Those who understand this are frightened because they know that "...when you lose power over the curriculum, you lose power over what children are taught and what they get to believe is the truth."[15] Thus, tests are a major factor in restructuring efforts.

The idea of a national test is distasteful to many, so some tests are being developed at the state level and are often shared among the states. According to the National Education Goals Panel, "Assessment systems would be developed by clusters of states that come together to define a shared curriculum framework and procedures for assessment. The cluster results would be linked together and to a common national standard, possibly with the use of a national anchor examination."[16]

We do have one national examination right now, the National Assessment of Educational Progress (NAEP), but it is administered to selected students and schools, and results are not reported at the individual level. Still, the NAEP lays the groundwork for a national examination, and this model is being copied in some states. In fact, Kentucky's assessment "shares about 80 percent of its content with the national examination," according to Edward Reidy, the associate state commissioner of education for assessment and accountability services.[17]

We are being manipulated into accepting the need for a nationalized curriculum and centralized school system, and the NAEP is one of the major tools. A national goals panel report on the NAEP says, "This assessment is intended primarily to support the policy process."[18] NAEP results are referenced by the national goals panel every year to summarize the nation's educational progress. These summaries and other data gathering vehicles such as the census combine to push policy makers in the desired direction.

At this time, most of the state level assessments differ from the NAEP because they are designed to support outcome-based education more than the larger policy goals as spelled out in Goals 2000. However, new assessments take a variety of forms; some of them look similar to standardized tests. For instance, multiple choice questions are still used on some tests, but they require students to explain their choices, allowing them to receive credit for correct reasoning processes. Some assessment questions are open-ended with a number of possible solutions. For instance, design a zoo that takes into consideration the habitat, diet, and other needs of the animals who will live here. In general, children do much more writing than they did on the old, computer-bubble standardized tests.

There are some content problems with the new assessments, but much of the criticism is aimed at scoring. Scoring is often based on the student's solution process, with minimal weight given to actual right or wrong answers. On language arts assessments, if students express themselves well, it seems to matter little what it is that they say or how proper their grammar or paragraph development is.

As you can imagine, these assessments have drawn some sharp criticism, and not just from opponents of restructuring. Dr. Richard Paul, director of the Center for Critical Thinking and Moral Critique, presents a devastating analysis of the new California Learning Assessment System (CLAS), showing how Hitler's ravings would earn top scores under the new system.[19]

California's Language Arts Assessments are prime examples of the worst of the new evaluations. For these tests, students are not expected to have studied and retained a body of content knowledge. They are seldom asked to draw on factual content but rather are directed to respond according to their feelings.

For example, the first question on a tenth grade language arts test is, "Was there ever a time when you or someone you know felt oppressed or trapped in a relationship? Write briefly about what happened and how the person felt about the oppression." A short story about a woman trapped in an unhappy marriage is then used as the basis for the rest of the test. Group discussion (another feature of these tests) begins with a sharing of ideas about whether or not this marriage can be saved. Part of the test includes the learner's evaluation of how well he/she felt they performed on this test![20]

A fourth grade CLAS language arts test is even worse in that it forces young children to role-play evil situations. It is based on a story titled "Priscilla and the Wimps." Priscilla is a large, strong girl, and her friend Melvin is small and weak. The school bully Monk confronts Melvin, but Priscilla intervenes. She manhandles Monk into her school locker, locks it, and leaves school with the other students. The story ends by saying, "It snows all that night, a blizzard. The whole town ices up. And school closes for a week." The children are supposed to tell what they think happens to Monk and what his thoughts are at the end of the story. They are asked to draw a picture of Monk being shoved into the locker. Students also get together in groups and take turns pretending to be bullies, saying things that bullies might say.

It is clear why opposition to the CLAS tests goes beyond the issue of poorly constructed assessments, because just the experience of taking the tests is likely to be psychologically harmful for many children. All of the new assessments are not as outrageous as those described, but enough of them fit this category that parents should be scrutinizing them beforehand. School officials, however, will not allow parents that opportunity, claiming that it will undermine the integrity of the tests.

One defense of the tests is that part of their purpose is to make them interesting enough to stimulate children to write, but this is ridiculous. It appears that, in attempting to correct weaknesses of the traditional tests, both subject-area knowledge and objective standards of measurement have been abandoned or minimalized.

Assessment Score Reliability

When these new assessments are employed in determining whether students meet the standards or outcomes, we cannot simply dismiss them as silly, experimental tests. They will be important in influencing and directing students' futures. Yet, the tests are so subjective that there are serious questions about score reliability.

Vermont is struggling with reliability problems with their new statewide testing program that was adopted in 1988:

> Under the program, 4th and 8th graders are assessed in writing and math in two ways. They are given a uniform test, which is a standardized test that includes multiple-choice questions and a longer, open-ended question or task, and they are asked to put together portfolios of their work that either include a set number of 'best pieces' in a specific area or a combination of best pieces and other samples of work completed throughout the year.

> The RAND study [studying the validity of scoring results with the new assessment system] used a standard statistical measure known as a reliability coefficient, which measures the extent to which two raters rank a student's work the same. Under such a measure, no agreement would be zero, while total agreement would be 1.00.
>
> The reliability of the scores for the writing portfolio was 0.56 for 4th grade and 0.63 for 8th grade, which, the report says, was only a slight improvement over the previous year and "low by any standards."
>
> For the math portfolios, the reliability of scores ranged from 0.72 to 0.79, which are roughly comparable to those for some National Assessment of Educational Progress tests.[21]

This points out one of the most important criticisms of new assessments—the subjectivity involved in their evaluation. While work is progressing to improve reliability, it is doubtful that we can ever reach a valid level when students are responding without specific guidelines of what is expected and what criteria will influence their scores. And from a student's viewpoint, it is unfair to evaluate them without those clear guidelines of what is expected. The most conscientious students say, "Tell us what it takes to earn an 'A' so that we can deliver that type of performance."

Many private schools have shied away from criticizing the new assessments, staying out of the debate and figuring that they will just stick with the old tests. However, that strategy will be worthless before long. The present standardized tests are all likely to shift to outcome-based education tests in response to state laws requiring performance-based testing, and publishers will discontinue the older tests because the demand will be too small.[22] Eventually, all who rely on testing will be forced to adopt the new assessments for the sake of accreditation

Does It Work?

Many criticisms of OBE and restructuring arise from gross violations of family and individual privacy. Children are asked to reveal private personal or family experiences. They are expected to fill in questionnaires about family habits. Schools are assuming responsibility for inculcating attitudes and beliefs that have traditionally been outside their jurisdiction. Still, some people are willing to sacrifice their liberties in order to get the school system fixed using these reforms. So it is fair to ask how successful the reforms are in improving learning. What we have seen so far tells us that the sacrifice will be pointless. The few successes have been limited in scope, and they are far outweighed by broad and significant failures.

Within every state, OBE is being implemented at some level, the lowest possible estimate being hundreds of schools using some form of OBE. Considering even these figures, a significant proportion of them should be available for review as successful examples. However, at a High Success Network conference, Bill Spady could come up with only nine examples of successful OBE implementation. He cautioned that none of them were actually doing the "real thing." It makes one wonder, if OBE is so great, shouldn't we have far more examples, including some that are "doing it right"?

I followed up on one of Spady's examples, the Lucia Mar School District in California. They openly acknowledge that they are not implementing Spady's version of OBE, but they are pleased with what they have. Test scores have improved dramatically, and more students are taking the SAT test and scoring higher on it. One of their most significant reforms has been creating a Technology Plaza. Major industries have created learning centers where students can use industry's own technology to develop academic and technical skills that ready them for high-tech jobs.

The Lucia Mar School District has written outcomes, but they have retained Carnegie units and grades. They are still teaching the basic academic subjects, but they have added eleven exit outcomes that all students are to demonstrate before they leave. Those outcomes include the typical fuzzy-affective outcomes seen elsewhere, such as "an understanding of our national identity, constitutional heritage, civic values and our rights and responsibilities as citizens."[23] It is impossible to determine how much attention is given to the outcomes, but it is apparent that in the Lucia Mar District, academic achievement is the major emphasis.

This sounds like a great success story, but we need to ask a few questions to know what Lucia Mar truly represents. If what they are doing is essentially beefing up the academics, pursuing motivation with real work-world experiences, and merely paying lip service to affective outcomes, then many would say that this is not OBE. On the other hand, Lucia Mar does claim to be using a form of OBE. If so, then their results make them an exception among the thousands (or more) schools using OBE that are unable to manage the time and resources to teach "proper" attitudes, values, and beliefs while simultaneously providing a strong academic foundation.

The Lucia Mar District illustrates a difficult problem in dealing with OBE. If everyone defines it differently, how do we evaluate it? If what one district implements conflicts with someone else's definition of OBE, is it still valid to call it OBE?

Peg Luksik tells us that when she called a number of schools listed as models for OBE, they denied that they are using that model. The only possible explanations are that they do not know what OBE is, they have something to hide (such as any association with OBE), or that they truly are not doing OBE. This situation makes defending OBE a nightmare for some school personnel.

Jayna Davis of NewsChannel 4 asked Oklahoma State Board of Education member Ray Potts, "Can you name a school district anywhere in this country where test scores have improved because of OBE?" He answered, "Well, I can't say that I can." Oklahoma State School Superintendent Sandy Garrett likewise would not identify any research that she had seen or evidence she had uncovered to support that OBE has been successful.

According to Davis's special report, test scores in the most prominent OBE model schools in Chicago, Johnson City (NY), and South Washington County (Minnesota) have failed to improve. In Pasco (Washington), the school district has fallen below the national average.[24] Forty-five percent of fourth graders, thirty percent of eighth graders, and forty-seven percent of eleventh graders scored in the bottom 25% of all students in 1992 statewide testing for math, reading, language, spelling, science, and social studies.[25]

Zane Bowman, superintendent of Ada Schools in Oklahoma, commenting on the implementation of OBE, said, "To change a complete philosophy with no data to support...with no stories of where is this really successful...to try to explain to your teachers that we're going to change to something that I can't even explain to you, made no sense."[26]

South Washington County, Minnesota, shifted into OBE nine years ago. Since then, test scores have dropped dramatically at every level. Still, student grade point averages are very high. The explanation for this anomaly is that no student is allowed to fail. A student "failing" a class is given an incomplete as a grade. So far they have given 15,510 incompletes, but no one is failing.

Littleton, Colorado, was one of the leaders in outcome-based education. They had thirty-six demonstrations that students must perform to graduate. Students still took high-school classes and received grades, but the grades carried no weight for high-school graduation. The impact of this policy was obvious: 533 students enrolled in algebra. Of those only 145 students completed the course. One hundred sixty students were scheduled to retake it in summer school. The other 228 dropped the course, receiving incompletes. There was no incentive to complete the course, because demonstrating knowledge of algebra was not a graduation requirement. (Eighth-grade math will do.) And since geometry was likewise dispensable, students did not need to complete algebra before tackling a non-existent geometry requirement.[27] Littleton has dropped their OBE graduation outcomes and returned to Carnegie units.[28]

Learning incentives are lost, and motivation also suffers from grade devaluation. Everyone who passes gets an A. It only requires 80 percent to pass, and there is more than one opportunity to attempt a score of 80 percent or higher. Eighty percent used to be a B or a C depending upon your grading scale. When everyone gets A's and they do so by doing B or C level work, A's become worthless. Most students feel no incentive to work harder and to improve when there is no reward for doing so.

Many parents and students are concerned about the effects of this method on college preparation. On a C-NET program, one father related that because of the high school's OBE program, his son did not receive the necessary English courses during high school, so he had to do a year of remedial English at college.[29]

In defense of OBE, Dr. Spady explains that no school in the country is truly implementing a complete OBE program.[30] He claims that partial implementation is itself responsible for some of the poor results, and the present system needs to be completely redesigned to support OBE implementation. The present situations might be compared to yoking a camel with a kangaroo. The combination can be crippling.

Although results thus far have been largely negative, it is still possible that OBE has something valuable to offer education. To find out if that is so, it would be best for a few schools to implement total OBE programs (called transformational OBE) to give it a fair chance to prove itself. In justice to the children and families involved, they should be free to participate or opt out. For a successful experiment, government-dictated outcomes would also have to be ignored, probably an impossible hurdle to overcome. Government interference tends to corrupt even the best ideas. Even if someone has a sound idea for educational reform, by the time government agencies get through inserting their agenda into the plan, the original idea has been mangled beyond recognition.

Confusion in the Ranks

Aside from lack of significant statistical support and positive results, there is growing confusion among educators and bureaucrats concerning OBE. A hearing of the Wisconsin Educational Goals Committee was set to "reach a consensus on the new goals needed to prepare our students for life in the 21st century." A serious dilemma cropped up at this hearing:

The Committee was in its final hearing on outcome-based education goals when...one committee member announced to all who had ears to hear that people ought not to think that the outcome-based education goals really meant "outcome-based education." That confused quite a few of those present, not the least of which were some committee members. Suddenly, after hearing testimony all day (and presumably for two solid months from many special interest groups who were trying to get their outcomes listed by the state), members of the committee began to draw distinctions between what others...meant by the program. Significantly, such disclaimers came only after, and in response to, the denunciations of this OBE program. Perhaps someone was being disabused of his innocence.

One ought not to be surprised to find educators scurrying for cover when OBE is mentioned. The controversial program has been opposed everywhere it has reared its "politically correct" head. OBE advocates throughout the country have regularly changed the name after finding opposition to the proposals. One ought not to be surprised that committee member, Dr. Charles Edwards, would suggest that the committee change the name to something like "results" in education... The wonder is that committee members were even suggesting that education in this state suddenly should become "results" oriented. What, pray tell, has been the purpose in education heretofore? Did no one seek "RESULTS" in education before this? And, after 13 hearings, why are they now suddenly suggesting a new name to announce their educational purpose?[31]

Who's in Control?

A point that is crucial to understand here is that setting goals and making plans to implement them is not a new idea. Schools and teachers have always had them, although sometimes they have been ignored. The more legitimate criticism is that some of the goals set in the past might no longer be valid. But schools are such cumbersome bureaucracies that change is as difficult for them as lowering taxes is for Congress. It might well be that some of the goals of education need to be reexamined and replaced, but the real issue remains: Who will decide what those goals will be? Consider the following description of goals:

[T]he goal of education must be greater than covering a set number of academic subjects. We must purpose to train up sons and daughters in such a way that they will be able to understand how to apply what they have learned to the challenges of life...In ATI, the Scope and Sequence Chart does not identify the subjects which are to be taught, but rather, the areas in which a young person must have a working ability for success in life's responsibilities.

The foregoing sounds like a description of an outcome-based education program, doesn't it? The emphasis is on what students know and can do rather than on covering specific subjects. It sets outcomes, then designs the curriculum to produce those outcomes.

Interestingly, it comes from the Advanced Training Institute, a conservative, evangelical, Christian educational program. If we read further, we spot the difference between it and outcome-based education. "The Scope and Sequence Chart provides the overall structure for integrating all learning around the five basic responsibilities of life: Being a mature man or woman; Being a successful businessman or home manager; Being a loving husband or wife; Being a wise father or mother;

[and] Being a dynamic leader or teacher of good things."[32]

While the general goal statement sounds like OBE, the specific outcomes not only resemble little those of the public schools, they reflect a markedly different worldview and interpretation of the purpose of life in general and education in particular.

But, the significant difference is that no one is forced to subscribe to ATI's goals. There are no choices available to those within the public school system who might prefer to pursue other goals.

Whose Agenda?

A revealing discussion about national goals was transcribed in a special edition of *Education Week*. Participant Richard Mills[33] said, "We didn't really ask the public what the goals of education should be. We got a lot of smart, powerful people together to write the goals. But we didn't ask the public, 'What do you want for your children? What are you willing to give up to get it?'"[34]

Recalling the numerous program and curricula problems that have encumbered school boards across the country without the presence of federal intervention, there is little question that dictating those decisions from on high will not make the protests go away. For example, the proposed science standards require that evolution be taught as a unifying theory of scientific study. Christian parents and teachers are not going to accept this simply because it comes from the federal level any more than they accept such determinations at the state or local level. The strategy seems to be to make protest more difficult by removing the local forum as the place of debate, robbing parents of the easy accessibility of the local forum and forcing them to a less accessible arena. In this way, some educational planners hope to impose their beliefs on all by default.

Religious differences are not the only fly in the ointment. A less controversial, but nonetheless important, clash of agendas centers around the academic curriculum. A good example is the preference for a curriculum designed to teach cultural literacy. Cultural literacy has been moved lower and lower on the totem pole in recent years because many people view knowledge of classical literature and history as less essential than reading, writing, math, and science. However, Dr. E.D. Hirsch, author of the book *Cultural Literacy*,[35] touched an extremely responsive chord in many parents when he championed a resurrection of cultural literacy within the curriculum. Millions of parents think it is so important that they have gobbled up Hirsch's guides for teaching cultural literacy for children in the early grade levels. What a signal to the schools—a marketer's dream come true! Yet, the national goals ignore cultural literacy and the wishes of those who would like to see a curriculum to support it. It's been said before and it's worth saying again. If schools were businesses, most would be filing for Chapter 11.

The Emasculation of Local School Boards

If parents don't want the schools teaching Johnny about condoms in fifth grade, what do they do? They show up at the school board meeting to register their protest. Until now, parents have had the opportunity to confront school boards over curriculum used in schools under their jurisdiction. They have not always been successful, but then they have usually had the right to try to replace unsupportive board members at the next election. Under the new system, school boards, if they continue to exist at all, will have little authority beyond deciding how to implement the federal agenda. There will be room for only one standardized agenda under the national education goal, and parents will be deprived of any say over that agenda, much less an arena in which to say it.

Restructuring advocates say that there will be more local control as the system moves to site-based management. However, school site teams will have very limited authority, being permitted to make no more significant decisions than selecting a company to resurface the playground.

David Hornbeck, author of restructuring plans for many of the states, member of the Goal 3 panel, and key player in Goals 2000, proposes robbing school boards of their authority from above and below. National goals will determine the over-all direction of a school's curriculum, and the classroom teacher and school staff will have control over implementa-tion. According to Hornbeck, school boards can take care of hiring, firing, and budgeting, but "decisions regarding instruc-tional practices should rest with school-based staff...decisions regarding discipline and classroom management techniques should rest with school staff." He summarizes, "Whatever actual governance structure is ultimately adopted for site-based decision-making, I strongly recommend that majority authority rest with the teachers."[36]

By rewording contracts, teachers' unions have been trying to increase the autonomy of teachers in regard to materials and lessons as well as protect them from parental objections. A proposed master contract between the teachers' union and the San Dieguito Union High School District stresses the need for academic freedom for teachers. It would allow teach-ers much greater latitude to share controversial ideas and materials with protection from disciplinary action. It says, "A unit member may introduce lawful political, religious or other-wise controversial material, provided the said material is relevant to the course description and within the scope of the law." There are cautions about balance and against indoctrination, but it says, "In performance of certificated duties, a unit member may express his/her opinions on all matters relevant to the course description in an objective manner." Try to express an opinion objectively, and you'll detect the self-contradiction in that statement. This labor group of purveyors of knowledge will stop at nothing—even nonsensical declarations—to achieve their self-serving ends. The union's desire for teacher autonomy is reinforced by the clause stating, "This agreement shall supersede any rules, regulations or practices of the Board which are or may in the future be contrary to or inconsistent with its terms."[37]

The federal government and teachers' unions will effectively squeeze out parents, preventing them from having any input in what their children will be learning. Parents who previously utilized recourse to the school board and the electoral process will be left with none at all.

Teachers and Administrators are Forced to Jump Aboard

Under Goals 2000, teachers' opinions about the validity of outcome-based education will be irrelevant; they will all be trained or retrained to operate within the restructured system. The fourth national education goal of the House version of the legislation is politely phrased, "By the year 2000, the Nation's teaching force will have access to programs for the continued improvement of their professional skills and the opportunity to acquire the knowledge and skills needed to instruct and prepare all American students for the next century." The objectives, again, spell it out in more detail:

1) Every State will establish opportunity-to-learn standards

and create an integrated strategy to attract, recruit, prepare, retrain, and support the continued professional development of teachers, administrators, and other educators, so that there is a highly talented workforce of professional educators to teach challenging standards;

2) Subgrants for preservice teacher education and professional development activity will be made to local educational agencies, institutions of higher education, private nonprofit organizations, or consortia of such organizations, to support continuing, sustained, professional development activities for all educators; and

3) Partnerships shall be established, whenever possible, between local educational agencies, institutions of higher education, local labor, business, and professional associations to provide and support programs for the professional development of educators, particularly in the area of emerging new technologies in education.

We are already witnessing the coordination of all of these elements with universities, and their role in the restructuring of new programs (with at least some of the funding coming from Department of Education grants). Business groups like the Business Roundtable are financing "advisors" like David Hornbeck to redesign education, and business consortia are working together on the SCANS projects for school-to-work transitions. With the ongoing development of the national data system, linked to school-based data gathering, employers (and others) will be able to access the "life history" of potential employees.

Teachers will have to know how to teach to the new standards using outcome-based education techniques, but on top of that, they will be forced to be the middlemen for implementation of the much larger social restructuring agenda.

Many teachers stand in opposition to the new agenda. The Philadelphia Federation of Teachers opposes Outcome-Based Education and expressed its opinion in a letter written on November 20, 1992, to all Pennsylvania state senators. In the letter Jack Steinberg, Education Director of the Philadelphia chapter of the AFT, stated: "OBE should be a pilot project at best, and tested in several schools as a welcome addition to the existing Carnegie Units. It should not be implemented statewide because it could be a costly disaster. OBE is really non-graded schools and non-graded classrooms. It is a very dishonest approach to slipping this whole structure into place. Parents, teachers, and students have a right to honestly discuss these very important educational plans."[38]

At an October, 1992, school board meeting, Robert Paserba, superintendent of the Butler Area School District criticized the State Board of Education's school reform plan. He stated the reform recommendations could force curriculum standards down instead of improving them. He noted that studies and reports of similar reforms in other states show that schools there had lower levels of competency in basic skills requirements. ...He said that the reforms would very likely fail to accomplish the primary goal which was defined by the State Board of Education as improving student competency in skills.[39]

A Littleton, Colorado, high-school English teacher, Linda Young, tells us that English literature was dropped from the curriculum, and emphasis on literature in general was replaced by what she terms "skills" classes. She asks, "How can students who have been deprived of a solid background in great literature become good critical thinkers and good writers?" Linda was also concerned about the many demonstrations and assessments related to "non-academic areas such as community involvement, human relations, personal growth, and personal health" as well as the subjectivity of the program.

According to this teacher, loss of students and staff were byproducts of Littleton High's outcome-based education: "Littleton High School has to face a distressing loss of students, which many teachers attribute to our complex experimental program. Seventy-three students from next year's 9th-grade class have opted either to enroll in our two other high schools or to homeschool, and over 20 upper classmen have chosen not to return to Littleton High School. We will lose seven staff members."

Teachers face tremendous pressure to support restructuring efforts. Linda Young recounts the story of an orientation meeting for teachers where "a guest speaker from the State Department of Education told us that teachers who support change are 'gold teachers motivated by love,' while those who oppose change are 'mica teachers motivated by fear.' She relates that two fellow teachers from other schools told her that "in their schools, teachers are labeled as 'eagles' or 'vultures,' and as 'owls' or 'buzzards.'"

When Linda took a public stand against OBE, her school district attempted to fire her.[40] Dozens of dedicated teachers are caught in the same bind as Linda. If they criticize OBE, they might lose their jobs, yet the alternative is to participate in or actively implement programs that are a disservice to students. The situation for these teachers will become more difficult with the passage of Goals 2000, because school boards and local districts will be forced to follow the national goals and accompanying standards.

Meanwhile students are pawns in the game.

End Notes:

[1] *Summary Guide, The National Education Goals Report, Building the Best,* National Education Goals Panel Communications, Washington, D.C., 1993, foreword.

[2] William G. Spady, "Dispelling the Myths About Outcome-Based Reforms," paper presented under the title "In Defense of Outcome-Based Reforms" at the 1994 National Convention of the American Association of School Administrators and personal meeting with Spady, April 29, 1994, Garden Grove, CA.

[3] John Champlin and Peg Luksik, "Debate-Resolved: Outcome/Performance-Based Curricula Should Replace the Carnegie Unit." (audio cassette), National Association of Secondary School Principals, New Orleans, LA, Feb. 18-22, 1994.

[4] Ken Hazelip, "Outcomes Interview," *Outcomes* , Syracuse, NY, Network for Outcome-based Schools, Fall 1993, pp. 23-30.

[5] Researched and compiled by Peg Luksik, *To Tell the Truth: Will the Real OBE Please Stand Up?*, PA Parents Commission, Johnstown, PA 15907.

[6] "Transforming Schools for 21st Century Success" seminar presented by the High Success Network in Anaheim, CA, April 28-May 1, 1994.

[7] Goals 3 and 4 Technical Planning Group on the Review of Education Standards, *Promises to Keep: Creating High Standards for American Students*, Nov. 15, 1993, pp. 11,15,16.

[8] "Educational Outcomes and Indicators for Students Completing School," National Center on Educational Outcomes, The College of Education, University of Minnesota, Jan., 1993.

[9] Albert Shanker, "Where We Stand: Outrageous Outcomes," syndicated column, written under the auspices of the New York State United Teachers and the American Federation of Teachers, Washington, D.C., 1993.

[10] Gregory Cizek, "On the Disappearance of Standards," *Education Week*, Nov. 10, 1993, p. 32.

[11] Ibid.

[12] Kurt Vonnegut, "Harrison Bergeron," reprinted in *Adventures in Appreciation*, Harcourt Brace Jovanovich, New York, 1980, pp. 158-162.

[13] *Potential Strategies for Long-Term Indicator Development*, National Education Goals Panel, No. 91-08, Sept. 4, 1991, p. 44.

[14] Ibid., p. 48.

[15] Millicent Lawton, "Differing on Diversity, *Education Week*, Dec. 1, 1993, p. 24.

[16] *Potential Strategies for Long-Term Indicator Development*, National Education Goals Panel, No. 91-08, Sept. 4, 1991, p. 52.

[17] Robert Rothman, "Kentucky To Link Assessment Results to NAEP's Scores, *Education Week*, March 17, 1993, p. 22.

[18] *Gauging High Performance: How to Use NAEP to Check Progress on the National Education Goals*, National Education Goals Panel, Jan. 24, 1992, p. 8.

[19] Richard W. Paul, Ph.D., *Pseudo Critical Thinking in the Educational Establishment: A Case Study in Educational Malpractice*, Foundation for Critical Thinking, Santa Rosa, CA, 1993, pp. 29-30.

[20] *Integrated English-Language Arts Assessment: Secondary Level, 1991 CAP Field Test Collection*, California Department of Education, 1991.

[21] Debra Viadero, "RAND Urges Overhaul in Vt.'s Pioneering Writing Test," *Education Week*, Nov. 10, 1993, p.18.

[22] Criticisms of the new assessments should not be taken as a defense of the old, familiar standardized tests, which have their limitations. Those tests measure knowledge in a very limited way. Good guessers and

strategists might do better than the creative, original thinker, given equal intelligence levels. Many of the tests also do a poor job of judging a student's actual writing skills, a key component of present and future educational success. Nevertheless, the old tests are more credible because they are attempting to measure objective information.

[23] Lucia Mar School District, *"Lucia Mar Unified School District, Mission, Exit Outcomes and Philosophies,"*Arroyo Grande, CA, undated published statement resulting from a task force formed in November, 1989.

[24] Jayna Davis, *What Did You Learn in School Today?*, NewsChannel 4 video report, Oklahoma, 1993.

[25] Peg Luksik, *Luksik Live*, OBE: *Chaos or Correction?* [video].

[26] Jayna Davis, *What Did You Learn in School Today?*, NewsChannel 4 video report, Oklahoma, 1993.

[27] C-NET, *Up Close: Outcome-Based Education*, [video] Sept. 8, 1993

[28] Christopher Hill, "Outcome-Based Education the Type of Reform That Could Do Far More Harm Than Good," newspaper article reprinted in *To Tell the Truth*, researched and compiled by Peg Luksik, PA Parents Commission, Johnstown, PA.

[29] C-NET, *Up Close: Outcome-Based Education*, [video] Sept. 8, 1993.

[30] "Transforming Schools for 21st Century Success," seminar presented by The High Success Network in Anaheim, CA, April 28-May 1, 1994.

[31] Rev. Wayne C. Sedlak, "When 'Outcomes' Become 'Results'," *Free World Research Report*, March, 1993, p. 13.

[32] *Advanced Training Institute Handbook*, Advanced Training Institute, Oakbrook, IL, 1993.

[33] Commissioner of education in Vermont and chairman of the coordinating council for the National Alliance for Restructuring Education.

[34] Richard Mills, "The Roundtable," *Education Week Special Report*, April 21, 1993.

[35] E.D. Hirsch, Jr. *"Cultural Literacy: What Every American Needs to Know,"* Houghton Mifflin Co. Boston, MA, 1987.

[36] Hornbeck, David W., "First Draft of Recommendations on the Iowa Initiative for World Class Schools," Sept. 19, 1990, pp. 22-23.

[37] Master Contract between San Dieguito Faculty Association/CTA/NEA and San Dieguito Union High School District, Effective July 1, 1991, through June 30, 1994, pp. 43, 58.

[38] Arras, Betty, "Parents Battle Outcome-Based Education in Pennsylvania, Washington, and Wisconsin," *National Monitor of Education*, Alamo, CA, March, 1993, p.1.

[39] Ibid., p. 2.

[40] Linda Young, "FOCUS: OBE: Unsuccessful Experiment," *Education Reporter*, Nov., 1993.

CHAPTER FIVE

GOAL 3: COMPETENCY? WHAT DOES IT MEAN?

G oal 3 of the National Education Goals says, "By the year 2000, American students will leave grades four, eight, and twelve having demonstrated competency in challenging subject matter, including English, mathematics, science, foreign languages, civics and government, economics, arts, history, and geography; and every school in America will ensure that all students learn to use their minds well, so they may be prepared for responsible citizenship, further learning, and productive employment in our modern economy."

The wording of this goal is so broad that it leaves plenty of room for interpretation. A few more specifics about the intent can be gleaned from the list of objectives for Goal 3:

> 1) The academic performance of elementary and secondary students will increase significantly in every quartile, and the distribution of minority students in each level will more closely reflect the student population as a whole.

2) The percentage of students who demonstrate the ability to reason, solve problems, apply knowledge, and write and communicate effectively will increase substantially.

3) All students will be involved in activities that promote and demonstrate good citizenship, community service, and personal responsibility.

4) All students will have access to physical education and health education to ensure that they are healthy and fit.

5) The percentage of students who are competent in more than one language will substantially increase.

6) All students will be knowledgeable about the diverse multi-culturalism of this nation and about the world community.

Still, even the objectives, with their sweeping generalizations of "what will be," leave us foggy about the goal's intentions. What is meant by demonstrating the ability to reason— choosing what clothes to wear or solving calculus problems? Who can tell? What about demonstrating personal responsibility? Does that mean remembering to wear a jacket when it's cold, turning assignments in on time, or being an independent learner? To discover the real intent, we need to investigate further.

Outcomes

For specifics about what the goals mean, sources such as the National Center on Educational Outcomes (NCEO) give us a window to the underlying agenda, identifying many "out-comes" for the national goals.

A number of NCEO outcomes reflect closely the third goal. However, they are still fairly general: "Demonstrates competence in communication...Demonstrates competence in problem-solving strategies and critical thinking skills [this actually sounds very similar to the second objective]...Knows the significance of voting and procedures necessary to register and vote [which takes the third objective a step further]."[1] The NCEO is not the only organization developing outcomes. "At least 30 States have identified essential student outcomes, according to the National Association of State Boards of Education."[2]

While outcome statements vary in wording from state to state, they are all essentially tied to the national goals. We will see why shortly, but first let's compare outcomes from two states, both presumably coming up with these on their own.

Oklahoma Outcomes*	Kansas Outcomes*
Teachers establish high expectatons for learning and monitor student achievement through multiple assessment techniques.	Teachers establish high expectations for learning and monitor student achievement through multiple assessment techniques.

Oklahoma Outcomes (Cont.)	Kansas Outcomes (Cont.)
Schools have a basic mission which prepares the learners to live, learn and work in a global society.	Schools have a basic mission which prepares the learners to live, learn and work in a global society
Schools provide planned learning activities within an orderly and safe environment which is conducive to learning.	Schools provide learning activities within an orderly and safe environment which is conducive to learning.
Schools provide instructional leadership which results in improved student performance in an effective school environment.	Schools provide instructional leadership which results in improved student performance in an effective school environment.
Students have the communication skills necessary to live, learn and work in the 21st Century.	Students have the communication skills necessary to live, learn and work in a global society.
Students think creatively and problem solve in order to live, learn and work in the 21st Century.	Students think creatively and problem solve in order to live, learn and work in a global society.

Oklahoma Outcomes (Cont.)	Kansas Outcomes (Cont.)
Students work effectively both independently and in groups in order to live, earn and work in the 21st Century.	Students work effectively both independently and in groups in order to live, earn and work in a global society.
Students have the physical and emotional well-being necessary to live, learn and work in the 21st Century	Students have the physical and emotional well-being necessary to live, learn and work in a global society.
All staff engage in ongoing professional development based on the outcomes identified in the school performance plan.	All staff engage in ongoing professional development based on the outcomes identified in the school improvement plan.
Students participate in life-long learning as contributing members of a community of learners.	Students participate in life-long learning.
*from Draft-Oklahoma Outcomes for Educational Excellence Accreditation "A Plan for Living, Learning and Working in the Twenty-First Century."	*from Kansas Quality Performance Accreditation (3-12-91) "A Plan for Living, Learning and Working in a Global Society."

Notice the terms "communications skills," and "problem-solving" repeated in NCEO, Oklahoma and Kansas outcomes. And you have probably already observed that the outcomes from the two states are almost identical; the biggest difference is that Oklahoma uses the phrase "21st century" when Kansas prefers to employ "global society." The vocabulary sometimes differs from national level to state level, as well as from state to state (the above two examples being an exception), but the basic ideas are consistent. It would take an enormous amount of confidence in the science of coincidence to believe that this has happened by accident.

The outcomes, supposedly developed at the local level, in reality reflect the objectives of the national goals. Thousands of schools across the country have had nearly identical experiences in developing outcomes. Parents, teachers, and community members are all invited to a meeting where their input will be requested and heard. They break up into groups, each of which develops outcomes they consider important. The leaders praise and thank them, then later produce a list of the outcomes they announce were developed by consensus. Too often the outcomes proposed by the group are mysteriously absent, while those appearing in the leader's notebook are all present. Amazingly, even though each school comes up with outcomes that sound just like the school across town, across the state, and across the country, the leaders actually go on record with the claim that these outcomes are unique to this school.

Should we be surprised to find that all of the outcomes satisfy the national goals? The whole thing has been orchestrated at higher levels with foregone conclusions, but the process is used to fool the public into thinking that this is a grass roots movement.

The national goals panel is straightforward about its intentions, assuring us that they are "working to develop voluntary nationwide standards that challenge all learners and indicate levels of accomplishment in major academic subject areas. The standards are intended to provide reliable, practical benchmarks for your communities and schools. The Goals Panel and a soon-to-be-created National Education Standards and Improvement Council will provide a 'seal of approval' and a form of checks and balances to assure all Americans that the standards are, indeed, top-notch...To succeed as a nation, all of us—parents, educators, and other citizens—must use the standards as guides for improving their local schools."[3]

The "standards" are the measurement by which we can know how much of any outcome is enough, or the type of outcome that is acceptable. According to Goals 2000 legislation, states will voluntarily submit their standards to the National Education Standards and Improvement Council (NESIC) for approval in hopes of qualifying for funding under the numerous government programs. If the individual standards do not line up with the national goals, then no funding is secured. This procedure ensures that state standards will line up with those desired by the federal government.[4] Why should we be surprised when we see outcomes that look almost identical from state to state?

Takeover by the Feds

Because the federal government is forbidden by the Tenth Amendment[5] to the Constitution from intruding in areas not specifically delegated to it, the states have held control over education until recent years. The Tenth Amendment prohibits the federal government from dictating curriculum, operating methods, graduation requirements, and other elements of education. Authority over these areas is supposed to be retained by the states. The prohibition was reinforced in 1970 by Public Law 92-318, Sec. 432, which spelled out the "thou shalt nots" for the U.S. Department of Education in detail. "No provision of any applicable program administered by the U.S. Department of Education shall be construed to authorize any department, agency, officer, or employee of the United States to exercise any direction, supervision, or control over curricula, program of instruction, administration, or personnel of any education institution, school, or school system, or over the selection of library resources, textbooks, or other printed or published instruction materials by any educational institution or school system."

Nevertheless, the federal government has overcome the prohibition by acting as an instigator by funding experimental or demonstration projects which develop new curricula, by disseminating information, by using the "government pulpit" to advance ideas, and by funding education through programs supposedly instituted to help the disadvantaged. Goals 2000 and the standards movement are the newest stealth method in their approach to control education.

Goals 2000 drastically alters the federal role in education, even though the prohibitions still exist. Legislation is worded to make it sound like participation by states is "voluntary," a smoke screen to mislead states into thinking that they remain in control. Literature from the national goals panels verifies the controlling role the federal government intends for itself. States are permitted to develop their own standards, but those must encompass the standards approved by NESIC. State standards can be more numerous, but the minimum will be those dictated from the federal level. (Some standards advocates prefer to describe the system as "national" rather than "federal," hoping that it will appear to be separate from the government, but semantics do not change the facts.)

It boils down to the federal government manipulating their pawns, the states, to establish the same basic outcomes for all students. The result will be transfer of educational control to the federal level—nothing less than the nationalization of our schools.

State standards are involved in that they are intended to "drive the system." Linked to State assessment programs and/or curriculum frameworks, they compel restructuring of day-to-day instruction at the local level in keeping with the standards.[6]

The important issue of defining the school's mission is taken over by the federal government, and the goals panels are candidly explaining how it will work. "States and communities will determine the best route for providing necessary assistance to schools; they will write their own roadmaps for achieving the standards."[7] It is the same as telling a group of people, "You will all make pineapple upside-down cakes, but you are perfectly free to do it any way you want." This directive has no provision for those who don't like or want pineapple-upside down cake.

All but one of the various educational and governmental groups working on developing the national standards, as far as I can determine, are funded by the U.S. Department of Education.[8] Does anyone really believe that any of them might come up with standards that will run counter to the plan already outlined by the government?

The problems with state-level educational mandates have been numerous, but we must realize that federal control of education makes the situation much worse.

"Government-Approved Feelings"

According to the outcome goals being developed in many states (subject to federal approval, of course), the target outcome underlying them all is the achievement of a plan, as Oklahoma and Kansas put it, "for living, learning, and working in the 21st century/a global society." The federal push behind these strategies means that every personal aspect of a child's life—including his feelings—will be scrutinized and assessed by the federal government.

How does your child deal with the bully on the playground? How many friends does he have? Does he handle stress well? If he falls short in any of these areas (as judged by his teachers, not his parents), he is unlikely to meet the outcomes demanded of students under the new regime.

Much criticism has been leveled at the affective standards. Some of them are just plain "mushy." The National Center on Educational Outcomes proposes a number of "indicators" to be used as evaluation standards. For example, to determine if a student is demonstrating personal and social adjustment (deemed essential for good academic performance), they will look for the following very subjective indicators:

- Copes effectively with personal challenges, frustrations, and stressors
- Has a good self image
- Respects cultural and individual differences
- Gets along with people[9]

Since traditional curriculum was not designed for teaching or evaluating these skills, we see a shift toward substitution of self-esteem, multi-cultural programs, alternative lifestyle programs, and group interaction programs so that students can meet these new outcome indicators. Parents are concerned that time spent learning the new curricula is time taken away from learning reading, writing, science, and math.

Their concerns are confirmed by the National Education Commission on Time and Learning (a commission created by Congress) which released a report about how government schools use their time. "The report notes that most American students now spend only 41 percent of their school days on basic learning—math, science, history, English, geography, foreign language, the arts, and the like...the report emphasized that an increasing amount of students' time and teachers' attention is spent on 'social functions' of schools, in classes and activities mandated by government bodies that see schools as the key to solving a wide range of society's problems." Among those classes and activities are education about personal safety, consumer affairs, AIDS, conservation and energy, and family life.[10]

What remains of traditional academic standards, instead of reassuring us, serves to prove how much even academic standards have changed. Consider an Oklahoma outcome for first grade reading: "The student plans and monitors his own reading progress." Oklahoma second graders are supposed to "Use fix-it strategies in order to continue reading." Fix-it strategies include: "ask a friend, skip the word, substitute another meaningful word."[11]

New outcomes relating to skills such as creative thinking and problem solving are especially hard to define and are too vague as to whether or not a student has learned whatever was deemed necessary. Yet, they are prolific in most State outcome lists. For instance, how would it be determined whether a student is able to "think creatively and problem solve in order to live, learn, and work in a global society" (a Kansas outcome)?

Skills sufficient for life in an African tribal village would be vastly different from those needed for a technological job in the U.S. How is it determined what constitutes approved creative thinking and who decides whether the outcome has been met?

Dilution of the academic curriculum with numerous social objectives draws criticism from those who prefer emphasizing academic goals, and rightly so, but there is a deeper problem involved. Is it possible to measure such elements as "self image?" How much good self image should a student have? If a student is conceited, is there a penalty for having too much good self image? What about the person who gets along with everyone but is totally peer dependent? What about Sociable Sue who spends so much time with her friends that she doesn't have time for academics? A gang leader no doubt has refined excellent social skills, so does he get extra credit?

Peg Luksik, a vocal critic of outcome-based education from Pennsylvania, made a pertinent point in a debate. She was first challenged with the statement that there must be values upon which we all agree. Then the question posed to her was, "Wouldn't you agree that you want children to learn that democracy is better than totalitarianism?" Her answer was, "No. We don't want children to learn [this]. We want schools to teach that democracy is better than totalitarianism. Once we mandate a child believe it, [we] have totalitarianism." Peg summarizes the difference between traditional education and OBE: in the first system we teach the information, and in the second we require students to believe it.[12]

Social Engineering

All of this social engineering should make us return to the question of the purpose of public schooling addressed in Chapter

3. Again, many people, mostly parents, believe that public schooling is primarily intended to be for the good of the child.

Some educators work under that assumption, but historically, public education has clearly identified the goals and needs of the State as dominant over the needs of individual children. "A national system of education was advocated by many American intellectuals during the late eighteenth century, and most of them left no doubt that this education was to serve State interests. 'Let our pupil be taught that he does not belong to himself,' wrote Benjamin Rush in 1786, 'but that he is public property.'"[13]

This attitude was evident in the remarks of nineteenth century educators such as the Illinois superintendent of schools who said, "There is one thing that we should have learned from the nations of Europe in respect to public education... [A]ll their systems, such as they are, are conceived, designed, and carried out with direct and persistent reference to the maintenance and stability of the existing political order of the government. And so it must be with us."[14]

The U.S. Bureau of Education, in a 1914 bulletin, said, "The public schools exist primarily for the benefit of the State rather than for the benefit of the individual."[15]

The recurring theme is almost like a mantra and reveals how critical the issue has become—Do children belong to the State? Plato taught that children belonged to the State, to be trained for war, commerce, or government as the State required. More than two thousand years later, the Prussians affirmed State ownership of children, and that idea was implicit early on in our duplication of their system. However, until recently, few have been willing to openly acknowledge it.

Recently, the Association of California School Administrators, prompted by the movement behind the private school voucher issue, said, "Parents' choice proceeds from the belief that the purpose of education is to provide individual students with an education. In fact, educating the individual is but a means to the true end of education, which is to create a viable social order to which individuals contribute and by which they are sustained. 'Family choice' is, therefore, basically selfish and anti-social in that it focuses on the 'wants' of a single family rather than the 'needs' of society."[16]

No one asked the parents how they felt about the purposes of education, and most families would not agree with the description of their concerns about their children's education as selfish. Instead, they generally view encouragement of individual excellence in their children as a responsible exertion of parental influence.

In 1925, the Supreme Court affirmed the traditional view that parents have primary control over the type of education their children receive in the landmark *Pierce v. Society of the Sisters* case. The court's decision read:

> We think it entirely plain that the Act of 1922 unreasonably interferes with the liberty of parents and guardians to direct the upbringing and education of children under their control. As often heretofore pointed out, rights guaranteed by the Constitution may not be abridged by legislation which has no reasonable relation to some purpose within the competency of the State. The fundamental theory of liberty upon which all governments in this Union repose excludes any general power of the State to standardize its children by forcing them to accept instruction from public teachers only. The child is not the mere creature of the State; those

who nurture him and direct his destiny have the right, coupled with the high duty, to recognize and prepare him for additional obligations.

Peg Luksik strikes a chord with parents all over the country because she addresses this bottom-line issue. She says, "As I travel, parents nowhere want outcome-based education implemented, and the bureaucracy everywhere wants it implemented." In one presentation, she details a list of experimental education failures such as open classrooms, new math, and look-say reading. She additionally criticizes the educational bureaucrats who brush off parents by saying, "We're educators. We know best. Trust us." She receives spirited applause when she continues, "...we as parents, taxpayers, grandparents, community members, and rank and file teachers need to start saying to the bureaucrats, 'Excuse me. We are talking about my children and my money. And unless and until you can prove to me that you are this time going to behave in a responsible fashion with both, keep your hands off of them!'"[17]

Those who agree with whatever the goals of the State might be at any given time are unlikely to identify the goals of education as being manipulative or harmful for children. The conflict becomes obvious to those who do not identify or agree with the goals of the State. Then we have to counter the questions: Should the government be involved in social engineering? What happens to individual rights when the government dictates social policy, particularly through the school curriculum?

Consider the goals of nineteenth century America. The flood of Irish Catholics frightened the Protestants. So much so, that the public schools were given the task of Americanizing the immigrants into a Protestant mindset.

The Indians posed a similar problem. Not only were Indians slaughtered and driven from their homes, but they were subjected to the "benefits" of government education as well. The House Committee on Indian Affairs reported in 1818 that "in the present state of our country, one of two things seems to be necessary: either that those sons of the forest should be moralized or exterminated." Accordingly, a "Civilization Fund" was established in 1819 to educate the "savages." Indian education, under the control of the federal government, was used not only to eradicate vestiges of Indian culture, but to manipulate Indians into compliance with government programs such as the infamous massive Indian removals during the Jacksonian era.[18]

Today other minority groups face milder, yet nonetheless exhaustive, efforts to eradicate their cultural mores. Hispanic families who follow a patriarchal tradition often view higher education for females as a waste of time. Consequently, Hispanic girls frequently lack the motivation to even graduate from high school. From the broader American cultural perspective, this might seem wrong, yet, who are we to dictate feminist rhetoric on family structure to another culture?

Conforming Diversity

The current emphasis on diversity arrives on the scene with an ironic twist on the movement for social and political conformity. Conformity and diversity appear to be opposites, but conformity in this case means that everyone will accept the politically correct attitude on diversity, which is that all cultures and lifestyles must be accommodated and tolerated non-judgmentally. Any judgments reflecting attitudes that one culture or lifestyle might be better than another are unacceptable. Arnold Fege, director of the National PTA, adds a word of warning to this discussion of diversity: "We must, however, be prepared to limit our tolerance when it could lead to the creation of intolerant policy."[19]

Inclusion of controversial topics, supported by questionable materials for teaching diversity, has already created problems in schools nationwide. But with the implementation of programs to satisfy the sixth objective of Goal 3, it will become an explosive issue —"All students will be knowledgeable about the diverse cultural heritage of this nation and about the world community."

When a few students laughed during the wrong scenes while watching Spielberg's movie about the holocaust, *Schindler's List*, "Oppression Studies" were mandated for all, including the panacea for putting an end to offensiveness, sensitivity training.[20]

Ben Griffith, father of two daughters in a southern California school district, shared his personal confrontation over a "diversity" issue. He was so incensed by what happened in one of his daughter's classes and the lack of suitable response by the school that he requested an independent investigation of code violations to be done by an out-of-district source. The problem apparently began when his daughter was shown a film containing nudity and lesbianism in Drawing I class. The film was not approved by the district. In his written statement, Griffith says:

> After the movie the teacher told the class that the movie may not have been entertaining, but it was art. He said that their (meaning teenagers) form of art, movies like Rambo killing people, are B___ S___ and he would rather watch two women embrace than people being killed. He told the class that they needed to learn

things from a different perspective. My question is what does any of this trash have to do with Drawing I?

...The teacher told the class that yes, the movie was uncomfortable, but we sometimes learn from being uncomfortable. He also said that just because you're raised to think one way, it doesn't mean that another way is wrong.

When Mr. Griffith attempted to discuss the issue with the principal, he was put off. The school board was also unresponsive. After two months, he finally got a meeting with the teacher, the assistant superintendent of instruction, a union representative, an attorney-friend, and his wife. Griffith reported, "This accomplished absolutely nothing. In fact, during the meeting, the teacher had the gall to say that he feels part of his job is parenting. The assistant superintendent of instruction never did give an opinion on the movie. Two and half months later this movie still has not been reviewed by the board."

Ben Griffith's daughter, Stacy, relates: "One of my biggest problems...is that we are encouraged to state our opinions; and yet if our opinions have anything to do with morals, we are verbally called down by other students. This is seldom stopped quickly by teachers. An African/American has his rights, which is good. A homosexual has rights...and yet a student with old-fashioned values no longer has the right to state his or her opinion without being condemned."[21]

Some parents are concerned with more fundamental issues, such as which worldview will dominate the curriculum. Mark Foreman, a parent, wrote to the school board expressing a number of concerns:

I am writing to express my concern regarding the required reading curriculum for sophomore Honors English. I write both as a concerned parent and as a counselor. My degree is in Guidance and Counseling (M.Ed.), and I am currently enrolled in a Ph.D. program in Psychology. Specifically, my concern is regarding the books: *The Man Who Lived Under Ground, Catcher in the Rye, I Know Why the Caged Bird Sings, Waiting for Godot,* also the supplemental reading by Jung and Freud, *Man and His Symbols,* and *The Interpretation of Dreams,* respectively. I am even more concerned about the timeless classics that are not read. I have four issues to discuss: purpose, emotional effect, values, and academic excellence.

First of all, I am curious to know the designed purpose of this class. The required reading reminds me of the material I read as an undergraduate in Sociology. This literature seems to accomplish the purposes of exposing the students to alternative or unhappy lifestyles and promoting self-awareness. Such a purpose is appropriate for Social Behavior but not for English. I believe that the purpose for an English class should be exposure to great and timeless literature.

The emotional effect upon students is my second concern. Many of these books follow a negative, emotional theme: hopelessness, despair, and alienation. One book would suffice, but I question the wisdom of pointing impressionable adolescents in this depressive direction. Although these emotions are real, and I appreciate the existential "aloneness" that each person experiences, still, they are not the sum total of human emotions. Where is the joy and happiness that many teenagers need and would appreciate reading about?

My third concern is values. As a parent I monitor what my children are exposed to. For example, I don't as a rule allow them to watch an "R" rated film without first previewing the film. I know it is difficult for our minds to forget vivid images. Some of the scenes in these books are beyond what I want my son dwelling on. Furthermore, the worldview presented in these books is definitely one-sided. These books are existential in nature, dwelling on some existential themes common from the 60's to the present: absurdity, despair, alienation, and relativity. I am not for censorship, but neither am I for the promotion of only one particular perception of life. Timeless classics provide a variety of worldviews without promoting any one particular philosophy or worldview.

Finally, I desire my son to have a well rounded education. I applaud the proposed use of Dostoyevsky and Sophocles. However, I think it unfair for one person or committee to decide that an English course will have a certain philosophical or psychological bent in the books it chooses. Philosophy and psychology are not the expertise of the teacher and a little knowledge is sometimes dangerous. Furthermore, Freud and Jung, listed as supplemental authors, represent only a portion of psychological theory. If two theories are to be presented, then present them all so that the students don't interpret these two as authoritative.

I am not opposed to promoting self-awareness in students but I am concerned about who is guiding this self-awareness. An Honors English Course should provide an excellent, well-rounded literary preparation for the future, not a certain psychological approach or philosophical theme.

These are my concerns: purpose, emotional effect, values and academic excellence. I request that those who chose the curriculum and those who teach it re-examine your purpose and shift from this potential emotional harm to impressionable students by dwelling so much on introspective themes without objective hope. Turn from presenting simply an existential philosophy without alternate worldviews. Return to a well-rounded approach, teaching English which includes the classics. I don't know what awaits my son in college and the 21st century, but certainly, it will require knowledge of more than this limited approach to English literature.[22]

Mark Foreman received no response, nor has anything changed at the school.

Schools should know by now that when parents are ignored and their complaints dismissed as unimportant, instead of disappearing, they often become open antagonists of school administrators and board members. Parents want to have some control over what is happening to their children in school.

Many parents have banded together to form Citizens for Excellence in Education (CEE) chapters. Robert Simonds, president of CEE, says, "While claiming to teach our students critical thinking, schools have trained them in the anti-American principles of atheistic socialism. In the process, our nation has outdone even the Soviets in the subtle but systematic destruction of children's faith in God and their sense of right and wrong. Of course, this is done under the guise of 'neutrality' in religion and morals. CEE parents have had it! A national injustice is being done to children and their future families, which must be corrected."[23]

School Wars

Curriculum attacks have multiplied in recent years, coming from a vast array of sources. Many of the attacks are perceived as coming from the religious right, so much so that special conferences are held to help school boards and educators deal with groups that reflect this point on the political spectrum. Unfortunately, personal attacks—*ad hominem* arguments—rather than honest evaluation of the criticisms seem to be the norm at these conferences. Speakers such as Frosty Troy and Michael Hudson stir up animosity against public figures like James Dobson of Focus on the Family, using biting satire, innuendo, and undocumented accusations.[24] The result of such demagoguery is an "us" against "them" mentality that has contributed to what we might soon be calling the "School Wars."

The religious right is a popular bogeyman at the moment, but I have found that criticisms and complaints about school policies cross religious and philosophic boundaries. Mark Foreman's concerns are shared by parents from different religious perspectives. They have little to do with any one belief system but reflect a desire for a practical, balanced curriculum that is not psychologically dangerous.

The continuing barrage of curriculum attacks has made school administrators gun shy. The simplest parental request is viewed with suspicion and, very often, hostility. Even though parents are entitled to look at materials used in their children's classrooms, school personnel do not always support that right.

Kelley Watt never set out to cause trouble. She heard that the school district was adopting new math texts for her child's grade level, so she asked if she could be on the review committee. She was told, "No, there's already one parent representative on the committee." At the school another time to pick up her child, Watt noticed the newly adopted texts in piles in the hallway outside the classroom. She picked up a book and thumbed through it. The principal saw her and told her she could not look at the book. She saw no justification for his attitude and insisted upon her right. The principal responded, "Do you leave or do I call the police?" Mrs. Watt answered, "Call the police." The police came and forced her to leave the building.

Mrs. Watt then called the superintendent and school board members to complain. Recognizing that her request was legitimate, the superintendent arranged for her to review the books, not at her local school, but at a school two miles away, where she was observed the entire time. Ever since, when she speaks up about any issue at the school, her past confrontation is used to label her as a meddlesome troublemaker who has been in trouble with the police. Thus, her concerns are dismissed.

When parents are ignored and complaints are addressed with defensive strategies rather than consideration, school wars will be inevitable. One battle plan is for rebuffed parents to try to elect school board members who will promote and defend their own viewpoints. Other parents then feel threatened and counter with their own candidates.

In Vista, California, Christian parents were upset because their requests that evolution be presented as theory rather than proven fact were rejected. They decided to back a slate of school board candidates who would support the teaching of evolution as theory alongside the theory of creation. Their candidates won the election. Opponents feared that more than teaching about the origins of man was at stake, and their fears might be justified. The new school board approved a new sex education curriculum, called *Sex Respect*, that "limits dis-

cussion of homosexuality, masturbation and birth control."25
This same curriculum already faces challenges from homosexual activists, Planned Parenthood, and others who prefer that
all aspects of sexuality be taught in schools. Now, parents on
the other side of the fence are up in arms, concerned that
their children will be religiously indoctrinated.

What is the role of government in the education of children and who controls the development of purpose, agenda,
implementation, and assessment are still the foundational
questions in this whole debate. But time after time, the
defense strategy of the educational bureaucrats is *dismiss*,
attack, ignore, or *redefine* the terms. With little hope of gaining
allies among parents concerned about their children, it's no
wonder school administrators and teachers, often caught in
the middle, have opted to accept the system's war propaganda
as truth, even though many of them know better.

In Vista, the school wars have already begun, but skirmish-
es are erupting all over and, in all likelihood, at a school near
you.

End Notes:

1 "Educational Outcomes and Indicators for Students Completing School,"
    National Center on Educational Outcomes, University of Minnesota,
    pp. 12-13.

2 John O'Neil, "Schools Pushed to Restructure Around Student
    Outcomes," *Update*, ASCD, Vol. 34, No. 10., Dec., 1992, p.4.

3 *Summary Guide, The National Education Goals Report, Building the Best*,
    National Education Goals Panel Communications, Washington, D.C.,
    1993, p. 11.

4 Debate about what those standards will be has caused serious conflicts between various interest groups. The mathematics standards are widely accepted, but standards for other disciplines are not. *Education Week* regularly publishes articles about the ongoing debates.

5 The Tenth Amendment reads: "The powers not delegated to the United States by the Constitution, nor prohibited by it to the states, are reserved to the states respectively or to the people."

6 John O'Neil, "Schools Pushed to Restructure Around Student Outcomes," *Update*, ASCD, Vol. 34, No. 10., Dec., 1992, p. 4.

7 Goals 3 and 4 Technical Planning Group on the Review of Education Standards, *Promises to Keep: Creating High Standards for American Students*, Nov. 15, 1993, pp. 3,8.

8 *America 2000 Community Notebook: Creating a New Generation of American Schools*, pp. 317-319.

9 *Educational Outcomes and Indicators for Students Completing School*, National Center on Educational Outcomes, University of Minnesota.

10 "Flunking the Schools," *Orange County Register* (editorial), May 9, 1994.

11 Jayna Davis, "What Did You Learn in School Today?," NewsChannel 4 video report, Oklahoma, 1993.

12 Peg Luksik, "Understanding Outcome-Based Education: Goals and Response," audio tape from the 1993 National Christian Home Educators Leadership Conference, Williamsburg, VA.

13 George H. Smith, *Atheism, Ayn Rand and Other Heresies*, Prometheus Books, Buffalo, NY, 1991, p. 264.

14 Ibid.

15 Ibid., p. 265.

[16] Crowell, Royal D., "How California Schools Denumb a Child's Mind," *The Orange County Register*, Santa Ana, CA, Oct. 31, 1993, p. 1-2.

[17] Peg Luksik, Luksik Live, OBE: Chaos or Correction? [video], National Parents Commission, Johnstown, PA.

[18] George H. Smith, *Atheism, Ayn Rand and Other Heresies*, Prometheus Books, Buffalo, NY, 1991, p. 266.

[19] Arnold F. Fege, "A Tug-of-War Over Tolerance," *Education Leadership*, Dec. 1993/Jan. 1994, p. 23.

[20] Michelle Malkin, Will the Age of Oppression ever end?," *The Orange County Register*, Feb. 14, 1994.

[21] Quotes from letters by Ben Griffith and Stacy Griffith.

[22] Quoted from letter written by Mark Foreman.

[23] Robert L. Simonds, "A Plea for the Children," *Education Leadership*, ASCD, Dec. 1993/Jan. 1994, p. 12.

[24] Tapes from I.D.E.A. conference, Denver, CO, 1993.

[25] "New Sex Education Program: Just Say No," *Orange County Register*, May 7, 1994.

CHAPTER SIX

PRISONERS OF THE SYSTEM

"Son, your mother and I have decided that you are going to learn to play the clarinet. We have decided that it will take you ten years to learn, so you will not be allowed to do anything else from 8:30 in the morning until 2:00 in the afternoon on weekdays. We will allow occasional vacations and sick days, but if you try to skip any other days, you will be in serious trouble. We also require that you demonstrate a positive attitude about learning the clarinet and prove to us that you have developed a life-long love for the instrument."

If parents treated their children this way, social workers would be pounding on the door, ready to defend the rights of the child quicker than police responding to a burglary call. And you can bet they would get support from the public for going after such abusive parents.

Substitute the words "math," "writing," "science," or other school topics for "the clarinet," and we have our modern school system. Strangely, few are concerned about child abuse in the classroom, because most of us believe that math, writing, science, etc., are important to learn and that the clarinet is optional.

Most parents would probably require their children to learn something about these subjects even if schools did not exist. So the fact that government schools have been "locking up" our children until they finish their learning has not seemed too offensive. Probably, many parents saw government schooling as taking a load off their shoulders, especially in the early days of public education.

When the schools change those words from "math," "writing," and "science," to "self-esteem," "environmental responsibility," and "good citizenship," parents are suddenly reacting negatively. They never asked the schools to teach this stuff. They want schools to teach the academic subjects. Angry parents are bad for public relations, so schools are busy trying to soothe parents' concerns. But has anyone stopped to ask students how they feel about all of this? Not likely. Many of us believe that parents have authority over their children, and that they have the right to require that their children do things that they might prefer not to do. In fact, many parents believe that parents have a responsibility to train children in responsibility, diligence, and perseverance, and they see the traditional work ethic of schooling as a means of instilling those qualities. Even if parental authority over children in the area of education is remanded over to the schools, we have to recognize the change that takes place under restructuring and OBE.

The student role in the scenario is going to be in a far different position than it has been up until now. Let's start with taking a look at the past to see why. Students have been forced to go to school ever since compulsory schooling laws were passed in the 1800s. Before compulsory schooling, education was viewed as a privilege, even though not all children thought learning a joy. Compulsory schooling laws removed the concept of privilege, because schooling was judged to be an experience to which all children must submit for a minimum amount of time. The classification as a privilege changed when the option to be involved was removed.

Children have been prisoners of the educational system ever since. Yet, until now, under compulsory schooling, the learner could still choose whether or not to absorb whatever was being served by the educational establishment. He retained the right to control his own mind. He could serve his time unwillingly, then be free, whether or not anything "stuck." Even though resistance was painful in the days of switches and rods, the learner retained the right to remain uneducated.

The learner loses that right under Goals 2000. And he loses it not to his parents but to the educational bureaucracy.

The new assumption is that "everyone...is capable of reaching the standard...[S]tandards will set targets for what all students should know and be able to do."[1] During a Goals 2000 Satellite Town Meeting hosted by Deputy Secretary of Education Madeleine Kunin, panelists "stressed that the core of the reform efforts is the agreement that all students can learn at higher levels."[2]

Most people react positively to statements like "all children can learn," because they sound compassionate and accepting of even the slowest learners. While, in all but the truly exceptional cases, children possess the ability to learn, the truth is that learning is something a learner *chooses* to do or not to do. The best learners are generally those who choose to learn. If a student chooses not to learn, we can attempt to motivate him. However, if motivation is insufficient, all that remains is coercion.

While educators are saying students can learn, what they really mean is that students *will* learn or face harsher consequences than choosing not to learn ever brought before. The chronological element will be removed, so serving a sufficient amount of time will no longer gain the student a diploma and release from the system. Students will now have to meet performance objectives before they are released. Compulsory schooling laws might still permit students to drop out at certain ages, but the option will be hollow, because a certificate proving that the student has met the standards will be required for higher education and, quite likely, for entering the job market. No certificate, no job. If students choose to opt out of the system they will cut themselves off from higher education options within the system, and they might well find themselves unemployable.

Realizing that such threats are still not enough to motivate some students, many states have considered, and some have passed, laws tying driver's licenses to school attendance. One newspaper reported that "Under Kentucky's optional 'high school dropout law' of 1990, students who quit school, have nine or more unexcused absences, or become 'academically deficient' (by failing to pass at least four of their classes) lose the right to drive unless they can prove family hardship." In 1993, 2,676 students lost their driver's licenses under the law.[3]

The school-to-work transition will be addressed in a later chapter, but the problem we need to examine is the assumption that the government can coerce not just attendance but learning. We are not arguing here the idea of whether or not all children are *able* to learn, but the shift from recognizing ability to requiring action. When those actions include demonstrating acceptance or approval of values, attitudes, or beliefs, we have moved far beyond the traditional education system.

In the Soviet Union, dissidents who had politically incorrect attitudes or beliefs were shipped off to Siberia to be "reconditioned." In the United States, we won't wait for children to turn into adult dissidents. We will make sure that they are "properly conditioned" before they grow up.

We, as a society, bought the idea that the government can coerce attendance (although many individuals still reject that idea), but we have balked at mind-manipulation. Yet, if we require students to meet affective outcomes before they can get their Certificates of Mastery, we effectively will be imprisoning both body and mind.

Even if we were not dealing with affective outcomes, but simply wanted to improve academic learning, would requiring more compulsory schooling be an effective way to accomplish that?

Spending More Time in Prison?

Requiring students to remain in school is hardly likely to improve the amount of learning that takes place. Memories of our own schooling experience should shatter that misconception. A few students will appreciate options where they can work and receive job training in place of some of their high-school classes. However, many students will still rebel at coerced attendance.

Dennis Evans, associate director of the Department of Education at UCI, California, says, "Schools are simply not seen as good places to be. Rather, as in Philadelphia, they are considered on a par with a police holding tank; a form of punishment; a way of reducing street crime." Evans is one of the few educators to question the very nature of compulsory schooling. He comments: "Sometimes, when things seem crazy and everything is going wrong, a good approach is to stop doing what you're doing and try the opposite!" Evans suggests that instead of requiring attendance of disruptive high school students, they be told that they *cannot* attend unless they agree to abide by the rules.[4]

Private schools have been doing this for years, and the effectiveness of such a policy is obvious. Yet, public schools are forced to corral even the most reluctant students into their classrooms, which downgrades the learning process for everyone else. Students are also getting a very mixed message about the value of schooling. Many of them ask, "If school is so good for us, why do you have to force us to be here?"

Few in the educational establishment or government are listening to Evans or others who raise questions about the value of compulsory schooling laws. Instead, they seem to be looking for ways to expand the length of time they can retain students within the system.

A recent First Circuit U.S. Court of Appeals' ruling seems to open the door for K-12 educational agencies to continue to provide educational services to adult students. Although the case itself dealt with a retarded student, the ruling itself says "disabled students"—a vague term that can readily be interpreted as learning disabled students, which can be used to encompass most students who need more time to learn. The court opinion said, "In order to give meaning to a disabled student's right to an education between the ages of 3 and 21, compensatory education must be available beyond a student's

21st birthday...Otherwise, school districts simply could stop providing services to older teenagers..."5

Oregon leads the way in opening the door for older students to receive government-paid education. Oregon's Educational Act for the 21st Century states that the "Certificate of Initial Mastery shall be required for entry into college preparatory and academic professional technical programs..." Recognizing that it will be difficult for some students to earn their certificates within the normal number of years, they are instituting learning centers that students can attend at government expense until age twenty-one.

The Association for Supervision and Curriculum Development, an NEA spinoff organization that is one of the key players in formulating education policy, advocates that the federal government expand its educational funding for both younger and older students. They support "funding of early childhood education, which includes nursery school, pre-kindergarten, full day kindergarten, and the primary grades." They also state that, "U.S. public education should be extended to include two years of post-high school education supported by federal, state, and local governments."6

It is very likely that we will soon have longer school days and longer school years as well as more years of schooling for each child. Parents will be encouraged to spend less and less time raising their own children. Families that crave more time together will find it more and more difficult to carve out that time from the few hours when children are not under government care. Family trips, soccer games, or whatever priorities families have rightly assumed will play second fiddle to the school's plans for students.

Values and Mental Coercion

While many of the troublesome issues with Goals 2000 are practical (Does it work? Does it cost too much?), the most problematic are those relating to values, cutting to the heart of parental rights. It is impossible to teach children without values becoming part of the picture in one way or another. For example, teachers uphold the value of honesty by forbidding students to copy each other's work. They condemn stealing when Johnny has to give back the pencil he stole from Christy.

However, parents do not want to send their children to school to have the value systems of the home undermined. When schools move beyond common values, into areas of value conflict, parents rightfully object. With an increasingly diverse population, values conflicts are becoming more and more common, even on the most basic issues, because any value system depends upon a philosophical foundation for its existence. That foundation answers the question, "Why does it matter?" If we teach children that it is wrong to lie, they want to know why. After all, sometimes lying saves them a lot of personal grief. We cannot even agree on honesty as a basic value, because some people believe that truth is relative, while others believe that there is such a thing as absolute truth. Yet the schools have no common philosophical foundation to provide the "why" answers for values. This baseless approach to values should make us very cautious when it becomes part of the curriculum.

When we look at some of the standards or indicators, realizing that students will not be allowed to escape from the school system without demonstrating mastery according to the educational establishment's definition, the values compulsion is obvious. The National Goals Panel "recommended three indicators for assessing citizenship. These were community service, voter registration of 18-to 20-year-olds, and knowledge of citizenship."[7]

In 1992, the Goal 3 Planning Subgroup recommended that the federal government use funding to reward states that developed systems for collecting data on community service. States that formerly saw no need for requiring community service suddenly decided that this was an essential part of schooling.[8]

We have already seen the results of this recommendation as many states and school districts throughout the country have made mandatory community service a graduation requirement. However, students in Bethlehem, Pennsylvania, sued the Bethlehem School District because they felt that it was unconstitutional for the school to force them into "involuntary servitude" and to require them to demonstrate a belief in the value of altruism. Their case was rejected. They will not graduate, no matter how good their grades, without having served their "mandatory volunteer" time.[9] As is usual when dealing with bureaucratic language, the form that community service takes is acceptable only on the school's terms. A student opting to satisfy that indicator by volunteering at a crisis pregnancy center, a church library, or on a building project mission team may find her time counted as unworthy. She might instead be compelled to be a volunteer in another community service project that is politically correct but inconsistent with her personal beliefs.

To check on voter registration, Goals Panel members decided that since many eighteen-year-olds are still in school, they will collect information on voter registration through the schools. Apparently, if a person chooses not to register to vote for ideological reasons, he is not exhibiting good citizenship.

Does this mean he cannot graduate? A freedom to abstain, long held precious in this country, could now hold a diploma hostage.[10]

Another interesting insight on what the citizenship requirement means comes from the Pennsylvania *Educational Quality Assessment (EQA)*, a test which has aroused vigorous parental opposition. The fifth goal of the EQA says "Quality education should help every child acquire the habits and attitudes associated with responsible citizenship." The rationale: "Responsible citizenship embodies a much more complex concept than commonly expressed in love of country and participation in the democratic processes. Viewed in its broadest sense, responsible citizenship implies a respect for law and proper authority, a willingness to assume responsibility for our own actions and for those of the groups to which we belong, respect for the rights of others and overall personal integrity."

The meanings applied to all of these behaviors can be relative to the district, the school, the classroom, or the teacher, and in light of the bureaucratic tendency to ascribe different meanings to words and phrases than the average person does, they should be clarified. However, the only item addressed in the following explanatory paragraph is the part about assuming responsibility for group actions.

It says, "Schools should encourage pupils to assume responsibility for their actions as well as the actions of the group. Opportunities should be provided for pupils to cooperate and work toward group goals and to demonstrate integrity in dealing with others. Pupils should be given the chance to take the initiative and assume leadership for group action as well as lend support to group efforts as followers." The clarifying language still leaves much to be desired.

One sample question in the assessment shows how testing for "citizenship" occurs: (A situation is described) "There is a secret club at school called the Midnight Artists. They go out late at night and paint funny sayings and pictures on buildings. A student is asked to join the club. In this situation, I would JOIN THE CLUB when I knew..." Following are three conditions: "1. My best friend asked me to join; 2. Most of the popular students were in the club; 3. My parents would ground me if they found out I joined." For each condition, students indicate "Yes," "Maybe," or "No."[11] Apparently, students who say *no* to the first two and *yes* to the third are not demonstrating a concern for group goals, so their citizenship "grades" drop.[12]

The Amish provide a classic example of a culture affected by values coercion. In 1968, in Wisconsin, three Amish fathers were arrested for failing to enroll their three children (two aged fifteen, one aged fourteen) in high school. Wisconsin law required attendance until the sixteenth birthday, but the Amish believed that their children should not attend public schools past eighth grade.

> The problem of Amish education is a clash between those who advocate the forced assimilation of minority cultures such as the Amish, and those who seek to maintain the identity and integrity of the cultural diversity in a pluralistic America; it is a clash between those who assert that the majority and the state bureaucracies should define approaches and values, and those who hold that progress and truth are best found when freedom and diversity prevail. Tied closely to this is the issue of the theoretical basis and the limits of a state's power to compel its citizens to get an education and conform to its values.[13]

The Amish wanted to raise their children to embrace their spiritual values, to be good and wise people. They shunned popular culture, technology, pride, and ambition. Attorney for the Amish, William B. Ball, said, "The State wants to enter the minds of the Amish young people, expose them to worldly education, fill up their minds with State-packaged learning, alien to the Amish way, threatening the privacy of their psyche, and causing a painful personality restructuring by placing them in a high school which places the stress upon competition, ambition, consumerism and speed."[14]

The Amish teens were excused from the compulsory attendance law in this case, which went to the U.S. Supreme Court (*Wisconsin vs. Yoder*), but the court was careful to point out that "the decision was based on the claim of religious belief— not philosophical, personal, secular, or cultural values."[15] So while the court extended limited protection of rights on religious grounds, it denied them for any other reasons. Those who have educational philosophies contrary to that of the government or those who hold value systems out of the mainstream are still captive to compulsory schooling laws.

Contrasting the Amish view of education with that of the American Association of University Women (AAUW) serves to highlight some extremes. Amish views of education for girls are even more out of step with the mainstream than are their views about young men. The Amish believe that young women need to be trained to maintain a household and care for their families. The idea of their daughters being trained to leave the Amish community to seek work in high tech industry is unacceptable.

The AAUW counters, "Girls must be educated and encouraged to understand that mathematics and the sciences are important and relevant to their lives. Girls must be actively supported in pursuing education and employment in these areas."[16] Since the AAUW promotes the implementation of their viewpoint in education and finds support in the National Goals,[17] the Amish are put in the untenable position of being forced to send their daughters to schools that teach them a fundamentally different view of their role.

Mandating acceptance of values is a violation of individual freedom. The value of tolerance (a word that shows up often in lists of goals) in today's politically correct society might be promoted in a situation similar to what occurred at a London school. A charity offered discounted tickets to students to see "Romeo and Juliet" at Covent Garden. Their headmistress refused the offer because the play is a "blatantly heterosexual love story." She said,"...until books, film and theater reflected all forms of sexuality, she would not be involving her pupils in heterosexual culture."[18] In the U.S., parents might have been in the strange position of suing because the school was teaching intolerance of heterosexuality. Truth be told, such a situation is all too plausible in our country.

Outcomes relating to diversity and tolerance appear in most states. For example, Arkansas requires that all students should develop a sensitivity to and an understanding of the needs, opinions, concerns, and customs of others." Statements like this too often translate at the political level into demands for the normalization of the homosexual lifestyle, which some people see as morally unacceptable.[19]

A Kentucky outcome demands the student "maintains an open mind to alternative perspectives."[20] Ohio's second goal under socials studies is "to enable learners to...exhibit respect for individual and cultural diversity."[21]

Such "outcomes" or goals are defended by many, naively so, because anything more than a general tolerance is unimag-

inable. They reject the notion that any sort of politically correct attitudes are involved. However, numerous examples to
the contrary abound.

Jamestown High School in Pennsylvania required
eleventh graders to take a mind-bending quiz with the following true-or-false questions (correct answers are in brackets):

1. In order to be part of a family, you have to be related to
   other people by blood, marriage, or adoption. [F]
2. You're not part of a family unless you and the other
   members live in the same house. [F]
3. A couple isn't really a family unless they have children.
   [F]
4. College roommates (two people of the same sex) could
   be considered a family. [T]
5. If a young person is living with his parents and sister but
   doesn't feel the group shares love, trust, and respect,
   then according to our definition, he doesn't really have
   a family. [T]
6. A family is a group of people who work together, solve
   problems and who never argue. [F]

In a "Life Stress Inventory" given to New York fourth
graders, various emotional events are given numerical stress
values. According to the inventory, pregnancy of a family
member (most likely to be the mother) is more stressful
than being robbed, feeling threatened (trouble with a bully
or a gang), or the death or serious illness of a close friend.
What message does that send to fourth graders regarding
pregnancy?

In Iowa, some high-school students were given the
Bettendorf Survey. The order in which questions are presented
tips us off that this survey is designed to elicit politically cor-

rect answers. It begins by asking, "Are you male or female?" and "What year are you?," followed immediately by "Do you regard yourself as a bigot?" The question about bigotry is succeeded by the following (in order):

Do you think homosexuality is a problem society must deal with as strictly as possible?

Do you think people are born homosexual or do you think they choose to be homosexual?

Do you think everyone who wishes to become a United States citizen should be made to speak a minimal/functional amount of the English language?

Do you think the United States was stolen from native Americans or do you think it was rightfully colonized by Europeans?

Have you ever rolled up your car windows in a predominantly minority neighborhood?

Have you ever rolled up your windows in a predominantly poor white neighborhood?

A Simplicity Survey was given to an Iowa high-school English class at the beginning and end of a unit in order to record any change in beliefs and attitudes. It said, "The statements below describe actions that have actually been taken by families and/or individuals in an attempt to simplify their lives. Assume that you are now about age 35 with or without a family. To determine to what degree you would commit yourself (and your family, if you have one) to 'voluntary simplicity,' indicate with an X in the appropriate square...." [Selected questions follow.]

I and/or my family will own no more than three sets of clothes and three pair of shoes per person.

I and/or my family will own only one automobile.

I will deliberately limit myself and /or my family to fewer material things than my family had while I was a teenager.

I will avoid working for any company that is so large that I cannot personally know the owner.

My family will have no more than two children.

My family and/or I will eat less meat, more [unclear in original]
vegetables and fruits, and no white sugar.

To save wild animals from extinction my family and/or I will
never wear fur or ornamental objects taken from these animals."[22]

Such surveys are blatant evidence that there is an agenda
behind the outcomes or goals, provoking confrontations over
whose views are correct.

Continual confrontations over values and intrusion into
personal areas prompted parent advocates to fight successfully
for protective language within Goals 2000. They were able,
through the Grassley Amendment, to amend Section 439 of the
General Education Provisions Act (20 U.S.C. 1232g) to allow
parents or guardians to inspect all resources used in connection
with any program funded by the U.S. Department of Education.
P.L. 103-227, Sec. 1017 amends Section 439 as follows:

(a) All instructional materials, including teacher's manuals,
films, tapes, or other supplementary material which will
be used in connection with any survey, analysis, or evaluation as part of any applicable program shall be available for inspection by the parents or guardians of the
children.

(b) No student shall be required, as part of any applicable
program, to submit to a survey, analysis, or evaluation
that reveals information concerning—

(1) political affiliations;

(2) mental and psychological problems potentially embarrassing to the student or his family;

(3) sex behavior and attitudes;

(4) illegal, anti-social, self-incriminating and demeaning behavior;

(5) critical appraisals of other individuals with whom respondents have close family relationships;

(6) legally recognized privileged or analogous relationships such as those of lawyers, physicians, and ministers; or

(7) income (other than that required by law to determine eligibility for participation in a program or for receiving financial assistance under such program), without the prior consent of the student (if the student is an adult or emancipated minor), or in the case of an unemancipated minor, without the prior written consent of the parent.

(c) Educational agencies and institutions shall give parents and students effective notice of their rights under this section.

The amendment also allows students to withhold personal information about themselves or their families. The catch is that the reviewable offensive programs (i.e., tests, surveys, resources, etc.) must have some connection to a federally funded program. States can, at present, ignore protests against intrusion and deny these guarantees of family and personal freedom in the majority of cases. (Passing legislation in each state that parallels the federal language should be a priority!) Meanwhile, Goals 2000 and Reauthorization of the Elementary and Secondary

Education Act, together comprising the carrot and stick approach, will force states to implement their own state-level programs to conform all students to the politically correct agenda.

A No-Win Situation For Public Schools

Battles continue to wage about the classroom practices leading to values conflicts, and they head the list of complaints about educational reform. Yet, public schools are in a no-win situation. Take the issue of multi-culturalism. Some parents object to their children being taught about the value systems of other cultures without some input on their validity. For instance, consider a lesson on an African culture that believes in many gods. The teacher is in a bind no matter what she does. If she comments on the possible falsehood of that belief she, will offend those who prefer that the belief be presented as valid. If she teaches that the belief in many gods is valid, she offends those who want their children to be taught that there is only one God or those who believe there is no God at all. If she makes no comment, she offends both who want their positions supported.

When schools select one set of values and require students to demonstrate acceptance of those values, the results will never satisfy, or even be accepted, by all. But the schools themselves are trapped. If they choose to take the cowardly way and teach no values at all, they are still in trouble. By opting to teach no values, as they have attempted to do in recent years, they send students the message that values themselves are not to be valued.

Children Caught in a Double Bind

Those who hold to the idea that it is appropriate for the State to determine which values will be taught have ignored the harm to children that occurs when they must sort out conflicting "truths" espoused by parents and teachers.

Consider this situation. Joe and Mary believe in being truthful with their children. They take this principle further than do most parents. They teach their children that Santa Claus and the Easter Bunny do not exist. In kindergarten class, their daughter Susie is handed a picture of Santa Claus to color. To the dismay of her teacher, Susie blurts out the truth taught to her by her parents. The other children still believe in the myth and turn to the teacher in desperation, so the teacher decides that she needs to defend their "innocence." She explains to the class that Santa Claus really does exist, but some people like to celebrate Christmas in different fashions. Susie's parents have simply chosen an alternative form of celebration. Poor Susie is now totally confused; the only part of the lesson that sank in was the rejection of her parents' "truth" by her beloved and all-knowing teacher. Who is right? Is this one of those deep things that only grownups understand?

Come Halloween and Easter, the problem gets worse as Susie has to sort out the reality of witches and the Easter Bunny. Pretty soon, Susie has learned that truth is one of those things that changes from person to person and experience to experience. Trapped in the chaos of relative thinking, the lesson transfers over into her moral life. Some of her friends think it is okay to shoplift, and others don't. Susie sorts out the conflict by only shoplifting when she is with friends who approve. And anyone who thinks the moral question of shoplifting will be the only conflict she will face as a result of this thinking is terribly deluded or naive.

Take this issue to the deeper level of fundamental world-views. A child is being taught a particular belief system at home and a conflicting one at school. Belief systems themselves, under such biased scrutiny, become unbelievable. A Muslim girl attending public school has to deal with the dress and behavior of her female classmates that is immoral according to the views of her parents. She desperately wants to be friends with other girls but finds the morality barrier a major obstacle. How long can she operate, torn between the need for friendship and the need to abide by her parents' teaching on morality?

A Christian boy is taught at home that the Bible is the source of all truth. The Bible tells him about the story of creation, the fall of man, and the need for salvation. School tells him that he is the result of accidental chemical and biological encounters. He learns that sin is only another name for self-imposed guilt, and that man can continually improve himself, reaching higher levels of consciousness and harmony with the universe. These issues deal with the purpose of existence and the fundamental decisions we make in life, and yet they are trivialized to the level of schoolroom lessons. Prisoners in this values-washing system, children from homes with conflicting worldviews resist the pit of relativity only if their parents' words reach more fertile ground than their teachers'.

When faced with totally irreconcilable worldviews, children can react in numerous ways. Some might reject all truth. Some will decide that they will determine their own truth. Some will reject the truth taught by their parents. Some will reject the truth taught by the school. Some will be easy prey for persuasive cultists who offer them answers they can live with. Some will try to escape the conflict via drugs or alcohol. Some will find the conflicts so unsettling that they become mentally unbalanced.

Many parents are alarmed because too often their children are choosing to believe the school truth and reject family values and beliefs. Sometimes that choice is not evident until the teen years, when it shows up as rebellion.

The schools may elicit sympathy because of the no-win situation they find themselves in, but parents, too, are put in an impossible situation. Author Thomas Sowell summarizes the situation:

> Parents who send their children to school with instructions to respect and obey their teachers may be surprised to discover how often these children are sent back home conditioned to disrespect and disobey their parents. While psychological-conditioning programs may not succeed in producing the atomistic society, or the self-sufficient and morally isolated individual which seems to be their ideal, they may nevertheless confuse children who receive very different moral and social messages from school and home. In short, too many American schools are turning out students who are not only intellectually incompetent but also morally confused, emotionally alienated, and socially maladjusted.[23]

End Notes:

[1] The National Education Goals Report 1993, p.186.

[2] "Sweeping Changes in Kentucky Schools Aim to Help Students Reach High Standards," *Community Update*, U.S. Department of Education, Dec. 1993, Jan. 1994.

[3] Simson L. Garfinkel, "Big Brother at the Wheel," *Orange County Register*, April 3, 1994.

[4] Dennis L. Evans, "Treating Schools Like Police Holding Tanks," *Education Week*, Feb. 9. 1994, p. 46.

[5] Sara Sklaroff, "Adult Eligible for Special-Ed. Services, Court Finds," *Education Week*, Dec. 8, 1993, p.6.

[6] *Developing Leadership: A Synthesis of ASCD Resolutions through 1993*, Association for Supervision and Curriculum Development, Alexandria, VA 22314, 1994, pp. 3-4.

[7] *Assessing Citizenship: The Goal 3 Technical Planning Subgroup on Citizenship*, National Education Goals Panel, July 31, 1992, p 2.

[8] Ibid, p. 6.

[9] Aaron Epstein, "Forced community service likened to slavery," *Philadelphia Inquirer*, Philadelphia, PA, April 4, 1993.

[10] *Assessing Citizenship: The Goal 3 Technical Planning Subgroup on Citizenship*, National Education Goals Panel, July 31, 1992, p 7.

[11] EQA Test, Section H, Goal V Citizenship, pp. 19-20.

[12] Test notes from the Pennsylvania Coalition for Academic Excellence.

[13] Dwight W. Allen and Jeffrey C. Hecht, *Controversies in Education*, W.B. Saunders Co., Philadelphia, PA, 1974, pp. 488-495.

[14] Ibid.

[15] Ibid., p. 493.

[16] "Gender Bias in American Schools: Problems and Solutions," from the AAUW Report: *How Schools Shortchange Girls*, American Association of University Women, Washington, D.C., 1994.

[17] The third objective of the fifth goal says, "The number of U.S. undergraduates and graduate students, especially women and minorities, who complete degrees in mathematics, science, and engineering will increase significantly."

[18] "'Romeo and Juliet too heterosexual?," *The Register*, Santa Ana, CA, Jan. 20, 1994.

[19] "Arkansas Learner Outcomes: A Vision for Outcomes-Based Education," Arkansas Department of Education, Sept., 1991.

[20] Kentucky's Outcomes, Excerpt from the *September 1989 Technical Report of the Council on School Performance Standards*.

[21] November 2 Draft of the "New State Model Curriculum for Social Studies," Ohio Department of Education.

[22] The above examples are all taken from *Preparing America's Children for the 21st Century*, compiled by PA Parents Commission, Johnstown, PA 15907, 1994.

[23] Thomas Sowell, *Inside American Education*, The Free Press, NY, 1993, p. x.

CHAPTER SEVEN

THE HEALTH EDUCATION CONNECTION

Grade school girls—that is, pre-teen girls—practice putting condoms on bananas. Chaste teenagers have to view pictures and descriptions of deviant sexual practices. Family values regarding sexual activity are undermined.

It's old news that these are the realities of health education today, which no longer concentrates on proper nutrition, exercise, and basic physical functioning. A powder keg with the potential to explode family values and parents' rights to pieces lies in wait for a match. Goals 2000 is johnny-on-the-spot. The health arena claims an important role in Goals 2000, mentioning intervention in a number of places.

The fourth objective of Goal 3 says, "All students will have access to physical education and health education to ensure that they are healthy and fit." The third objective for Goal 7 says, "Every school district will develop a comprehensive K-12 drug and alcohol prevention education program. Drug and alcohol curriculum should be taught as an integral part of health education. In addition, community-based teams should be organized to provide students and teachers with needed support..."

Though the National Goals outline the program, they don't stand on their own. Several additional pieces of legislation, such as the Reauthorization of the Elementary and Secondary Education Act (which wields the power of the purse), the Comprehensive Services For Children and Youth Act of 1991 (S.1133), the Healthy Students-Healthy Schools Act (S.629, 1994), and Clinton's health plan detail the plan fully. Should these particular pieces of legislation not pass, the intent of the federal government regarding health and health education has been revealed. Failure to pass any or all of these pieces of legislation will not daunt our government nannies— it is too integral a part of their agenda. Their bag is full of tricks to revive and supply the power behind the programs.

There are two primary avenues for the health education push: comprehensive health education curriculum for kindergarten through twelfth grade and school-based clinics.

Comprehensive Health Curriculum

Dr. Joycelyn Elders, the surgeon general appointed by President Clinton, sees schools as the natural center for health education, although she does not limit herself to schools to promote her agenda. According to an article in *Education Week*, "If this 60-year-old pediatrician had her way, every school would have a comprehensive health-education course, all children would be planned and wanted, and AIDS education in the form of condom advertisements would blare on every television network... She said her game plan calls for pooling the federal monies slated for drug-free schools, AIDS education, and nutrition education into one comprehensive health-education program. An aide calls it 'a sort of one-stop shopping.'"[1]

The philosophy behind the health agenda reads like this: In the last few decades, health education in the schools has mushroomed in importance. Care for the bodies of their children has always been recognized as the domain of the family. However, government agents like Dr. Elders, assisted by educators and health care experts, have decided that parents were not doing a proper job, so they must fulfill their responsibility by taking over.

If the specter of widespread parental neglect of health issues isn't enough to get people to buy into the agenda, the Healthy Students-Healthy Schools Act (S.629) provides an additional, albeit twisted, rationale for federal involvement in health education. It says, "...given the international dimensions of the health and education challenges facing the United States, the federal government should play a key role in the national effort to equip all American children with the intellectual and physical skills needed to compete in the new and rapidly changing global marketplace." Now the health education plan is made a necessity for economic survival!

Of course, it is physically impossible for the federal government to personally "equip all American children," so this really means that once they determine the needs, local agencies will be forced to carry out the actual work of "equipping the children." "Equipping" is one of those special, new "power" words. Here it means a "comprehensive health education," defined as "a planned, sequential, kindergarten through grade 12 curriculum that addresses the physical, mental, emotional and social dimensions of health."

The curriculum described in the Healthy Students-Healthy Schools Act includes "a variety of topics such as personal health, family health, community health, consumer health, environmental health, family life, mental and emotional health, injury prevention and safety, nutrition, prevention and control of disease, and substance use and abuse . . ." The curriculum will "be designed to assist students in developing the knowledge, attitudes, and behavioral skills needed to make positive health choices and maintain and improve their health, prevent disease, and reduce health-related risk behaviors." (S.629, Sec. 3)

The curriculum described above is so broad that it could include studies of rain forests and whales under environmental health, and lessons in using power tools under injury prevention and safety. These topics might be worthy of study, but the mandate here is much too broad to accomplish within the schools.

To reinforce the idea that health education is not limited to traditional concepts, consider that Healthy Students is not intended to be run by the Department of Education but by Donna Shalala's Department of Health and Human Services. Even stranger, the Centers for Disease Control is designated to carry out the actual programs, research, and training. One function of this office will be to "integrate health education programs with health and social services for school-age youth."

Further indication of the effort to shuffle children through social service agencies once they are captured by the education snare lies in the use of the term "Interagency Task Force" in the legislation, echoing the title given the oversight group in the Healthy Tomorrows program described in Chapter 1. Recognizing that these programs and the legislation are all pieces of the Goals 2000 puzzle, we should not be surprised to see such overlaps in purpose and language. In fact, most suggested federal cures for the health care problem in the U.S. encompass a number of the National Education Goals. Part of the Task Force's job will be to "review and coordinate all federal efforts in school health education, including drug and alcohol abuse prevention education [Goal 7], HIV prevention education, physical fitness, school services [Goal 1], and nutrition."

As was mentioned earlier, the federal government is prohibited from writing or selecting curricula, but we see evidence in the Healthy Students-Healthy Schools Act that they intend to overcome the prohibition by indirectly influencing curriculum. When it says that a second assignment of the Interagency Task Force will be to "provide scientific and technical advice concerning the development and implementation of the model framework comprehensive school health education programs and curricula..." (Sec. 6), it means that through the provision of scientific data—perhaps selected for their biased conclusions—again the federal government puts its thumbprint in the plan. And the impression made is neatly cemented when money becomes a factor. As with most federal efforts related to education, funding is offered to qualifying schools that agree to teach the prescribed comprehensive health education, financial incentives most schools find difficult to reject (Sections 8 and 11).

We can verify the changing shape of health curricula by looking at the proposed standards or indicators of the comprehensive health curriculum. The National Center on Educational Outcomes suggests evaluating a student (and subsequently the school's access to funding) according to whether he "makes healthy lifestyle choices"; "[i]s aware of basic safety, fitness, and health care needs"; and "[i]s physically fit."[2] In the curriculum, because of political pressures, this translates into already existing AIDS education, support for alternative lifestyles, and invasive personal sex questionnaires. An example of the latter was the 1993 Rand "Sex Survey" executed in California. The Rand survey asked students extremely personal questions about their sexual activity, used sexual slang terms that were offensive to many, and described acts that most people would consider sexual perversion.[3]

Further evidence of the radical direction the health curriculum is heading appears in the report from the National Center on Educational Outcomes. It describes the types of data that will demonstrate whether or not students have achieved the desired outcomes. For example, to determine if students are meeting physical health outcomes, they say that we must find out if "...they use tobacco products...make good nutritional choices...have abused alcohol or drugs in the past year...indicate they have had unprotected sex in the past year..."[4] As usual, when the terms "use," "abuse," and "good" are used without limited definition, nearly any agenda could be applied to the above framework and still achieve the desired outcomes. One outcome is clear, however. Sexual encounters are acceptable; "unprotected sex" will result in a poor evaluation.

Whatever is being evaluated is what will be taught.

School-Based Clinics

When government gets into the health business, controversy is inevitable. The curriculum, as described above, poses a significant problem on its own. However, the expansion of school-based clinics promises to arouse even more parental fury than such clinics have caused in the past. They dispense birth control aids to our children and arrange for abortions, all without parental consent, and parents rightly claim that family authority and autonomy has been violated.

As schools become the center for health services for the entire family through federal programs and Clinton's health care plan, the problem is exacerbated. Strong pressure for school-based clinics is coming from the Oval Office directly and through the surgeon general, Dr. Elders, who "...is the Administration's point person on the controversial topic of school-based clinics, which she argues are an ideal way to tackle many of the health problems young people face...She helped write the section of the health plan that proposes to fund the creation of school-based health centers in low-income, underserved areas. Dr. Elders said the Administration hopes to spend $450 million on the effort over four years."[5] Considering Dr. Elder's promotion of condoms, "safe sex," and a teenager's unobstructed access to abortion, the philosophy of government-financed clinics is obvious.

So far, the agenda behind the establishment of school-based clinics has been primarily about the dispensation of contraceptives, abortion referrals, sexual counseling, and treatment for venereal diseases. "Clinic planners openly admit that the comprehensive character (physicals for sports teams, weight-loss clinics, etc.) is primarily a smokescreen for ensuring privacy while delivering contraceptives to the children. As one advocate explains, virtually all new clinic patients—whatever their reason for contact and whether male or female—are asked if they are or plan to be sexually active."[6]

Indirectly, Goals 2000 makes school-based clinics a fundamental part of school restructuring. If present legislative attempts to further this goal should unexpectedly fail, Senator Edward Kennedy (D-Mass.) will be ready to introduce yet another health-education bill when necessary. One way or the other, the Administration is determined to make clinics a reality.[7]

Sexual and reproductive services generally provoke the most controversy surrounding school-based clinics. Add to this brushfire the circumvention of parental rights, and the situation promises to become explosive.

Parents Lose Control

As I discussed earlier, in some states, once parents sign a form allowing the school to provide services to students—usually through a school-based clinic—that permission is afforded virtual power of attorney status. And although permission is often given with limitations in mind or as a result of special circumstances, it remains in effect even though parents frequently have forgotten about it.

Kentucky is the only state in the Union which is "completely restructured," having implemented many of the programs we have discussed. According to a report from Parents and Professionals Involved in Education (PPIE) in Kentucky, government clinics do not have to notify parents.[8] They quote the law:

> Any physician, upon consultation by a minor as a patient, with the consent of such minor may make a diagnostic examination for venereal disease, pregnancy, alcohol or other drug abuse or addiction and may advise, prescribe for and treat such minor regarding venereal disease, alcohol and other drug abuse or addiction, contraception, pregnancy or childbirth, all without the consent of or notification of the parent, parents, or guardian of such minor patient, or to any other person having custody of such minor patient."[9]

California, although not as far along in this area as Kentucky, already offers some students reproductive health care without parental permission. A good example is the surgically implanted contraceptive, Norplant.

In San Fernando, California, a school arranged for girls to be taken off the school premises to a doctor, where surgery was performed to implant Norplant contraceptives. This despite the fact that Norplant remains controversial as a method of birth control since adequate studies on side effects are not complete. Even the National Women's Health Network, a group which normally promotes birth control, announced that they were opposed to Norplant's approval and marketing until more research has been done.[10] So quick were the proponents of this California program to deny parents any and all right to knowledge about the care of their children that even a possibly dangerous procedure is pursued in a manner which cannot be described as anything but deceptive. (Every cause needs its martyrs—willing or not.)

See how cautiously Julia Scott, director of the public education and policy office for the National Black Women's Health Project, treads around the consent issue while decrying the implantation of Norplant on these girls:

> There is an added concern that this drug was not tested on teen women...If you're talking about putting Norplant in 13-, 14-, 15-year-olds, we need some discussion, we need some study. While students must have parental consent to use the school health clinics, once that consent is given, students no longer need parental consent for any treatments received there...[I]f parents sign a consent form for the clinics but place no restrictions on the services offered, they would not be notified if their children receive Norplant or any other type of birth control.[11]

In addition, it seems that neither patients nor parents are advised that removal of the Norplant a few years down the road is a costly business, not covered once the student leaves school.

In Baltimore, Maryland, Norplant is now available through a number of high-school health clinics. "The district does not require parental notification or consent before dispensing contraceptives, including Norplant, to minors, and some city leaders fear parents will be excluded from the process." Karl Stokes, a city councilman opposed to the program, summarizes the action, "The health department has decided they want to do surgery on girls without parental consultation."[12]

In the Norplant situation, it seems that the social engineers were the instigators of its development rather than educators whom we have assumed have the best interests of the young women at heart. Social engineers had the cause but they had to link up with educators who had access to the necessary martyrs. "Norplant was developed by a small non-profit group concerned with population problems and issues, the New York-based Population Council."[13] It would take a stretch of logic to find the connection between this stated purpose for the development of Norplant and what most Americans would define as the purpose for education. The only viable link is the school-based clinic, and contraceptive dispensation has served as a proving ground. Any behavior that can be categorized as medical care—regardless of how accurately or legitimately—will be similarly linked to education. Thus the schools are made to serve the purposes of those who have hidden agendas.

Back in Kentucky, this blurring of the lines caused Judy Paternostro, the only parent representative on the Interagency Task Force on Family Resource/Youth Services Centers, to submit her letter of resignation from the Task Force. In that letter she highlighted some concerns. Here are a few excerpts:

1. Parental Rights—The circumvention of parental rights through government intrusion is an increasing threat. Services are being offered through the centers that do not require parental consent. The result is that control of minors is being taken out of the hands of their parents, where it rightfully belongs, and placed into the hands of government employees, where it does not belong.

2. School Accountability and Authority—After serving on the Task Force for over 2 years, it is still unclear to me who has the final authority over the centers. In Danville, for example, a center was denied the right to establish procedures providing for parental consent for its services by the Cabinet for Human Resources. If schools are to exercise local control, then they should be able to establish such procedures in their own localities, yet according to the Cabinet, they have no such discretion.

3. Family Privacy—Parents are unaware of the kind of information that can be gathered on their children and their families through the centers...[14]

From the School to the Clinic to the Welfare Office

In the twentieth century, medical care has come to include most forms of social services, and the latter are included in school-based clinics' one-stop-shopping and referral programs. However, social service agencies have earned bad reputations for operating with autonomy, as if they are answerable only to themselves, and for too often causing problems worse than those they are attempting to solve.

The Nunno Family

Although a stable, traditional family, the Nunnos were no more immune to the mistakes of their children than most other families. Both of their unmarried teenage daughters, ages 15 and 16, became pregnant. Both chose to keep their babies. Although the family had health coverage under their father's employer's health plan, the new babies would not be covered. Because the expense of adding them would be considerable, the family decided to seek help from Medi-Cal (California's medical assistance program) to defray the costs for the babies. Candy Nunno, the mother, was told by the social service worker that, technically, her daughters were the ones seeking aid; therefore, the parents had no voice in the matter.

The girls were informed they were eligible for Medi-Cal, food stamps, and financial aid (Aid to Families with Dependent Children). They also had the choice of where they wanted to live—at home, with their boyfriends, or on their own. Even though both daughters were under age, Candy's preference that her daughters remain at home was overruled. Aid was granted to both girls, who believed that there would be no obligation of repayment. They both moved out.

Many months later, the Nunnos were served a subpoena. The subpoena server told them that they were being charged as unfit parents for not providing for their children. The county claimed that only that portion of the government aid that provided for the babies was "free money." The rest was providing for the girls who were really the responsibility of their parents, so the parents must pay back that money. Even though the parents had not sought and even objected to the extra money which took their daughters from their home, they were forced to repay it.

The other, more significant, problem was that the social worker overruled Candy's objections to any aid for her daughters that assisted in anything other than medical costs, obligating the Nunnos to assume an unwanted financial burden. The fact that they did not realize what had happened to them until well after the fact makes it worse. Further, the district attorney's staffer with whom they dealt was emotionally detached about the situation, dismissing their concerns with the excuse that the Nunnos were lucky that the district attorney went after them so soon after the aid was dispensed. Apparently, some people do not get contacted for up to three years, by which time they owe a huge amount of money.

One of the most frustrating aspects of the story is that neither of the Nunno daughters would have taken financial aid if they had understood that their parents would have to pay it back. Candy Nunno sums up their experience: "The State abducted my children financially and mentally. It's wrong. I felt completely betrayed by my own country."[15]

Candy was willing to share her family's story because she worries that other families will be enticed into the welfare system through Medi-Cal, school-based clinics, and other government health care systems, where social workers await unsuspecting individuals. Too often, welfare/social service agents bring harm to families with their policies and their actions as we have already seen in Chapter 1. When social workers offer financial incentives for young, unwed mothers to leave home, with or without parental consent, they are breaking up families, denying parental authority, and creating (sometimes hidden) financial burdens for parents. When it happens in spite of parental objections, the State is, in effect, saying that it has primary authority over our children—but no responsibility for any of its own errors.

Social workers justify such actions by claiming that it is for the good of society, but they have unwittingly created far worse sociological problems. Ben Wattenburg, syndicated columnist and senior fellow at the American Enterprise Institute, talked with a group of six welfare mothers, most of whom were African-American and in their twenties. He began the conversation: "Some people say that teen-age girls are having out-of-wedlock babies in order to get welfare; now I don't think that's so, but isn't it likely that the package of welfare benefits reduces the restraints against such births, and makes them more likely?" The women jumped in before he could say anything more. "Right, there are women out there just having children just to get it . . ." "That's what they'd rather do, is sit at home and do nothing." "Young girls out there that will brag that 'I have four kids so I get this amount of money and this amount of food stamps.'"[16]

While many young women getting financial aid come from a sub-culture that supports this attitude, the Nunnos did not. It is frightening to think that society's attempts to be helpful, popularly exercised today by the provision of health care in school-based clinics and referrals to social services agencies, are actually encouraging dependence upon government where it did not previously exist. More devastating is the practice of undermining families by offering very young women incentives to leave home prematurely.

All one-stop shopping centers include health care and social services. By making these options more easily available, the government will greatly increase the number of people who use these services. The research showing that dependence upon the government reduces individual responsibility is rich. Consider the evidence compiled by Charles Murray[17] and others, and it is clear: the health-care connection becomes one more strike against Goals 2000.

End Notes:

[1] Jessica Portner, "Elders Offers Health-Care Prescription for Youths," *Education Week*, December 1, 1993, p. 12.

[2] "Educational Outcomes and Indicators for Students Completing School," National Center on Educational Outcomes, The College of Education, University of Minnesota, Jan., 1993.

[3] "High School Student Survey," Rand, Santa Monica, CA.

[4] "Educational Outcomes and Indicators for Students Completing School," National Center on Educational Outcomes, The College of Education, University of Minnesota, Jan., 1993.

[5] Portner, Jessica, "Elders Offers Health-Care Prescription for Youths," *Education Week*, December 1, 1993, p.12.

[6] Allan C. Carlson, *Family Questions: Reflections on the American Social Crisis*, Transaction Books, New Brunswick (U.S.A.), 1990, p. 93.

[7] Portner, Jessica, "Elders Offers Health-Care Prescription for Youths," *Education Week*, December 1, 1993, p.12.

[8] According to KRS214.185.

[9] "Brown Bag Condom Program in Kentucky Raises Ire," *Free World Research Report*, June, 1993, p. 6.

[10] Philip J. Hilts, "The Birth-Control Backlash," *Daily News*, Los Angeles, Dec. 16, 1990.

[11] Diana E. Lundin, "School Clinic Implants Contraceptives," *Daily News*, Los Angeles, March 25, 1993.

[12] Jessica Portner, "5 Baltimore School Clinics To Offer Students Norplant," *Education Week*, Oct. 20, 1993.

[13] Personal conversations with Candy Nunno, 1994.

[14] Philip J. Hilts, "The Birth-Control Backlash," *Daily News*, Los Angeles, Dec. 16, 1990.

[15] "Brown Bag Condom Program in Kentucky Raises Ire," *Free World Research Report*, June, 1993, p. 6.

[16] Ben Wattenburg, "Welfare Dialogues," *Orange County Register*, Dec. 19, 1993.

[17] Charles Murray, *Losing Ground*, Basic Books, 1984.

CHAPTER EIGHT

THE SCHOOL-TO-WORK TRANSITION

Hi-ho, hi-ho. It's off to work we go. But, forget it if you don't have the blessings of the bureaucrats.

One of the major features of restructuring and Goals 2000 is the school-to-work transition. Here, just as in parenting, health, and education, a fundamental shift in societal roles takes place. Until now, schools were expected to offer students a basic education that would prepare them for life. Schools were not held responsible for mapping out the future beyond graduation. That was beyond their scope. Students were expected to research their options, make their own choices, and plan their own futures. It has been the graduate's (or dropout's) responsibility to determine what jobs are available, then go through the application process. Some help has been available, but self-determination has predominated.

Now, the government plans to eliminate one more layer of uncertainty and risk in our lives by taking over that transition from school to work. While the intent is at least partially to help more students graduate and get jobs, the interests of business are very evident. The School-to-Work Opportunities Act of 1994 (H.R. 2884), written to help implement Goals 2000, has the Secretary of Labor and the Secretary of Education working together, meshing the interests of business and education. One of the purposes of this legislation is to "offer young Americans access to a performance-based education and training program that will enable them to earn portable credentials, prepare them for a first job in a high-skill, high-wage career, and increase their opportunities for further education...." (Sec. 3 [C])

The portable credentials are intended to serve as evidence of high school or higher education completion and as evidence of training for particular employment. Ideally, business will save millions in training expenses for new employees who will have already received training, including on-the-job learning, at taxpayers' expense.[1]

There is nothing particularly astounding about businesses preferring that hirees have the necessary skills for entry-level jobs, courtesy of the government school system. Preparing young people for the work force was probably a major reason that many taxpayers were willing to finance government schools in the first place. But, until recently there was always a large element of self-determination and personal responsibility involved. Both of those features are largely missing from the new school-to-work plan for education. Under Goals 2000 and school-to-work legislation, the government narrows the options by setting up performance standards that all students must meet to "graduate." Graduation will include obtaining a Certificate of Mastery which will serve as a key to the work world.

Under the new system, students will work to achieve a Certificate of Initial Mastery by the end of tenth grade. They will then choose to move into a vocational or apprenticeship program, or else into a college preparatory program. Once the system is in place, a Certificate of Advanced Mastery from that program will be required for employment.[2]

Students must select "a career major not later than the beginning of the 11th grade." (H.R. 2884 Title I, Sec. 102/P.L. 103-239) Eleventh and twelfth grade students, according to the legislation, are supposed to follow a "program of study designed to meet the same challenging academic standards established by States for all students under the Goals 2000: Educate America Act, and to meet the requirements necessary for a student to earn a skill certificate." Here lies a major part of the problem.

If the academic standards are truly challenging, it is hard to imagine how students will have time to simultaneously earn their skill certificate. Examples of methods of integrating work-related skills into basic subject areas are given in the federal publication, *Teaching the Scans Competencies*; yet, those examples do not include specialized skills. Students are supposed to be spending some time in on-the-job training and developing very specialized skills. There is not enough time to cover both academics and job training and do them both well, at least within our present educational system. Something has to give, and it will probably be academic standards.

Germany, which already has in place a system such as that proposed for the U.S., separates students into college prep and vocational tracks as early as age ten. They have arrived at the realization that students can participate in apprenticeship programs or prepare for college, but there is not time for both.

With Goals 2000, the U.S. is trying to come up with one set of outcomes for all students, so offering choices of tracks becomes difficult. What we find is that new learner outcomes seem to be leaning toward apprenticeship rather than college preparation.

We get a clear picture of these outcomes from the U.S. Department of Labor's Secretary's Commission on Achieving Necessary Skills, more popularly known as the SCANS Commission. They identified a three-part foundation of skills and personal qualities:

- *basic skills*-reading, writing, mathematics, speaking, and listening;
- *thinking skills*-creativity, decision making, reasoning, and problem solving;
- *personal qualities*-individual responsibility, self-management, and integrity.

SCANS also describes five "competencies" that are to be built on this foundation. They are the ability to productively use:

- *resources*-allocating time, money, and people;
- *interpersonal skills*-working on teams, teaching, negotiating, and serving customers;
- *information*-acquiring, evaluating, and processing data;
- *technology*-selecting, using, and applying technology;
- *systems*-understanding social, organizational, and technological systems.[3]

These skills, competencies, and personal qualities are utilitarian compared to the traditional content and goals of education. Although reading, writing, and mathematics are included, they are taught in the limited context of the work world.

Within the SCANS competencies we also run into a problem we encountered earlier—how do we evaluate "creativity," "responsibility," "integrity," and other subjective traits? A hypothetical resumé from the SCANS Report, *Learning a Living*, has an entire section for evaluating the "personal qualities" of responsibility, self-esteem, sociability, self-management, and integrity/honesty. An averaged rating is given, derived from ratings by a variety of people with whom the student has been in contact.[4] Considering that students are unlikely to have lengthy contact with more than a couple of people, these ratings can easily be skewed by the level of rapport established between a student and just one rater. Including such subjective ratings as part of a resume is unlikely to be useful to employers.

Oregon Leads the Way

Oregon has already passed legislation (HB 3565) implementing Certificates of Mastery. They resolve the conflict with the regular school curriculum by saying, "State curriculum frameworks should be based on the CIM [Certificates of Initial Mastery] outcomes and be revised to support them. Outside of these frameworks, there should be no required state curriculum." They go on to say, "The State should prescribe outcomes and assessment processes. Local districts should then have significant flexibility to design instructional programs that will address CIM outcomes."[5]

Oregon is not alone in getting a jump on the implementation of school-to-work legislation. "About 15 states—including Arkansas, Georgia, Maine, Oregon, Wisconsin, and Pennsylvania—have already passed school-to-work bills. Jobs for the Future, a nonprofit group that specializes in work-force issues, says many more states are considering doing so."[6]

California's proposed legislation (AB 2583) typifies school-to-work bills across the country. It requires state (and local) programs to be coordinated with federal. A school-to-work council is directed to come up with recommendations for changing the curriculum to integrate workforce preparation, establishing skill and hiring standards consistent with Goals 2000 and related state and federal legislation, and implementing Certificates of Mastery.

While many concerned citizens have been concentrating on outcome-based education, they have missed the Certificate of Mastery tie-ins. Vocational or job training is not a bad idea in itself. But we have two major problems: government treating people as human capital, and the coercive and limiting nature of the program.

People As Human Capital

The whole school-to-work agenda assumes that people are no more than human capital. Reading through the literature from the SCANS commission and the legislation, I get the feeling that the authors see themselves as "factory operators" and all others as raw material for their operations. Students seem little more than plastic blobs to be molded into useful forms for the purposes of society.

Perhaps the analogy is a little extreme, but their autocratic attitude is the inevitable result of paternalistic government programs. Once government agencies assumed responsibility for individuals through welfare and other government "support" programs, they then put themselves in the role of a parent caring for a dependent.

If parents knew that they would be burdened with supporting their own children through adulthood should their children not master the skills needed for getting jobs and functioning in society, they would be greatly concerned about the training they provide those children. It follows naturally, that since the government has assumed responsibility for those who grow up irresponsible and skill-less, it is now claiming the right to train citizens to prevent such dependence. So now job training has become another government responsibility.

The only new concept here is the breadth of job training programs. The government has sponsored job training programs for many years, but just as with other programs that the government intends to expand, we should take a careful look at the success of previous efforts. Have they accomplished their goals? The original job training programs were intended to reduce the numbers of unemployed and welfare recipients. Contrary to expectations, job training thus far has failed to do either.[7] Senator Nancy L. Kassebaum, ranking Republican on the Labor and Human Resources Committee, refused to back the federal school-to-work legislation saying, "My opposition is based on my conviction that it compounds rather than corrects the deficiencies of current federal job-training efforts. Just consider the fact that we already have 154 separate job-training programs on the books. By passing this bill, we will have 155."[8] Kassebaum's remarks remind us that good intentions too often prevent objective evaluations of government programs.

The JOBSTART program operated in thirteen communities from 1985 to 1988. The goal was to provide "relatively intensive basic-skills education, job training, placement assistance, and support services to low-skilled dropouts." A four-year follow-up and evaluation of the program revealed that "JOBSTART youths participated more heavily in education and training programs than did a randomly selected control group. Forty-two percent of the JOBSTART youths attained a general-equivalency diploma within the follow-up period, compared with 29 percent of those in the control group. In general, however, the study found no real payoff in earnings for JOBSTART participants." If the goal had been to increase the number of students who earned their GED certificates, the results would be encouraging. However, the established goal was more long-range—to improve their employment opportunities. With or without GED certificates, these youths somehow still lacked qualities sought by employers.[9]

Now that job training is part of Goals 2000, the results are supposed to improve. But the planners ignore philosophical and psychological aspects of the situation they are creating.

Enforced Attendance

It used to be that unwilling students could bide their time until they reached the age when they were free from compulsory attendance laws. The latest thinking has taken a more coercive bent. The second National Education Goal says, "By the year 2000, the high school graduation rate will increase to at least 90 percent. The objectives are: 1) The nation must dramatically reduce its dropout rate, and 75 percent of those students who do drop out will successfully complete a high school degree or its equivalent; and 2) The gap in high school graduation rates between American students from minority backgrounds and their non-minority counterparts will be eliminated."

Government officials know that verbal encouragement will not be enough to coax the system up to a 90 percent graduation rate, so coercion through the Certificates of Mastery will be the method. Rather than trying to patch dropouts back into the system after the fact through job training or GED courses, potential dropouts will receive job training through the educational system before they will be allowed to leave.

The job market will be closed to them through regulations or laws such as Oregon's Department of Education's regulation (ORS 335.125, OAR, 581-XX-XXX) which says, "A student who has not earned a Certificate of Initial Mastery and is not 18 years of age may not he employed while school is in session."

Oregon forestalls other options by saying, "A Certificate of Initial Mastery shall be required for entry into college preparatory and academic professional technical programs leading to the appropriate endorsement." Without the Certificate of Initial Mastery, students will not be able to choose other options.

Graduation from the educational system changes for all students, not just the dropouts. Students will no longer graduate when they have accumulated a certain number of Carnegie units. Instead, they must demonstrate the required outcomes. Evidence of graduation will no longer be a diploma; instead it will be the Certificate of Mastery. The Certificate of Initial Mastery is unlikely to be sufficient for most employers since most students will be able to earn it after completing the equivalent of tenth grade. (It might be viewed on a par with the present GED certificate.) But that certificate will be required before students will be allowed to seek the real graduation diploma—the Certificate of Advanced Mastery.[10]

What Choices Do We Have?

The Certificates of Advanced Mastery will be earned through either vocational or college preparatory programs. Promoters of the school-to-work agenda point to vocational training and apprenticeships as major opportunities for individualizing the school experience. Undoubtedly this will be true for many students, yet schools can accommodate only so many options for vocational training.

If schools do not have a local computer company willing to apprentice or train future computer programmers or technicians, those students might be out of luck. What if a student wants to become a religious minister? Schools are unlikely to tackle the church/state issues involved in sponsoring a religious education in any form. What if a student is interested in a very specific and unique career goal that does not fit in with what is offered? Will those students be shunted into vocational training according to the needs of local businesses? What if a student sees no benefit in the education being offered by the school, and he prefers to drop out and learn what he needs to learn on his own? Certificates of Mastery are intended to act as gatekeepers to the work world. Students who choose not to comply with the program might well be cut off from the traditional job market.

OBE and Certificates of Mastery

Outcome-based education is very much a part of the Certificates of Mastery system. Students will have to satisfy outcome requirements to get their certificates, and the outcome-based education facets of the certificates take us back to the same problems of subjectivity we discussed earlier. The outcomes reflect attitudes, beliefs, and values. By requiring conformity in these areas, government is claiming control over the minds and hearts of students. The control issue is crucial.

We must recall that desire for control is not new to our educational system; in fact, control was the reason for its very existence. The present restructuring is simply an expansion of the Prussian model upon which we have built our public school system. John Taylor Gatto, former New York Teacher of the Year, tells us that "modern forced schooling" was begun in Prussia to create for the State obedient soldiers, mine workers, "well subordinated" civil servants for government and clerks for industry, and citizens who agreed with the State. Schools would be tools for creating a consensus predecreed by those in control. The Prussian goal of creating a form of state socialism replaced the traditional American goal of preparing individuals to be self-reliant. Prussians feared intellectual independence which might encourage citizens to disagree with State purposes and policies. Ninety-four percent of Prussian students were relegated to the Volksschule where "socialization" to State purposes was the goal. Only one or two children out of every two hundred were educated to develop higher levels of thinking and analysis—to be the policy makers. The remaining five percent were trained to be the second tier who supported the policy makers and implemented their ideas. The real purpose of Prussian education was not intellectual development, but socialization—training in obedience and subordination.[11]

Under Goals 2000, the control extends beyond the doors of the public school system. Students from private and home schools will be brought into line one way or another, illustrated by Oregon's law. They say that allowances are to be made for those in private schools and those coming from out-of-state, but there is a big catch. Sec. 25 (4) says, "A high school diploma issued by an *accredited* private or out-of-state secondary school as signifying successful completion of grade 12 shall be considered acceptable in lieu of a Certificate of Advanced Mastery for purposes of any rights or privileges that attach to the holder of a Certificate of Advanced Mastery" (italics added). The word accredited is crucial. For a school to be accredited these days, they have to agree to a host of controls over their curriculum and day-to-day operations. Some schools and home schoolers who wish to make their own curricula and operations decisions refuse to seek accreditation. Yet, students with diplomas from unaccredited sources are likely to find their diplomas invalid.

Learning Centers

Educational controllers have even figured out a way to hold on to students who are past compulsory schooling age but have not attained the CIM. Students who are unable to attain the certificate in a regular school must then go to learning centers or youth centers. In an article by Hillary Rodham Clinton and Ira Magaziner, they recommend state/federal partnerships to create and fund "alternative learning environments" for those who cannot attain the Certificate of Initial Mastery in regular schools. They say, "Youth Centers should be established to enroll school dropouts and help them reach that standard...The idea of Youth Centers, the Commission's strategy for recovering school dropouts and bringing them up to a high academic standard, is an essential component of the whole strategy for national human resource development."[12]

Oregon's legislation authorizes student attendance at learning centers at State expense until age twenty-one or until they receive Certificates of Initial Mastery. At age twenty-one, students can continue, but must pay their own tuition.

Employment Barriers?

While, at this point, employers cannot be forced to require potential employees to present Certificates of Advanced Mastery, the potential for this happening is great through two avenues. The first avenue is wording in the School-to-Work Opportunities Act of 1994 (Sec. 5) which says that, "...the

Secretaries shall jointly provide for the administration of the programs established by this Act, and may issue whatever procedures, guidelines, and regulations...they deem necessary and appropriate to administer and enforce the provisions of this Act." This leaves the regulatory door wide open, although there might be constitutional challenges and subsequent barriers to government dictation of hiring practices. Such protests, however, might be overcome by the second avenue, financial incentives.

Employers stand to gain many low-or no-wage employees, along with government funds for mentoring, if they participate in the school-to-work program. However, there is much debate about whether it will be possible to have unpaid or below-minimum-wage apprentices in the United States. Germany, the model for U.S. apprenticeship programs, has a powerful employer incentive since German youth-apprentices can be paid less than the minimum wage, allowing businesses to obtain labor at lower costs than otherwise possible. U.S. minimum wage laws would have to be altered to put businesses on the same footing as their German counterparts.[13] Still, U.S. businesses will save on training costs they would have had to cover themselves under the old system. Overall, the costs of taking on untrained labor might well be offset by government subsidies. We must remember that businesses stay in business by making money. Stockholders have little sympathy for charitable endeavors that hurt the bottom line. So we can be sure that employers will not be enticed into the system unless there is some sort of financial advantage.

Government Tells Business How to Be Efficient

For employers it will not be all gain with no pain. The driving ideology behind the school-to-work agenda says that,

"American business has to be restructured for high performance..." and we need to reshape our work force as we create more jobs requiring high skills.[14] Hillary Rodham Clinton and Ira Magaziner explain (yes, Hillary has her hand in this too!):

> We can do this only by reorganizing the way we work in our stores and factories, in our warehouses, insurance offices, government agencies, and hospitals. We can give our frontline workers much more responsibility, educate them well, and train them to do more highly skilled jobs.
>
> If we do this, we can streamline work. We will need fewer supervisors, fewer quality checkers, fewer production schedulers, and fewer maintenance people, so organizations will become more efficient. Because they will be more efficient, they will be able to sell more. Because they sell more, they can expand. Because they can expand, they can employ more people. Although each operation will require fewer people, society as a whole can increase employment and wages can go up.[15]

The above statements reflect a belief in a planned economy—a basic supposition of socialism. Marc Tucker, president of the National Center on Education and the Economy, says:

> If we want to maintain our current level of income in this country, our whole work force has to be vastly better educated than it is. Most of the companies in the United States these days are not competing with Japan and Germany; they're competing with the Philippines, with Mexico, with Thailand. If we are not better educated than they are, by a lot, we will end up working for their wages at their hours. We can either be a high-skill and

high-wage country or a low-skill and low-wage country."[16]

Unfortunately, Tucker ignores the fact that Germany's unemployment rate is around 12 percent and rising, and they are discussing reducing the work week or creating job-sharing to provide jobs for more people. Hillary Clinton and Ira Magaziner were simply echoing Tucker's ideas from *America's Choice: High Skills or Low Wages!* where he decries the old organizational structure with six front-line workers backed up by eighteen support staff. His new organizational structure would have eight front-line and six support staff. We have just lost ten jobs in this brave new world.[17]

If the economic planners have their way, businesses will no longer be able to determine their own objectives. Planners would like to compel businesses to not only compete with Japan and Germany but to look like them.

Planners like Marc Tucker have already begun to reshape American businesses by pressuring employers to rewrite job descriptions and retrain workers with the goal of eliminating low-paying jobs. In at least one proposed piece of legislation, the government would require employers to chip in at least one percent of payroll costs to pay for some of the retraining costs,[18] a "tax" idea borrowed from Germany. "Albert Shanker, the president of the American Federation of Teachers, notes that the highly acclaimed German apprenticeship system is not voluntary. Employers who do not participate in training youth apprentices have to pay a tax that supports government-sponsored training programs."[19]

The justification that government programs will make businesses more efficient makes it sound like businesses up until this point have had no incentive to be efficient on their own. Perhaps the confusion is merely a reflection of something government employees know all too well—inefficiency; and they are transferring their experience in inefficient bureaucracies to the business world. They ignore the fact that most for-profit businesses already try to function as efficiently as possible. Some of them might have determined that hiring cheap labor for some low-skill jobs, and hiring more expensive labor for other specialized jobs is the most practical solution. If it is more efficient to do away with low-skill jobs, is it not likely that businesses would have figured this out?

The question of whether or not such a shift is more efficient, although interesting, is really not the crucial issue. The real issue is the freedom of businesses to make their own choices about how they operate. Our government definitely lacks both credibility and constitutional authority for telling businesses how to function.

High Skill/High Wage Fairy Tales

"Students need to be prepared with the skills necessary for the high skill/high wage jobs of the 21st century." This theme repeats itself over and over again in Goals 2000 and other restructuring efforts. Since preparation for high skill/high wage jobs is a cornerstone of the school-to-work restructuring, we need to examine the truth or falsehood of predictions about such employment opportunities. A U.S. News & World Report article, "White Collar Wasteland,"[20] describes the dramatic drop in white collar jobs with the down-sizing that is occurring in many major companies. While companies have been cutting jobs, they have also demanded higher productivity. With fewer jobs available, workers have no choice but to produce at higher levels with no increase in wages since employers are in the enviable position of having a surplus of workers.

Pat Farenga writes, "The most disturbing thing about the schooling + diplomas = jobs equation is the assumption that these 'high skill, high wage jobs of today' really do exist in abundance...Like architects, English majors, and engineers in the '70s, our children may spend time and money getting diplomas for school-defined jobs, only to find that the market is glutted with graduates like themselves." Farenga goes on to quote from a *New York Daily News* article entitled, "Schooling is Out. '90s Job Forecast is for Less Education." "'More than three-quarters of all jobs in New York State during the 1990s will require a high school education— or less—with most of the growth in the service sector,' Samuel Ehrenhalt, regional commissioner of the U.S. Bureau of Labor Statistics, said yesterday." Farenga followed up by checking the U.S. Department of Labor's statistics, which verified that service sector jobs will add the largest number of jobs by the year 2005. "The jobs highlighted for fastest growth in the service sector are correction officials, firefighters, guards, police, detectives and special agents, chefs, cooks, kitchen workers and 'food and beverage service workers,' salespersons, clerks, cashiers, receptionists and secretaries, nursing and home health aides, childcare workers, janitors, groundskeepers."[21]

In 1993, 255,000 manufacturing jobs were lost, while 294,000 restaurant industry jobs were added. A realistic look at the future make-up of the workforce reveals that a small percentage of new jobs will require a significantly higher level of training.[22]

One has to wonder about the honesty of those who are hyping high skill/high wage jobs. After all, the menial tasks will not simply disappear; there are always some that need accomplishing. No intelligent employer is going to cross train his computer expert in janitorial work and vice versa so that everyone gets a high paying job. And no matter how many times we say that everyone can achieve high standards the fact remains that there will always be those who can only achieve low standards and are not competent to hold high skill/high wage jobs. In fact, Thomas Bailey and Donna Merritt of the Institute for Education and the Economy at Columbia University say, "The vast majority of U.S. employers remain firmly committed to traditional production processes that depend on low-wage, low-skilled workers."[23]

Like specialized fields of the past which have experienced ebbs and flows in popularity and demand, it looks like there will be little job security for those who spend the extra time getting business, engineering, and marketing degrees for the foreseeable future. This situation should give us pause in making statements about the need for a workforce of highly trained workers for the 21st century.

Those selling the high skill/high wage scenario know about labor department predictions, but they are being less than forthright to the public. One writer says, "In the last few years, discussions of education and education reform have been marked by a dreary instrumentality about jobs. The dread vision of 'competition in the global economy' has replaced the terror of the Red Menace as a scare tactic to keep Americans in line."[24]

Whether predictions about the future of the job market are right or wrong, freedom is the real issue here. Young people need the freedom of self-determination. Businesses need the freedom to determine their own goals, hiring, training, and labor practices. Dictating these details from the federal level is the type of micro-management that is disastrous for businesses and workers alike. Requiring businesses to pay for government-imposed restructuring of their work-place practices adds insult to injury.

Apparently some large businesses feel that benefits to them outweigh the disadvantages, because a number of them have weighed in as strong supporters of restructuring.

Collusion between Government and Big Business

Whoever pays the piper calls the tune. As long as both government and business fund educational reform, both gain control. Government control we have already examined. Businesses will be in a position to dictate the outcomes they desire from the educational process. And by controlling job training opportunities available to young people, they will be able to effectively shape the work force to reflect their particular needs.

This is exactly what has already happened in Germany. About one-third of the students are in college prep programs, while the others are on vocational tracks. Tracking begins as early as age ten. At age sixteen, the non-university students begin their three-year apprenticeships. "Companies decide how many openings will be available in what areas..."[25] Americans, already unhappy with our own present system of limited tracking, are unlikely to embrace a system that separates students at such young ages into vocational/education tracks that will determine their future. Debate and protest over any such system will likely plague it from the planning to the implementation stages.

When businesses exert influence, if not control, over the number of people trained for various jobs, they can effectively keep wage scales down by creating more competition for particular jobs. For example, if they know that there will be a big demand for computer programmers in the next five years, they will try to channel more than the required number of students into studies for that field. If there are more applicants than jobs, lower wages can be offered than when there is a scarcity of applicants. Some of the highest paid workers are those in high skills-technological fields. If businesses can create a surfeit of workers in this field, they can cut wages significantly. Overqualified workers can usually handle jobs that call for less skill (or the government can retrain them to do so). Businesses which enjoy the financial freedom to play the numbers game like this—not your typical small or moderately sized company —will enjoy an even greater advantage than when engineers were laid off in defense cutbacks and downsizing.

Businesses are not the bad guys in this situation. Any responsible businessman owes it to the owners or stockholders to keep production or operating costs as low as possible, so it is good business practice for him to take advantage of the opportunity to influence job training and career preparation. But for government to, in effect, sponsor such a situation with their programs and scarce tax dollars is a travesty. Although business participation in the school-to-work transition programs might be best for business, it might very well be bad for students and employees.

In Germany, the recession has taken such a financial toll on businesses that they have been unable to maintain the number of apprenticeships they had previously. Talk now is of changing to a totally government-financed system. If that happens, businesses will have more difficulty calling the shots, but will have to use political patronage to achieve their goals.

Many of the questions in the U.S. about apprenticeships hinge upon the question of financing. It appears that we are moving toward a system where government pays most of the costs with some assistance from businesses. Yet, many initial efforts are business-sponsored and, consequently, shaped to directly meet the sponsors' needs.

Education for the Workforce

The needs of the workplace dominate discussions of secondary education goals. A utilitarian approach to education is replacing any personal goals that students or parents might have. The latter simply are not efficient or wage-producing.

Many educators and academicians believe that traditional ideas about education—its value in shaping the inner man and developing an appreciation of knowledge for its own sake—are no longer necessary or desirable. The ability to function is enough. According to literacy researcher T.G. Sticht (who now works for Secretary of Labor Robert Reich), "Many companies have moved operations to places with cheap, relatively poorly educated labor. What may be crucial, they say, is the dependability of a labor force and how well it can be managed and trained—not its general educational level, although a small cadre of highly educated creative people is essential to innovation and growth. Ending discrimination and changing values are probably more important than reading and moving low-income families into the middle class."[26]

If we interviewed the average parent, do you think that he or she would place ending discrimination and changing values on a higher level than reading or improving economic status? Unlikely! Yet, the government planners have the gall to plod forward in restructuring our schools (and, soon, the work place) to fit their notions.

End Notes:

[1] The Association for Supervision and Curriculum Development, a major player in formulating government school policy, advocates government-paid education for an additional two years beyond high school in *Developing Leadership: A Synthesis of ASCD Resolutions through 1993*, ASCD, Alexandria, VA, 1993, p. 4.

[2] Oregon's HB 3565, Sec. 20 is one of the first in the country to implement this requirement.

[3] Arnold H. Packer, "Taking Action on the SCANS Report," *Educational Leadership*, March, 1992, pp. 27-28.

[4] *Learning a Living: What Work Requires of Schools*, SCANS, July, 1992.

[5] *Certificate of Initial Mastery Task Force Report, January, 1993*, Oregon Department of Education, Salem, OR, p. 15.

[6] Lynn Olson, "Bridging the Gap: The nation's haphazard school-to-work link is getting an overhaul," *Education Week*, January 26, 1994, p. 21.

[7] Charles Murray, *Losing Ground*, p. 19.

[8] Lynn Olson, "School-to-Work Bill Set for House-Senate Conference," *Education Week*, Feb. 16, 1994, p. 17.

[9] "News in Brief," *Education Week*, Jan. 19, 1994, p. 18. Full report: "JOB-START: Final Report on a Program for School Dropouts," Publications Department, M.D.R.C., 3 Park Ave., New York, NY 10016, 212-532-3200.

[10] At present, schools are using both Carnegie units and performance outcomes. Certificate of Mastery systems are in their beginning stages of implementation.

11 John Taylor Gatto, "Bootie Zimmer's Choice," Keynote speech delivered at Conference on Private Initiatives in Education, Indianapolis, IN, Nov. 13-14, 1992.

12 Ira Magaziner and Hillary Rodham Clinton, "Will America Choose High Skills or Low Wages?," *Education Leadership*, March, 1992, pp. 10-14.

13 Lynn Olson, "Bridging the Gap: The nation's haphazard school-to-work link is getting an overhaul," *Education Week*, January 26, 1994, p. 24.

14 John O'Neill, "On Education and the Economy: A Conversation with Marc Tucker," *Education Leadership*, March, 1992, p.19.

15 Ira Magaziner and Hillary Rodham Clinton, "Will America Choose High Skills or Low Wages?," *Education Leadership*, March, 1992, pp. 10-14.

16 O'Neill, p. 19.

17 Gerald W. Bracey, "What If Education Broke Out All Over?," *Education Week*, March 30, 1994, pp. 33, 44.

18 Ira Magaziner and Hillary Rodham Clinton, "Will America Choose High Skills or Low Wages?," *Education Leadership*, March, 1992, p. 13.

19 Olson, "Bridging the Gap" p. 24.

20 "White Collar Wasteland, *U.S. News & World Report*, June 28, 1993.

21 Pat Farenga, "Schooling + Diploma = Jobs?," *Growing Without Schooling*, Jan./Feb., 1994, p. 33.

22 Bracey, pp. 33, 44.

23 Olson, "Bridging the Gap," p. 21.

24 Bracey, p. 33.

[25] Charles J. Hanley, "Apprentices at Work," *Orange County Register*, May 12, 1994.

[26] T.G. Sticht, The Congressional Record, October 23, 1989.

CHAPTER NINE

THE COMPUTER CONNECTION

One of the most oppressive features of Orwell's 1984 society was the computer telescreen. These mechanical spies could see, hear, and record almost everything. Privacy was nonexistent.

In February, 1994, FBI director Louis J. Freeh said that Americans must give up some personal privacy in exchange for safety and security. He was promoting the Digital Telephony and Communications Privacy Improvement Act of 1994. This act, instead of protecting our privacy as the title implies, turns "the nation's telephone network into a vast surveillance system." It allows the government to "gather a wealth of personal information by monitoring citizens' calling patterns and credit-card transactions over the telephone network and over the two-way cable-television networks being planned by cable and phone companies." "What kind of movies we watch, what kind of commerce we engage in, what kind of political parties we want to communicate with—all of these things are going to be on the information highway," said Jerry Berman, of the Electronic Frontier Foundation, a lobbying group."[1]

Surveillance efforts will be aided by the government-designed computer chip, known as the clipper chip, that facilitates police agencies' interceptions of coded computer communications. To add insult to injury, taxpayers would pay the $500 million cost to develop and deploy the system.[2]

All of this sounds like adult technobabble unrelated to Goals 2000. After all, babies do not talk on the telephone and operate computers. But data tracking is part of a cradle-to-grave system, and it begins at birth. If the Clinton health plan or a similar, government-controlled program passes, everyone will have a "health security card," which will quickly become known as a "national identity card." At first, its use will be limited to health care. Doctor visits, prescriptions, hospitalization, and medically-related counseling will all be recorded in a massive national data bank. We are assured that those records will be private and that only "authorized people" will have access. Of course, most government bureaucrats will be authorized. And no one has been able to eradicate the threat of unauthorized hackers who figure out how to invade the system.

Once in place, it will be impossible to "close shop" on the technology. The card is here to stay. In fact, the temptation will be overwhelming to expand the card's oversight, probably using social security numbers, to correlate all personal records for easy access and cross checking by government agencies. Even if Clinton's health plan is killed, computer tracking and national data banks on all citizens will likely be implemented through another type of legislation. The seemingly harmless push for mandatory vaccination legislation might provide the vehicle that makes it possible to track citizens from the time of birth. The scenario is simple to construct: As soon as children begin breathing, they are assigned a number and entered into the data system. The system ostensibly records their vaccination records, with "bells and whistles" going off when vaccinations are skipped. If children are not presented on schedule, someone tracks them down. After all, good parenting includes following the government's policy for medical care. The vaccination/tracking program is so appealing that numerous bills have been introduced in Congress. If one does not pass, others are waiting.

Whether the enabling legislation is a special vaccination bill, part of Clinton's health care plan, part of the Parents As Teachers program or something else, the intent behind tracking at birth is obvious. The data in the national system will encompass far more than bare statistics. Since at least 1974, a plan has been in place for a detailed coding system. The *Student/Pupil Acounting Handbook V* issued by the then U.S. Department of Health, Education, and Welfare and the National Center for Education Statistics lists categories and codes to be used for students. Some of the categories are: family economic information; family social/cultural information; physical health, sensory, and related conditions; student medical record number; and mental, psychological, and proficiency test results and related student characteristics. Under this last category, there is a sub category for specific mental and psychological characteristics.[3]

A crucial component of Goals 2000 is the notion that everyone must participate, and computer tracking helps overcome the difficulty of attaining that outcome. There will be no escapees. Private and home schools must also meet the goals and become accountable to the system. One goals panel report says, "Any system designed to assess progress toward the National Education Goals must take account of those students who do not attend public elementary and secondary schools. Approximately one student in eight is enrolled in a private school, and others are enrolled in adult education programs outside the traditional K-12 system. It simply does not make sense to exclude such schools and programs, and the children and youth who attend them, from our measures of progress."4

The goals panel outlines a plan whereby all schools are required to offer identical instructional opportunities so that all students will meet the same goals. To ensure compliance with this plan, they judge that it will be necessary to monitor "instructional experiences" at all grade levels.5 This goes beyond requiring students to meet specified outcomes. It reaches into the classroom and controls what is taught, justifying the intrusion with the high-minded guarantee that all students have the "opportunity" to meet the outcomes. The opportunity-to-learn rhetoric and the standards that back it will excuse intervention into the classroom, not occasionally, but systematically and at all grade levels. This agenda is presented within the same report that requires private school participation in the system. Essentially, the government plans to dictate the curriculum and instruction in both public and private schools!

SPEEDE/ExPRESS

The national goals panel encourages "all states to move as rapidly as possible to include all institutions, public and private, into the reporting system."6 What is the reporting system they refer to? The SPEEDE/ExPRESS Electronic Transcript System, already in place, is actually a combination of two systems. SPEEDE stands for Standardization of Postsecondary Education Electronic Data Exchange. ExPRESS stands for Exchange of Permanent Records Electronically for Students and Schools. The combined system is intended to facilitate and expedite the transfer of electronic files between educational institutions, agencies, corporations, or other receiving entities. They propose expanding even further by seeking permission for international data exchange in the future.[7]

States have been pressured to devise electronic data systems compatible with SPEEDE/ExPRESS:

> Even before the establishment of the Goals and the subsequent America 2000 strategy, the National Cooperative Education Statistics Systems was established by the Hawkins-Stafford Education Improvement Amendments of 1988 (P.L. 100-297) to involve state and federal governments in a mutual effort to produce state-comparable and nationally-uniform data on public and private school systems...The National Center for Education Statistics (NCES) has been overseeing the progress of the above efforts toward the improvement of education data.[8]

NCES awarded a contract to the Council of Chief State School Officers to work on implementation. The ExPRESS system is one result of that contract.

A number of computer-data system projects are already underway. The School District Data Book is a federally funded project designed for "vast stores of information from the 1990 Census, the Census Bureau's school-finance data, and the Education Department's Common Core of Data...[A]ll of the information in the new system will be packaged on CD-

ROM's...that will enable anyone with access to a personal computer and disk player to use it." *Education Week* quotes George Grier, a statistician with the MESA Group, the Alexandria, Virginia-based, firm that is producing the electronic book for the education department: "The goal is that anybody can sit down in front of a computer, flip a switch, and be guided through the process of getting the data he or she needs." Although Grier's use of the word "data" is sterile and unalarming, let's not forget we're talking about private information, going far beyond vital statistics, making public information that which has never been anything but private.

Users will have access to information about both public and private schools, as well as individual students. Grier also said that, "anything you can ask about a kid, a parent, a household" could be found on the data base. The $5.2 million project is financed by the National Center for Education Statistics, an arm of the Department of Education.[9]

Privacy Disappears

Many citizens are concerned that centralized computer systems under the control of government agencies represent a gross intrusion into personal privacy. Citizens lose the right to choose who has access to information about them. Certainly a great deal of privacy has already been lost because of computerized information kept by Social Security, credit history bureaus, Departments of Motor Vehicles, Social Services, and others. Without granting that the present situation is acceptable, we must realize that creating a data system based within the school establishment which communicates with all the other systems vastly multiplies the amount of data compiled on any one person. It also enhances the file in a more personal dimension with the incorporation of reports on achievement of attitudinal outcomes, health history, and family data.

When a national goals panel studied data collection systems, they encountered local level concerns about how a state's department of education might use the data. Accountability, control, and confidentiality, and the phrase "Big Brother" recurred frequently.[10] Unfortunately, in most cases, the public is unlikely to realize their loss of privacy and autonomy until after the fact.

The data system will be one integrated system for students, teachers, district staff, etc., and eventually be united with other governmental agency data systems. Everyone will have a unique identifying number. Social security numbers seem the most likely option right now.

Delaware typifies states that have a data system already up and running. Students are assigned unique identification numbers. Information from student assessments and demographic data (e.g., family information such as income, race, employment, participation in federal programs, etc.) are combined with student records such as report cards and scheduling. The information is shared with state and federal agencies. It is also used to do long-term studies of students, including follow-up studies of high-school graduates. This goal of tracking individuals long-term recurs in descriptions of many state data collection systems.[11]

When information is freely shared by a number of agencies, citizens have a right to be concerned about their privacy. However, a bureaucratic memorandum defending Pennsylvania's right to disclose personally identifiable information tells us that all states have the right to share such data. They quote: "Federal regulations 34 CFR part 99 (FERP), section 31, permit an education institution to disclose personally identifiable information (name, address, SSN, etc.) from a student's educational record without prior parental consent..." While they list numerous authorized recipients of such information, they conclude that "we have no evidence that would lead us to believe that this information is being provided to any individuals other than those permitted under Federal regulations, and therefore, we do not believe a violation of the FERP regulations has occurred."[12] Citizens are supposed to believe that government agencies are above using such information improperly—after all, they are going to all of this trouble for our benefit, aren't they?

Kentucky was another of the first states to implement such a system. "A fundamental KETS principle is easy and open access to all applications and services that are appropriate for a given user." They came up against the confidentiality issue though, noting in their Master Plan that "data security is required to comply with the Privacy Act of 1974..." Their disclaimer should be in fine print: "Current state-of-the-art network security systems cannot guarantee compliance with the Privacy Act. The effectiveness of a network security system is measured by its ability to detect breaches of security, track down the offender(s), and effect punitive measures to prevent further transgressions. Password control is the primary mechanism for prevention and is only as effective as the users of the system are responsible." Even worse, they say, "The possibilities for abuse extend even beyond the boundaries of the system's ability to detect or control the abuse...Users of the system that have gained access via stolen passwords can copy sensitive data to their local hard-drive or workstation for later consumption or dissemination. Although access to the data may be logged to the audit file (unless there is reason to suspect foul play) the breach may never be detected."[13]

If Kentucky admits that it is impossible for a statewide system to maintain system integrity and confidentiality, what
happens when each state's system becomes part of the federal
network? This is frightening to any person who values his or
her privacy.

Recognizing that a centralized data system lacks integrity
should cause all of us concern about what type of data might be
entered into that system. Many of us think that educational
records consist only of test and school performance results.
However, many tests or assessments intrude into personal family
areas: family reading habits, attitudes toward education, income
levels, etc. A national goals panel recommends that schools also
use a uniform national school entry form that asks parents or
guardians about "their child's birth, health, language or languages, *household and family life*, as well as about their child's
daycare or preschool experience" [italics added for emphasis].[14]

The sources for data multiply as children advance through
the school years. Add data from health and social services,
which will all be entered into the same integrated system, and
link it to Department of Motor Vehicles, Social Security
records, and credit history records. All of this sounds scary
enough, but it gets worse.

"The White House is pressing for legislation to force telephone and cable TV companies to install computer software
on their networks that would enable law-enforcement agencies to eavesdrop on phone calls and computer transmissions...
This is the previously mentioned clipper chip that the government wants computer manufacturers to install on every computer so that they can intercept and decipher computer communications. Supposedly needed to combat criminals, the
clipper chip makes it all too easy for government agencies to
intercept phone conversations or electronic communications.

Considering that 'telephone and cable companies are building advanced networks that also will be used for shopping, education and personal business, ...more than tapping telephone calls is at stake.' Entertainment, commerce, political alignment will all be topics about you, available for monitoring, on the information highway."[15]

It will become extremely difficult to hang on to our privacy in the face of such massive exposure of the minutiae of our lives.

End Notes:

[1] "U.S.: Ease wiretaps on phone and TV cables," *The Orange County Register*, Feb. 12, 1994, and John Markoff, "FBI Wants Capability to Eavesdrop on Par with New Technology," *The Orange County Register*, Feb. 28, 1994.

[2] "Decoding the Electronic Future," *U.S. News and World Report*, March 14, 1994, pp. 69-71, and John Markoff, "FBI Wants Capability to Eavesdrop on Par with New Technology," *The Orange County Register*, Feb. 28, 1994.

[3] *Student/Pupil Accounting, State Educational Records and Reports Series: Handbook V*, U.S. Department of Health, Education, and Welfare/ National Center for Education Statistics, Revised 1974.

[4] *Potential Strategies for Long-Term Indicator Development*, National Education Goals Panel, Sept. 4, 1991, p. 37.

[5] Ibid., p. 56.

[6] Ibid., p. 37.

7 "A Guide to the Implementation of the SPEEDE/ExPRESS Electronic Transcript," American Association of Collegiate Registrars and Admissions Officers, National Center for Education Statistics, and Council of Chief State School Officers, March 31, 1992.

8 "Education Data System Implementation Project," Council of Chief State School Officers, Washington, D.C., undated paper.

9 Robert Rothman, "Electronic Data Book to Expand Access to Vast Storehouse of School Information," *Education Week*, Jan. 13, 1993.

10 *Statewide Student Record Systems: Current Status and Future Trends*, National Education Goals Panel, March 26, 1992, p. 14.

11 Ibid., pp. 23-41.

12 H.M. Monaghan, Regional Inspector for Audit, U.S. Department of Education, memorandum to Leroy S. Rooker, Director, U.S. Family Policy and Regulations Office, July 29, 1993.

13 "Kentucky Education Technology System Report," Office of Education Accountability, KY, July, 1993, pp. 42-43.

14 *Measuring Progress Toward the National Education Goals: Potential Indicators and Measurement Strategies*, National Education Goals Panel, March 25, 1991, p. 10.

15 "U.S.: Ease wiretaps on phone and TV cables," *The Orange County Register*, Feb. 12, 1994.

CHAPTER TEN

NATIONAL STANDARDS, ENFORCEMENT, AND MONEY

We have good reason to be wary of governmental control. It never seems to stop where logic dictates it ought.

A recent situation concerning rights for the disabled is all too typical. The Disabled Access Division of Los Angeles Department of Building and Safety decided that the Odd Ball Cabaret was out of compliance. The problem? They had a shower enclosure where nude dancers performed while customers watched, and the shower enclosure had no wheelchair access. Those who are wheelchair-bound did not have equal opportunity to perform nude dances while "showering." Never mind that no one in California was aware of even one wheelchair-bound nude dancer whose right to equal access was being thwarted. [1]

Legislators soothingly reassure us that states need not worry about federal control through national standards because Goals 2000 makes all standards voluntary. Their use of the word *voluntary* is a perfect example of doublespeak. Don't be fooled into thinking that *voluntary* means that states will be free to choose whether or not they want to adopt the standards. *Voluntary* doesn't mean *voluntary* in the dictionary sense, only in the political sense—you can choose to cooperate or not, but the government will impose severe consequences if you choose not to.

David Hornbeck, a key player in the business of selling restructuring to the states, wrote a report for the state of Washington that repeats the same themes found in his reports to Iowa, Pennsylvania, Kansas and Oregon, among others.[2] He says, "In 1989, National Education Goals were established by the President and the nation's governors. These goals have stimulated 'outcome' based education reform efforts in many states, including Washington. [The original six goals are then listed here.] To meet these goals, substantial reform and restructuring of Washington's and the other states' education systems is required."[3] So, according to Hornbeck, the goals have been set, and the states will be "required" to cooperate.

While Hornbeck is honest about the agenda, others continue protestations of innocence. A look at the proposal version of the legislation for the Reauthorization of the Elementary and Secondary Education Act reveals the truth. "To help all children reach high standards, all parts of school systems will be aligned to the challenging standards states are developing."

They spell out even more clearly the directive that state and local education will submit to federal mandates: "Under our proposal for ESEA, Title I, bilingual education, and dozens of other federal programs will become integral to, not separate from, state and community education reforms that center on high standards...*To ensure clear accountability, information on performance will be built into efforts at all levels.* Assessments of student learning must focus on high standards, not the minima of norm-referenced, multiple-choice tests. Rather than having separate accountability systems for federal purposes, states must be able to use results from their high-standards assessment systems to fulfill federal accountability requirements. Schools must use assessment results to continually improve. And there must be consequences for their performance recognition for exemplary progress, and assistance when schools are stalled." [italics in original][4]

While states are told that they can choose whether or not to adopt standards aligned with the federal standards, the choice is hollow. First of all, the National Goals Panel is supposed to report on the progress that states make toward achieving the National Goals. They are to "...report on State opportunity-to-learn standards and strategies and the progress of States that are implementing such standards and strategies..."[5] The Goals Panel is empowered to review the "...voluntary national content standards, voluntary national student performance standards and voluntary national opportunity-to-learn standards certified by the National Education Standards and Improvement Council [also created by Goals 2000 legislation], as well as the criteria for the certification of such standards, and the criteria for the certification of State assessments certified by the National Education Standards and Improvement Council..."[6] What happens if states choose not to have their standards certified by the council or choose not to play the "standards" game at all? Their access to the federal money trough will dry up. Opting out at any stage means ineligibility.

Education Undersecretary Marshall Smith told educators and standard-setters that, "ESEA is going to come right behind Goals 2000, and it's going to reinforce it with $10 billion in Chapter 1 and other compensatory education funds to ensure that disadvantaged students meet the same standards that other kids in the state should be meeting."[7]

In this same article, Kathy Hand, an educator from Washington state raised questions about local autonomy. She queried whether school districts, autonomous under local structuring, who chose not to operate by state-set standards or curriculum frameworks, would still get federal funding to operate programs. "'You decide whether to opt in,' replied Shirley Malcolm, a leader in science standard-setting and the head of a standards review panel for the goals panel. But when Hand asked how Chapter 1 money would hinge on state or local standards, Malcolm referred her to Congress and the Education Department. 'That's so far down the track, I don't even see it now,' Malcolm said. Hand, however, thought she saw it all too clearly, and brought up the issue at the goals panel meeting...'This country was founded on local control,' she said in an interview later, fretting that 'federal funding is going to be tied to compliance,' and districts would be forced to bend or forego funds."

Still, Goals 2000 proponents point to the references to voluntary state standards, insisting that the federal government will not force its standards on anyone. This is the classic bureaucratic strategy to diffuse opposition: return the argument to the language of "doublespeak" and imply that the opponent is in some way deficient if he cannot comprehend such simple terms.

The best way to judge who is telling the truth is to look at the standards being developed in the states. We find that they are all curiously cut from the same cloth and all imprinted with the pattern of the federal goals. We see common elements appearing over and over, often with identical word-ing—curious for supposedly grass roots efforts springing up in each state independently.

Accountability to the Feds

We find out why the state goals look like they all come from the same source by reading the Reauthorization of the ESEA. According to Section 1111, those states that desire grant money must submit their plans, reflecting implementa-tion and assessment standards aligned with Goals 2000 criteria as well as the School-to-Work Opportunities Act of 1994 and the Carl D. Perkins Vocational and Applied Technology Education Act. (See Chapter 8 for more explanation of these legislative pieces.) To monitor states' adherence to the stan-dards described in their plans, the Reauthorization of the ESEA also requires states to use yearly assessments aligned with those approved standards.

To add teeth to the accountability, schools are subject to "alternative governance arrangements" or take-overs if they don't meet the standards:

> Each Title I school [schools receiving money under the ESEA] will be required to demonstrate, based on the state assessment, adequate yearly progress toward attain-ing the high state performance standards. Schools failing to make adequate progress will be identified for improve-ment and receive technical assistance from their LEA [local education agency]. If after two years in school improvement, the school still fails to make adequate progress, its LEA must take corrective actions, such as instituting alternative governance arrangements or authorizing student transfers to another school; the LEA,

however, could take such actions any time after a school is identified for improvement.[8]

The Department of Education probably picked up on the idea of accountability from David Hornbeck, whose restructuring recommendations to a number of states include Iowa. In his report, "First Draft of Recommendations on the Iowa Initiative for World Class Schools," issued September 19, 1990, Hornbeck advocates a reward and punishment system to make schools toe the line. He would establish "threshold levels of performance." "If the proportion of successful students in a school did not reach the threshold denoting satisfactory performance, assistance would be available to that school and the staff related to instruction in that school would be subject to penalties. Rewards and penalties would both be financial, but penalties would also include outside intervention and, if the situation continues, de-facto takeover by the State Department of Education's 'Iowa Mentoring Educators.'" Hornbeck's recommendations to the state of Washington are almost identical.[9]

Hornbeck is heavily into the notion of social engineering, the major theme of the larger Goals 2000 plan. In advancing the idea of a comprehensive, government-run system, he says, "One illustrative approach to accomplishing this objective would be to abolish the present State Board of Education and local boards of education and replace them with Boards of Children and Families at the state and local levels. One could then establish results for children we wish to achieve that cut across education, health, and social services."

Kentucky

Kentucky was the first state to buy into this type of plan, passing the Kentucky Education Reform Act (KERA) in 1990, which implemented total restructuring. Schools were required to demonstrate academic improvement and either be rewarded or penalized for results. Many schools have failed to perform as required. Under KERA, those schools should be getting "state assistance, some teachers should be losing their jobs, and some students should be allowed to transfer to better schools."

Kentucky Commissioner of Education Thomas C. Boysen, acknowledging that there have been numerous problems, said that schools who have made progress will be rewarded, but those who failed will get another chance. Meanwhile, they will attempt to "fix" low test scores resulting from students concluding that there is no need to perform well on tests that have no personal impact. They will also reimplement gifted and talented programs to answer criticisms that the program focuses on slower students to the detriment of those who are advanced, and address the difficulty of accurately measuring character traits such as self-sufficiency and responsible group membership.[10]

Court-assisted Takeover

What would happen if a state came up with standards and got them approved, but all of the local school districts simply ignored them? It could be embarrassing. The solution: change the funding structure for schools so that both control and funding come primarily from the state level.

Every state has its own formula for funding education, and a common, important variable in most states' formulas is property taxes. In wealthy areas, taxpayers pay more, and schools receive more. Consequently, in poorer areas where less money is collected and spent per pupil, the complaint is that school funding is inequitable. Although they have complained for many years, only recently did such low income districts seek remedy in the courts.

Recent state court decisions demonstrate that most states are thinking alike on this issue. New Hampshire's state constitution exemplifies the wording in most state constitutions when it says that the state must provide adequate and equitable funding for the public schools. The courts are tossing out present funding systems and sending legislatures to the drawing board to come up with plans that guarantee "equitable" funding.

Replacing property taxes with sales taxes and other statewide levies as sources for school funding are the popular solution in states such as New Hampshire, Idaho, Alabama, Michigan, and Wisconsin. New Hampshire is doubling the state contribution to schools. Wisconsin is increasing the state share of spending from 40 to 65 percent. Interestingly, the president of the Wisconsin Federation of Teachers said, "We would like to have at least 60 percent state funding, but would like to leave some local control through property taxes."[9] But as we have seen, whoever pays the bills (or most of them) gets to call the shots. Local control is the sure loser when funding moves to the state level.

California inadvertently led the way in turning school funding on its head with an initiative designed to cut property taxes. When Proposition 13 passed in 1978, most people were totally unaware of what it would do to school funding. Prior to the initiative's passage, local property taxes had covered approximately 50 percent of school funding. In the eight years preceding Prop 13 (1971-1978), the state's share ranged from 31 to 38 percent of the total. The next year, after implementation, state spending jumped to 65 percent of the total. According to a Claremont Institute study of California's spending on education, "The state is now driving the education system."[12]

Other states that transfer funding responsibility to state legislators will also find that local control becomes a thing of the past. But by silencing local opposition with the financial stick, they now find it much easier to implement Goals 2000.

England's Experience

England has cleared the path of educational restructuring for us. Christopher Thatcher, head teacher or principal at Potters Green School in Coventry, England, was a visiting administrator to the U.S. for six weeks under an exchange program administered jointly by the U.S. Information Agency and the Central Bureau in London. He was visiting Glenmont School in Bethlehem, NY.

An interview with Thatcher was printed in *Education Week*:

> Several reform strategies now gaining momentum in the United States such as site-based management and school choice are already firmly entrenched in Britain, where a 1988 education-reform law "fundamentally changed" the way schools are managed and children are taught there, Thatcher says.
>
> The law reduced the middle tier of the British education bureaucracy, a move akin to diminishing the powers of local school districts in the States...every school in the country set up its own on-site governing body composed of parents, staff members, and city-council appointees. Now, each school handles its own budget, makes hiring decisions, and contracts for services.

Thatcher then exhibits the same confusion about independence that is expressed by many Americans. He says, "Schools can become completely independent by applying for 'grant maintained status,' which provides the school with a direct grant from the central government...In addition to changing school governance, the law established a national curriculum in 10 subject areas and mandated a daily, 15-minute 'act of worship' in schools." Amazingly, Thatcher defines schools with government-mandated curriculum and government funding as being completely independent.

The principal of Glenmont School, Donald Robillard, recognized the contradiction. He views proposals for a national curriculum as being distinctly un-American. "There's something wrong with a national curriculum, a national testing format, because it smacks of conformity," he comments. "Diversity is the way to go."[13]

It Will Only Cost . . .

As with all government-proposed solutions, these "reforms" will require a great deal of money. Goals 2000 dishes out somewhere between $393 and $400 million.[14] The Reauthorization of The Elementary and Secondary Education Act is an $11 billion-a-year investment in education that dwarfs even the Goals 2000 millions.[15]

Millions more are authorized under a number of other related bills, making it difficult to put a price tag on the whole. As is typical of most federal programs, costs are slated to rise in coming years. Already, President Clinton has requested $700 million for Goals 2000 for 1995 (fiscal year) and plans to up the yearly ante to $1 billion.[16]

Local Level Budget Busting

Perhaps it is easier to look at the cost of reform efforts from the opposite end—the local level. Farrell, Pennsylvania, will serve as our example. Farrell is an old steel town where the unemployed constitute about 25 percent of the population. The Farrell Area School District runs an outreach project, which coordinates fifty-seven different programs for families and children. Pennsylvania's Governor Robert Casey says that the range of social services might be the most extensive offered by any district in the nation.

The district, with 1,285 students, has a budget of $8 million, not enough to cover the added expenses of this gigantic program. Officials decided to seek grant money. While it was expected that some of the grant money might come from private foundations or organizations, the bulk of it is provided by the government. Grants are the carrot-and-stick method the government uses to accomplish many of its goals. If they want programs that develop child care options, they offer grant money for those who establish such programs. If they no longer wish to see such programs, they dry up the grant money. The trouble with grant money is that it comes from taxpayers. So, when the Farrell District won $3 million in grants this year to fund these programs, much of the money came from taxpayers' pockets. Three million dollars is 37 1/2 percent of the district's original budget, thus, their costs are 37 1/2 percent higher.

As Richard Glean, a Pennsylvania executive director of student services, said, "Many of the services that Farrell provides already exist in some form in the school system...but to make them available to all students requires lots of money. Farrell is only one, relatively small, school district. If we increase school district budgets by 37 1/2%, even if we limit it

to districts with high unemployment, the cost is astronomical." Then Glean said, "...what is going on in Farrell is what
we're trying to achieve on a large scale in Philadelphia."[17] Can
Pennsylvania afford to implement such a program in a huge
district like Philadelphia?

Now let's look at how this translates when applied to other
states. California is essentially bankrupt, yet they keep approv-
ing spending for school reform. The new California Learning
Assessment, like other "authentic assessments" or outcome-
based education tests, costs far more than the previously used
tests—a projected nearly $47 million per year. That figure
(which is *only* for testing) makes Farrell's $3 million look like
peanuts. The cost of other restructuring and goal implementation programs in California is bound to be, as Richard Glean
described it, "astronomical."[18]

Kentucky, which is the first state with border-to-border
OBE, originally asked for $19.5 million for testing. The OBE
engineers had to go back to the legislature and raise that to
$29.5 million. Then, realizing how poorly they miscalculated,
they went back yet again, asking for $80 million.[19]
"Kentucky's new testing system is four times as expensive as
the old multiple-choice tests."[20]

A return to England, where outcome-based assessments
have been used for a number of years, offers an even better
estimate of testing costs. There, the cost for developing, pilot-
ing, and administering such tests for *one* level is $175 million.
Considering that the U.S. proposes to educate about four and
one-half times the number of students that England has, the
figure for a single level is bound to be higher. Now, get out
your calculators and multiply that by the number of levels, or
school grades. The result is in the multiple billions of dollars
just for testing.[21]

Several European countries use "essay-on-demand" tests with older students which require hand scoring, at a cost of $135 per student. This would be the minimal amount, since tests being developed here are much more complex. Applying even the minimal cost to students in the U.S., the least such assessments to older students alone will cost is $750 million.[22]

Each student will have a portfolio—the new test being only one component—that will contain samples and records of all work done to meet outcomes accumulated, assessed, and evaluated throughout their school years. It is expected that the portfolio contents will be linked to other personal information on the new data system. Some discussions of portfolios include plans to computerize and integrate all information into the national data system. However, portfolios at present often include video or audio tapes plus other evidences that cannot be readily computerized. It remains to be seen if students will have both a physical and a computer portfolio. The point is that compiling portfolios is another very time-consuming task for teachers, and many of them spend out-of-school hours completing them. It is not practical to expect all teachers to donate the extra hours, so the additional cost of maintaining portfolios must be factored into restructuring costs.[23]

Alabama faces almost insurmountable financial hurdles to implement court-ordered education reform, a plan that is expected to cost nearly $1 billion. There is no popular support for the reforms or increased spending for education, and legislators are extremely reluctant to raise taxes in an election year to cover costs. "I think we'll have a reform package done without complete funding of it," was the summation of Representative Taylor Harper, chairman of the House Ways and Means Committee in Alabama.[24]

Extending government services into the school-to-work realm will cost $300 million in the first year and unpredictable millions more after that. There will be a whole new layer of bureaucrats to act as liaisons among employers, schools, teachers, students, and parents, providing technical assistance and services to employers; assist schools and employers in integrating school-based and work-based learning; train teachers, workplace mentors, and counselors; match students with employers' work-based learning opportunities; and assist students who have completed the program in finding jobs.[25]

One-stop service centers, assessment, school-to-work programs, not to mention education itself, will all require major increases in expenditures under restructuring. The legislation for all of these new programs contains some interesting wording; specific sums are allocated for the first year of the programs, then typically they say, "There are authorized to be appropriated...such sums as may be necessary in each of the...succeeding fiscal years for allocations to carry out this Act." Nobody knows what this is going to cost! Yet, our legislators pass these bills as if the pot is bottomless.

Some districts try to hide actual costs. The Daniel Boone District in Pennsylvania bragged that it only cost them an extra $40,000 to implement OBE. What they forget to mention was the extra $300,000 in grant money that they also received, but the truth was exposed by the wife of a school board member.[26] One can only surmise that true costs are not readily acknowledged because they might raise unanswerable questions.

Can any state or the country as a whole afford these programs? Education and transfer payments (welfare, unemployment, etc.) already require the lion's share of government money at all levels. Some advocates of expanded programs say that coordination of agency services requires merely shuffling the money around, but assigning parent educators and social workers to each family, and assigning case managers to individuals at the high-school level and into adulthood costs a great deal more money. It is irresponsible not to ask, even if we want the services, whether we can afford them. From a purely fiscal perspective, the answer has to be "No!" In fact, financial limitations might bring a halt to government ambitions without the philosophical issues even being addressed.

The problems with federal aid to education were ably addressed by five congressmen in relation to the National Defense Education Act Amendment of 1961 (87th Congress, First Session, Rept. 674, pt. 2.) Their statement was lengthy, but it is worth reading because it so clearly foretold what happens when the federal government pays for education. They said:

> We, the undersigned members of the committee, believe that the respective States have done and are doing an outstanding job to meet the challenge of the sixties in the field of education.
>
> We hold that the record of accomplishment by the States and local communities in the last 10 years has been remarkable. The advocates of Federal aid to education have failed to prove the case of need. The figures speak for themselves.
>
> Public school expenditures alone have risen 1 1/2 times as fast as national income in the last 10 years. These expenditures have also risen much faster than spending for personal consumption.
>
> Public school enrollment had its greatest growth of all time during the past 10 years with a rise of 43 per-

cent, but over the same period public school revenues increased 152 percent in actual amount and 98 percent in dollars of constant value.

In the matter of construction of classrooms, the classroom needs are being met without Federal aid. Since the 1954-55 school year, the classroom inventory across the Nation has increased by 30 percent while enrollment was increasing by 20 percent.

In the matter of availability of teachers, teaching staffs grew to such an extent that the number of pupils per teacher dropped from 28.4 in 1953-54 to 26 in 1960-61. The record seems clear that outstanding progress is being made by the States and local communities in the field of education, and it is our opinion that a Federal aid program would only serve to stifle this healthy initiative already being shown at the local level.

We reject, furthermore, the philosophy that there can exist Federal aid to any degree without Federal control. We further hold that there should not be Federal aid without Federal control. It is the responsibility of the Federal Government to so supervise and control its allocations that waste and misuse is kept at a minimum.

Since we do not desire such Federal control in the field of public education, we do not desire Federal aid to education.

We should never permit the American educational system to become the vehicle for experimentation by educational ideologies. A careful analysis of the writings and statements of vocal and influential spokesmen in the governmental and educational fields indicates a desire on the part of some of these individuals to utilize the

educational system as a means of transforming the economic and social outlook of the United States.

We point to a statement by Dr. Harold Rugg, for
many years professor of education at Teachers College,
Columbia University, who declared in "Frontiers of
Democracy" on May 15, 1943 (pp. 247 to 254) concerning the teacher colleges, "let them become powerful
national centers for the graduate study of ideas and they
will thereby become forces of creative imagination
standing at the very vortex of the ideational revolution.
Let us make our teacher education institutions into great
direction finders for our new society, pointers of the way,
dynamic trailblazers of the New Frontiers."

We could supply pages of documentation analyzing
the type of new frontier planned. It is indeed a Socialist
frontier. It had been hoped that the philosophy of education expressed by Dr. Rugg and his cohorts back in the
early forties, had long since been repudiated. However,
in April of 1961, the U.S. Department of Health,
Education, and Welfare published a booklet entitled, "A
Federal Education Agency for the Future." Anyone who
doubts that the Federal aid to education bills now before
Congress would mean eventual Federal control of education should carefully read and analyze for himself what
the Office of Education is planning for tomorrow's
schools. They openly predict their "need" for new powers on the passage of the multimillion-dollar aid legislation now before us. They recommend that their Office of
Education be elevated to the status of U.S. Education
Agency, "to reflect the more active role of this unit of
Government." They envision the new Agency's mission
as one of "leadership" (p.42), "national policy making"
(p. 43), "national planning" (p. 47), a broadening of

"Federal interest in curriculum and improvement of instruction" (p. 49), "to prepare students to understand the world of tomorrow" (p. 40).

The Office of Education writers further say, "along with these responsibilities should be included that of stimulating and participating actively in the process of formulation, examination, and reformulation of the goals of our society in the terms of educational objectives" (p. 43).

In our opinion, this quietly circulated publication of the U.S. Department of Health, Education, and Welfare entitled "A Federal Education Agency for the Future" shows that there has been no basic change in the plans of the professional political educationists who, like Dr. Rugg, see the educational system as a means of remaking our society to fit their ideas of what is right and proper.

H.R. 7904, as proposed, is more than an expansion and ballooning of a department of the Federal Government. In our opinion, it is a clear attempt to take command and control of the American educational system. Under the cry of "emergency," the Department already has its toe in the door with the National Defense Education Act of 1958, which does not expire until June 30, 1962. H.R. 1904 is disguised as an extension of the NDEA. The original NDEA bill was born of the Sputnik panic as an emergency measure to provide temporary programs. It was designed to step up opportunities for needy students of engineering, science, and languages, and it provided for liquidation after 1966 (Public Law 85-864).

H.R. 7904, however, would redefine the purposes of the Act. It would put the Federal Government into the permanent business of teacher training at all levels of education, both public and private (sec. 205 b 3). That inevitably must result in specifications, standardized courses, and controls. This places State certification of teachers subject to Federal control, the key measure of all.

The document was signed by William H. Ayres, Edgar W. Hiestand, Donald C. Bruce, John M. Ashbrook, and Dave Martin.

In further floor discussion of the amendment, Congressman Ashbrook said,

> "We can assist local schools by a system of tax remission with no controls. We must remember, however, that the Federal bureaucrats control the expenditure of Federal funds. I think what we are faced with here is the complete domination of our State and local school systems by educators in Washington. I think anyone who reads 'Federal Education Agency for the Future' will certainly conclude that it represents a blueprint for Federal control and can readily lead to indoctrination of our students according to the political, social and international beliefs of our Washington bureaucrats."[27]

Prophecy or Common Sense?

The remarks of these five congressmen appear prophetic when reading them more than thirty years later, but they needed no supernatural assistance to see where the legislation would lead. A review of the history of our country reveals how laws are interpreted and/or applied.

The income tax serves as a familiar example. When the first income tax law was passed (aside from the temporary and unconstitutional income tax levied during the Civil War), it was both unpopular and unconstitutional. The Sixteenth Amendment to the Constitution permitting income taxation was ratified in 1913, although there have been numerous constitutional challenges ever since. At that time, the income tax ranged from 1 percent (on incomes up to $20,000) to a top rate of 6 percent on income over $500,000. (Remember, these are 1913 dollars.)[28]

Legislators made placating speeches, promising that income taxes would never go beyond 1 percent for the average family. We are all reminded how far beyond it has risen every April. On top of that, the Sixteenth Amendment never authorized a graduated or progressive tax on income, but only a uniform tax.[29] This is an example of how, when all three branches of the government agree to an idea in principle, constitutionality and individual rights seem to become irrelevant.

We began this chapter talking about being wary of government control. After all we have discussed, we have no reason to trust that the mammoth Goals 2000 legislation will not be used to expand government control beyond that which is clearly stated—as bad as that is likely to prove to be. The president's signature was barely dry on Goals 2000, and the Carnegie Corporation initiated their push for further control. They immediately pressed for expanded programs "for ages birth to 3 years" that would "provide new federal aid to improve child care for children under 3...[and] offer home visits to all first-time mothers and more comprehensive programs for at-risk families...[and] provide comprehensive programs to encourage planning for parenthood by all couples to avoid unnecessary risks and promote a healthy environment for child development."[30]

Hillary Clinton was a keynote speaker at a meeting sponsored by the Carnegie Corporation soon after the release of their report about the "crisis facing our youngest children." According to a report in *Education Week*, "Mrs. Clinton said the children's movement has been thwarted by a 'false debate' between one camp that believes families should be held solely accountable for children's outcomes and another that says society must assume responsibility for downtrodden families." She says that the real targets are interrelationships between families and society. She went on to pitch government solutions, such as the Clinton health care plan and a host of other programs.[31]

On another front, the National Center on Education and the Economy, a key instigator of the school-to-work legislation and its inclusion in Goals 2000, is pushing to replace traditional diplomas with the Certificates of Mastery as soon as possible. Although six states are working with the certificates thus far, the NCEE argues that the certificates are worth far less if they are not accepted everywhere. Their answer is nationwide use of the Certificates of Mastery and the requirement that all students must meet the standards set by the New Standards Project.[32]

At a conference of the Council for Exceptional Children, speakers described how Goals 2000 serves as the model for "other legislative actions." The upcoming reauthorization of the Individuals with Disabilities Education Act was used as an example. That legislation will be crafted using Goals 2000 as the blueprint, with the aim of providing special resources and accommodations for all special needs students so that they, too, can pass the tests and obtain Certificates of Mastery. Such accommodations must be made within the regular classroom for almost all special needs students, according to leaders in the inclusion movement.[33]

The message from those who designed a National Goal to read that U.S. students will lead the world in science and mathematics achievement now implies that, if the price for mainstreaming these students is a slowing of educational accomplishment for all others, so be it. Try explaining that to a teacher whose performance will be evaluated according to how well he accomplishes these conflicting goals. If the enabling legislation for full inclusion comes from Washington D.C., then local districts can no longer make decisions about the practicality of such programs in their schools.

We can find similar examples of chaos and contradiction for every tentacle of Goals 2000. The monster was given birth with the passage of Goals 2000, and, like any infant, it will grow.

End Notes:

[1] "Disabled-access Law Douses Shower Show," *Orange County Register*, April 21, 1994.

[2] Judy McLemore, "Educational Excellence or Social Experiment," *Free World Research Report*, August, 1993, p. 4.

[3] David W. Hornbeck, Milt Doumit, Ronn Robinson, "Washington Gap Analysis," prepared under the auspices of the Business Roundtable, July 29, 1992, p. 4.

[4] "Improving America's Schools Act of 1993: The Reauthorization of The Elementary and Secondary Education Act and Amendments to Other Acts," *Education Week*, October 20, 1993, pp. 1-2.

5 *Goals 2000: Educate America Act*, Conference Report, Title II, Part A, Sec. 203 (a)(2).

6 Ibid, Sec. 201 (3).

7 "Leaders Mull Voluntary Nature of National Academic Standards," *Education Daily*, Vol. 26, No. 222, Nov. 17, 1993. Chapter 1 and Title 1 refer to a section of the Elementary and Secondary Education Act authorizing funds for special-needs programs. It was originally called Title 1, changed to Chapter 1, and, now, changes back to Title 1.

8 "Improving America's Schools Act of 1993: The Reauthorization of The Elementary and Secondary Education Act and Amendments to Other Acts," *Education Week*, October 20, 1993, p.24.

9 David W. Hornbeck, Milt Doumit, Ronn Robinson, "Washington Gap Analysis," prepared under the auspices of the Business Roundtable, July 29. 1992, p. 35.

10 Lonnie Harp, "Kentucky Officials Announce 'Corrections' to Reform," *Education Week*, January 26, 1994, p. 13.

11 Peter Schmidt, "Wis. Conferees Appear Close on School-Finance Overhaul," *Education Week*, March 30, 1994, p. 14; "Wis. Legislature Clears Property-Tax Reductions," *Education Week*, April 6, 1994, p. 13.

12 "California's Education System: Where Does All the Money Go?," Golden State Center for Policy Studies, The Claremont Institute, Sacramento, CA, Feb. 1992, pp. 2-3.

13 Joanna Richardson, "A Trans-Atlantic Tale of Two Principals," *Education Week*, Nov. 17, 1993, p. 30.

14 Mark Pitsch, "Next Stop for Goals 2000 Bill: House-Senate Conference," *Education Week*, Feb. 16, 1994, p. 18.

[15] "Improving America's Schools Act of 1993: The Reauthorization of The Elementary and Secondary Education Act and Amendments to Other Acts," *Education Week*, October 20, 1993, p.1.

[16] Mark Pitsch, "E.D. Form for Goals Funding Sent to States," *Education Week*, May 4, 1994, p. 19.

[17] Denise-Marie Santiago, "Low-Income School District Leads Nation in Innovation," *The Orange County Register*, Nov. 25, 1993.

[18] Bill Honig (State Superintendent of Public Instruction), *A New Statewide Student Assessment System: Five-Year Cost and Implementation Plan*, California Department of Education, 1992, p. 39.

[19] Eric Gregory, "Boysen Seeks $80 million to test students," *Lexington Herald Leader*, Lexington, KY, July 30, 1991.

[20] "The Perfect School," *U.S. News and World Report*, Jan. 11, 1993, p. 57.

[21] George F. Madaus and Thomas Kellaghan, "The British Experience with 'Authentic' Testing," *Phi Delta Kappan*, Feb. 1993, p. 467.

[22] Ibid.

[23] "The Perfect School," *U.S. News and World Report*, Jan. 11, 1993, p. 57.

[24] Millicent Lawton, "Reform Bill's Prospects In Ala. Appear to Dim," *Education Week*, Dec. 1, 1993, p. 11.

[25] H.R. 2884 "School-to-Work Opportunities Act of 1994.

[26] Marsha Hulshart, "Beware of OBE's hidden cost," (letters) *Daily Local News*, West Chester, PA. This is reproduced in *To Tell the Truth*, researched and compiled by Peg Luksik, PA Parents Commission, Johnstown, PA, 1993.

27 Text reprinted in *Wisconsin Report*, Vol. XVII, No. 41, Oct. 22, 1992.

28 J. Steven Wilkins, *America, The First 350 Years*, Covenant Publications, Monroe, LA, p. 99.

29 Clarence B. Carson, *Basic American Government*, American Textbook Committee, Wadley, AL, 1993, pp. 378-79.

30 "Starting Points: Meeting the Needs of Our Youngest Children," Carnegie Corporation of New York, NY, 1994, and Deborah L. Cohen, "Carnegie Corp. Presses Early-Years Policies," *Education Week*, April 13, 1994, pp. 1, 13.

31 Deborah L. Cohen, "Report on 'Quiet Crisis' for Young Children Stirs Loud Response," *Education Week*, April 20,1994, p. 7.

32 "A New 'Social Compact' for Mastery in Education," article in "By All Measures: The Debate Over Standards and Assessments," a Special Report from *Education Week*, June 17, 1992

33 Sara Sklaroff, "Goals 2000 Seen Spurring 'Inclusion Movement,' *Education Week*, April 20, 1994, p. 5.

CHAPTER ELEVEN

RISK, RESPECT, AND RESPONSIBILITY

Robert Marzano had assumed that Christians were the "bad guys" and it was necessary to stop them. When Christians attacked his thinking skills program, he decided he was going to figure out what was wrong with those people. After examining the controversy from both sides, he concluded, "I now see them as fundamentally different from me in some of the basic assumptions that underlie their worldview. The assumptions on which their worldview is based are as unprovable as the assumptions on which my worldview (and that of most educators) is based."[1]

Basic assumptions about freedom, individual responsibility, religious or philosophical values, and the purpose of life are present in the National Education Goals and all of the associated programs. While some citizens might agree with those assumptions, many do not.

Worldviews collide on a number of points in the goals. While the debate regarding varying worldview perspectives is wide-ranging, we will simplify by concentrating on the contrast between conservative Christians (often falsely generalized as Fundamentalists) and the secular humanist worldview that dominates modern education.

What most people fail to recognize is the irreconcilable nature of these conflicts. For example, schools often try to instill self esteem in students, based on the philosophical belief that people are innately good, and society and other influences cause them to do bad things. The Christian belief is that all men are sinners and need salvation and God's grace to even attempt to be good. When schools teach self esteem in a way that contradicts a parental message about the need for salvation, the parents have no room for compromise. It would be silly to say, "We'll only tell the children that they are good three days a week instead of five."

Values clarification presents a similar dilemma. In values clarification, children are presented with various situations, then urged to determine right courses of action in each. There are no right and wrong answers to such exercises, because they are based on the belief that each person must develop his own value system. Meanwhile, Christians are teaching that there are absolute standards of right and wrong based on the Bible, and that man is a poor source of values because he has limited knowledge. If schools teach children that they must determine their own values rather than accepting those of their parents, they are directly undermining traditional parental authority and beliefs.

Many secularists would not intentionally undermine parents, but their assumptions about schools, authority, and education blind them to the nature and validity of criticism from the Right. Typical is the comment by Thomas Boysen, Kentucky commissioner of education, who does not believe that parents offended by assaults upon their religious beliefs have a legitimate grievance. He says, "We will continue to have attacks on public education, and people who feel this is an assault on religion...but there are also people who have a grievance, and we need to make adjustments based on their concerns."[2] Statements like these provoke us to wonder what does constitute a grievance.

Some Christians have determined that the solution to these attacks on their worldview is to reclaim authority over the schools by electing majorities to the school boards. While Christian majorities on school boards are restrained legally from making major changes in the schools, they can do as the Vista, California, school board did when it required that evolution be taught as unproven theory rather than proven fact. They can drop self-esteem programs and other curricula with "New Age" content. These actions spur modern educators to rise up, condemning the new oppressors for imposing their worldview on all the children. Curiously, secularists view condom distribution, sex education, and self-esteem programs as values neutral, but if Christians prefer to teach abstinence rather than self-esteem, they are "inappropriately forcing their beliefs on others."

Two of the most visible antagonists in the School Wars have been Citizens for Exellence in Education (CEE), headed by Dr. Robert Simonds, and Citizens Project, a Colorado Springs-based group. Dr. Simonds says, "The separation of church and state is another myth the ACLU, NEA and NOW have sold the public. Secular humanism is a self-pronounced one-world religion. It has control of public education. It is the state church right now."[3]

CEE assists parents and concerned citizens in forming local CEE chapters. "Chapters are intended to *reshape public school education* by promoting and encouraging academic quality, morality based on Biblical principles, conservative American traditions, family values, and overall excellence in public education. Each CEE chapter strives *to promote an excellent education in their local public schools* through the sound and thorough education of children for the challenges of the twenty-first century; and to protect them from harmful programs, curriculum, and teaching techniques which undermine family values and Godly morals."[4] [Italics in original]

Citizens Project decribes the origins of their group: "In the Pikes Peak area, we are seeing a push toward prayer in the schools, pressure to modify school curriculum to reflect religious views, the rise of stealth candidates in elections, increased anti-gay activity, and growing religious intolerance. Citizens Project was formed to challenge those trends."[5] Citizens Project counters CEE efforts with their own newsletter, *Freedom Watch*. They, too, instruct people on "Getting Involved in Public Schools," including how to get elected to the school board, but with an emphasis on challenging the "religious right." Their September/October 1993 newsletter says, "Nationally, local school board elections are getting more attention as controversy flares over issues such as prayer in school, outcome-based education, sex education curricula and creationism. Our local school board elections may reflect this clash over the classroom as the gulf widens between the worldviews of the political mainstream and single-issue advocates wishing to promote their religious agenda in public schools." The article continues with warnings about possible "stealth candidates" backed by Pat Robertson's Christian Coalition and CEE. It ends, "As concerned parents and members of the community, we should not underestimate what might happen if the religious right gained control of our local school boards. If you are interested in working to maintain balanced school boards through informing voters, please call Citizens Project..."[6]

The question begs to be asked but goes unanswered: if the Religious Right constituted a majority in a small town, would their antagonists accept a "balanced" board on which the Religious Right held most of the seats?

In a society such as ours, made up of widely diverse cultures and worldviews, the clashes are likely to increase, rather than decrease. Within our public school system, the only way to stop the worldview wars is to rewrite the Constitution, impose a standardized worldview upon all children, and muzzle complaining parents. If the next generation could be shaped to one, broad, "tolerant" worldview, the problem would be solved, and opposition would be heard no more. There might be a few people who do not cringe at the idea of thought-control, but most of us find the idea absolutely abhorrent.

The worldview problem cannot be solved within the present system, unless we choose to chuck the Constitution and take a totalitarian approach—"You will abide by this state-approved worldview." Unfortunately, the authors of the Goals 2000 do not realize that this is the solution they have chosen.

Is Choice in Education the Answer?

Some claim that the answer to this dilemma is the school voucher or choice in education. The arguments follow this reasoning:

The public schools are a disaster. They are not providing an adequate education in many cases. Public schools are unresponsive to parental demands for improvement, whether by inherent design, mismanagement or neglect. Public schools are also unresponsive to parental complaints about the curriculum and teaching methods.

Some parents feel that they are prisoners to the system—after paying taxes they cannot afford private schooling, yet the public school is inadequate. Other parents pay taxes for education, then pay again, often making extreme sacrifices, to send their own children to private school—an unfair double-barrel expense.

Vouchers seem to be the perfect solution, allowing parents to select from among public or private schools, with part or all of the cost of the private school option paid for by the government. They back up their conclusions with arguments that the competition offered by private schools will force public schools to improve. This community-interest sidecar gains the self-interest motivation a smoother ride.

If we ignore history, economics and the Constitution, we can accept these arguments. However, it is dangerous to do so. The principle at work here is the age-old "He who pays the piper calls the tune."

Setting aside arguments about taxation itself, the government is supposed to ensure that tax money is spent for approved purposes. They are not to give it away without any accountability. They don't always do this well, but this principle has been applied to the extreme in the public school system, with miles of red tape attached to every dollar. If private schools wish to receive government money, they, too, will be subject to the same controls as public schools. Attempts have been made to restrict government regulation of voucher-receiving schools, with protective language in some voucher intiatives and legislation. However, mismanagement, educational neglect, perceived racism or other missteps by even one voucher-receiving school are likely to prompt a burst of regulation.

Witness the cry for increased regulations of universities after the exposure of widespread Pell Grant fraud. Or, consider Milwaukee's limited-choice program which encompassed seven schools the first year of operation. One of those schools filed for bankruptcy protection in the middle of the year. Immediately a list of legislative accountability measures was drawn up to prevent such situations from recurring. That particular school's intentions were probably honorable, but not all schools will be founded by people with the best interests of children in mind.

Envision a con artist moving into an area where few of the parents speak English. He convinces them to enroll their children in his wonderful private school, but the parents, because of the language barrier, do not see that instead of receiving an education, their children are being used to help the proprietor collect their "school stamps." One such case would almost force the legislature to increase governmental oversight.

The potential for fraud in a voucher system would be immense because of the amount of money; the number of children, families, and schools involved; and the difficulty of tracking all of these elements accurately. Consider from this single angle: we want the government to make sure that children slated to receive voucher money actually exist. We all know about phantom welfare recipients, and we do not want to create an army of phantom voucher recipients. This would require data tracking on individual children and families to ensure that they are collecting only one voucher for each authentic child. More monitoring of private lives would be instituted, keeping tabs on every voucher-receiving child and family. Private schools would also have to open their enroll-ment records for government perusal as well as submit their curriculum for inspection and approval. The trade-off of fami-ly, individual, and private school privacy is a serious sacrifice of freedom, but one that would be necessary to prevent fraud.

In attempts to avoid regulation of private schools, some vouchers specify that money goes directly to parents rather than to the school. However, there is legal doubt that this will circumvent government intervention. Chester Finn, chief architect of the national goals and a voucher advocate, was asked, "Can legislation be drafted with appropriate language to insure complete autonomy of participating private and Christian schools?" He answered: "Some to be sure, like to think they can have it both ways; i.e. can obtain aid without saddling themselves with unacceptable forms of regulation. But most acknowledge the general applicability of the old adage that he who pays the piper calls the tune, and are more or less resigned to amalgamating or choosing between assis-tance and autonomy."[7]

Richard Mitchell in an article titled "Voucher, Smoucher," said, "It is simply naive to imagine that our government, or any government anywhere, will construe tax credits or vouch-ers as a way of letting its citizens keep, and spend as they please, some of their own money."[8]

Indirect Regulation

Regulation is not always direct. Requiring voucher-receiv-ing schools to meet outcome standards or administer outcome-based education tests is not direct control in the sense of dictating specific curriculum, but it is indirect regula-tion because standards and testing will themselves dictate the curriculum. According to Eva Baker, director of the Center for the Study of Evaluation at the University of California at Los Angeles:

> The "standards" have become a code word for what we used to call curriculum...For political reasons, it's seen as inappropriate to call this entity "curriculum" in a national context. So those backing national standards have softpedaled the "national curriculum" connotation while insisting that adoption of the standards by local districts and states will be voluntary...The major philosophical barrier to a national curriculum, concern over local control and flexibility in curriculum matters, has fallen by the wayside...[9]

Tests (now more commonly called "assessments") are key to implementation of the national goals. "...[A]ssessment systems would be developed by clusters of states that come together to define a shared curriculum framework and procedures for assessment. The cluster results would be linked together and to a common national standard, possibly with the use of a national anchor examination."[10]

"The Resource Group...continues to recommend that a nationwide system including several examinations in each subject matter, all calibrated to a single national standard...be developed."[11]

"The proposed nationwide assessment system is intended not only to provide a means of monitoring progress, but to contribute to the major changes in the nation's education system that are needed to achieve Goal 3."[12]

"The proposed nationwide assessment system is based on a vision of assessment that is closely linked to learning and instruction. Assessments would be based on clearly defined curriculum frameworks. The end-of-decade system would be radically different from testing programs that are currently in use in states and local districts throughout the country."13

All of this tells us that tests shape the curriculum, forcing schools to change the content and methods of teaching so that their students will achieve better test scores.

Most voucher proponents sincerely desire to improve education. They also want to increase parental authority and strengthen private schools. However, when the voucher concept was first proposed, federal control was not the major issue it has become in the years since. Nationalized curriculum and standards were unthinkable. Even when the 1993 voucher initiative in California was written, the term "national standards" loosely implied that we would raise the level of learning for all learners. Few realized that "national standards" would become synonymous with outcome-based education. When voucher authors included a requirement for testing tied to national standards, they were thinking computer-bubble, standardized testing, not the affective, subjective tests being developed for OBE. The ensuing federal legislation has made voucher proposals far more dangerous than proponents envisioned.

Enlarging Government Dependency

Good intentions aside, the voucher encompasses a larger political issue that few recognize. If the government began a program that benefitted you personally, would you be likely to vote for more funding for that program in the future? I think that very few of us could honestly say "no." Even when the budget gets tight, we each want "our share." And we also find it more difficult to do without something we have become accustomed to receiving than to turn down something we have not yet received.

Vouchers encourage more citizens to expect their "share" of government money. By cycling taxpayers' money through government hands, then back to parents, vouchers would create a new category of people who will become dependent upon government largess. This plays into the educational bureaucrats' hands because voucher recipients now join the lobby defending and promoting increased expenditures for education at all levels because they benefit from it personally. When the educational bureaucracy has more dollars under its control, it also increases its control over the form of education. Although vouchers were originally intended to provide more freedom to parents and children, they will end up accomplishing the opposite.

Regulation of Colleges and Universities

Funding has been a trap for institutions of higher learning. Many voucher advocates have pointed to colleges and universities as an example of the free-market education we can have at elementary and secondary levels under voucher plans. But few people realize how much freedom institutions of higher learning have lost since the government began assisting students with aid from the GI Bill, Pell Grants, and other programs.

In the 1980s two famous confrontations let slip how strong government intrusion had become. Bob Jones University and Grove City College both refused to sign compliance forms which would have indicated their agreement to abide by a number of federal regulations. These regulations were written to apply only to government institutions, but the courts decided that any institution receiving government money, even indirectly through student tuition, must comply with all federal regulations. Other colleges and universities have been challenged and have chosen to give in to the government muscle. Bob Jones University and Grove City College both refused. To this day, neither accepts one cent of government money, because that is the only way to stay free of government regulation.

Jerry Falwell's Liberty University was one of the more recent victims which succumbed to the lure of federal money. Liberty is an overtly Christian university, but they caved in on a number of important issues. One of the most crucial was the right to require students and faculty to agree to abide by their doctrinal statement. Liberty can no longer control what teachers teach in their classrooms.

Accreditation is another tentacle of federal control. Most universities and colleges are accredited by one of a number of accrediting agencies. These agencies set standards, review academic programs, check out the financial situations of institutions, etc. (There are similar accrediting agencies for other levels of education.) Accrediting agencies already have a significant amount of control over colleges and universities. Institutions of higher learning want to be accredited because it gives them credibility, and it also makes their students eligible for government aid. The power of accrediting agencies has grown through the years, reaching a point of confrontation over a number of issues, including "diversity guidelines."[14]

But accreditation has not prevented multi million-dollar fraud in federally funded student-aid programs. The fraud revelations have led the education department, in January 1994, to release a draft of new regulations to strengthen its control. The regulations would "increase accrediting agencies' responsibilities and would also establish State Postsecondary Review Entities to tighten oversight of institutions' finances and academic programs." Even more regulations are due under which "accrediting agencies would be required to establish standards for assessing institutions in 12 areas, among them recruiting and admissions practices, program lengths and tuition, curriculum, and graduation rates."

Colleges and universities are left with little choice in the matter, since compliance is required in order for their students to receive federal aid. Yet, private institutions of higher learning are strongly concerned that the new regulations will open the door even further for government intrusion into their internal affairs.[15]

The history of higher education in the U.S. only serves to prove that government money never comes without strings attached. Viewed alongside health care, social security and welfare programs, we see a consistent pattern of federal funding linked to mandates, regulations, and controls.

If we are able, we should take a mental step away from the situation and consider a comparison. What if we were the ones with all of the money, and it was our responsibility to dole it out? How would we do it? Would we hand it out with no strings attached? It is highly unlikely that any of us would answer "yes." One might assume that the government is simply doing what it ought—trying to require accountability from recipients of its largess.

A Socialist By Any Other Name...

Unfortunately, government efforts to fix problems and require accountability generally have made things worse. Government-run schooling and social-welfare programs have caused more harm than good. As the problems and the panic mount, people feel insecure. Paradoxically, the typical reaction is to look to government for even more fix-it programs. We keep falling back on the false assumption that more government spending, and with it more government control, will solve all of society's ills.

In our grab for security, we have sold more and more of our rights and our freedom to the government—so much so that soon we will no longer be able to claim that we are a free people. When we allow the government to tell us how to parent, we will have violated the autonomy of our families. When we allow the national government to dictate curriculum for the entire nation, we will have given up the right to influence that curriculum. When we rely on the federal government for health care, we will have given up the right to make decisions about what type of care we will use. When we rely on the government for job training and placement, we will have given up the freedom to determine our careers.

Children naturally look to parents to provide a reasonable level of security in their lives. They expect that they will be fed today, tomorrow and the next day. They don't usually live in fear that they will suddenly be thrown out onto the streets alone. But there is a price to pay. The security of belonging to a family carries with it some restrictions. Children do not have total freedom; they must follow the family rules to whatever extent they are enforced. Those bright enough to analyze this situation usually conclude that the price of family-imposed restrictions and controls is a reasonable trade-off for the security they enjoy. In the long run, it's a pretty good deal.

Adulthood should be a time of assuming self-responsibility, of accepting increased risks and responsibilities in exchange for a great deal more freedom. Unfortunately, too many adults are rejecting risks and responsibilities and, because you can't be a dependent child forever, they are opting for dependency upon the government. These pseudo-adults expect the government to provide that same security that they experienced as children. They view all sustenance as a right rather than something that requires effort on their part. Hungry? The government should make sure everyone is fed. Jobless? The government should make sure everyone has a job. Hurt? Medical care is your right. Homeless? You have the right to government-subsidized housing.

Such security demands a steep price: that we revert to the role of children and accept the restrictions and controls of governmental "parents." As millions of citizens clamor for security, those formulating governmental policy have responded by giving them what they have asked for—security at a price. We are not the first country to choose to sacrifice freedom in search of security. And we won't be the first to find out that this is the path to ruin.

Western European countries are farther down this path than the United States. A newspaper editorial describes their plight:

> As Western Europe digs itself ever more deeply into a recession, with soaring unemployment and no recovery imminent, it's becoming increasingly apparent that too much government is to blame. These countries, after all, comprise the cradle of modern 'social democracy,' where governments from Sweden to Italy, from the United Kingdom to Germany, for generations have promised cradle-to-grave coverage through assorted social services.

The editorial went on to quote from the *Wall Street Journal:* "Some of the social and labor policies put in place over the past 40 years to ward off poverty, it now turns out, are in fact increasing social misery. That is because the status quo, with its tangle of labor regulations and rising costs for employers, acts as a major disincentive to job creation and a powerful incentive to moving production elsewhere."[16]

In *Animal Farm*, George Orwell's thinly veiled critique of socialism, the animals revolted against the farmer's treatment of them and took over the farm. The animals merely wanted a reasonable level of security with food, shelter, and kind treatment. It wasn't long before the pigs, deemed more intelligent than the other animals, took responsibility for running the farm. Soon the pigs convinced the animals that they needed to make sacrifices for the security and welfare of the farm. Before long they had sacrificed themselves into a state worse than when they were under Farmer Jones. Of course, the pigs needed to live in the warm house and have first claim on the best food because they had such vital responsibility. No matter how difficult things seemed, the animals were still under the illusion that they were now free and all animals were equal. They failed to realize that they had become slaves to the pigs who offered false promises of security.

In the United States, citizens are rapidly becoming slaves to the government. Government bureaucrats, usually well-intentioned, claim to know what is best for the rest of us, even if we do not perceive the results of their efforts as being for our benefit. By assuming the roles of children or slaves, people have given up the right to object to how the government makes use of them. Just as in families, parents make decisions based on their priorities; and on plantations, owners run the show; so do the needs and desires of the government take priority. Because this state of affairs has been accepted without controversy for some years, individual and family rights are now treated with contempt, as being of no importance in light of the state's interests. The result is best described as socialism.

I doubt that most of the social engineers set out to impose socialism upon us. Many of them were confident in their ability to help solve problems. Unfortunately, most of them valued their programs more than the people they thought they were helping. Marvin Olasky says:

> Let's be concerned for the poor themselves, for the missed opportunities in relation to helping them, and for the harm which is done to them by means of bad public policy which feeds upon Socialist myth. In this area, good intentions are simply not enough. They can bring disaster upon the people we want to help if hopes are not informed by wisdom and prudence. Ignorance is not harmless; in the real world our illusions can have awful consequences.
>
> In short, we must learn to look closely at practicalities, at real outcomes. It is a wicked thing, for example, to weaken a society which holds some promise to raise the poor from deprivation, and to give suport to a self-styled utopia which does not. Such activity is not just an intellectual error which can be brushed aside: It inflicts real pain upon those least able to bear it. A 'good' ideology, like a good bridge, carries vehicles across the valley; a 'bad' ideology harms people, including the poor.[17]

When we discuss solutions to problems, we must guard against those that make bad situations worse. The immensity of the problems we face is daunting, and many conclude that each one is so big and so complicated that the only way to proceed is in increments—step one will fix one part of the problem, step two will address another, and eventually we will have the whole thing fixed.

Picture trying to unravel the maze of socialistic bureaucracy that was the Soviet Union, in increments. The factories will be turned over to the people this month. If they prove that they can handle that responsibility, then we will remove wage and price controls. OOPS! The factories went bankrupt the first month because of wage and price controls.

When the situation has become hopelessly snarled, unraveling it is a waste of time. When people talk about fixing the schools, the big snarl is the education code, and nobody wants to even attempt to unravel that! To even suggest such a thing arouses the ire of each special interest group whose personal fiefdom depends upon a piece of the education code. Special education proponents defend all the language alloting money and staff to their agenda. Science teachers fight to keep that fifty-minute block of time devoted exclusively to science. And so on.

To avoid fiefdom wars, the Goals 2000/OBE solution includes an end run around the education code by doing away with input requirements, such as regulations on hours, schedules, facilities, curriculum, etc., and substituting much simpler output requirements, i.e., students will be able to perform task A and reflect attitude B. In this case, the fix is no fix at all. We are tossing out the tangled ball of string and replacing it with unyielding steel cable.

That cable does more than imprison the educational system; it entwines itself throughout the entire social fabric. It leaves no man free from governmental control.

Separation of School and State

As we have discussed, when the federal government passes inappropriate legislation, states are often forced to implement it because of funding pressures. Some states have reached the breaking point over federal control, both because of financial impracticability and for reasons of principle. Governor Casey of Pennsylvania refused to implement federal regulations on abortions in Pennsylvania. As the first case of outright rebellion, it will be interesting to see how it is resolved. But consider what might happen if states refuse to implement parts of the restructuring program. Will opting out be an acceptable choice even if states are willing to forego federal money? California, where some school districts have refused to administer the state-mandated CLAS test to their students, provides a small-scale foretaste of the potential battles.

If the situation gets a lot worse, will states be allowed to secede if they disagree with the federal agenda? If you consider the ostensible reasons for the Civil War—ending slavery, economic issues, states' rights—none of these hold a candle to the enormity of the issue of family freedom and parental control over their own children. If people were willing to go to war over reasons that were important but less so than the freedom to raise a family without government intervention, how can we believe that people will not react violently over the enslavement of our children?

Revolution or Resolution?

Major conflict looms, but it is not too late to prevent it. We have to turn the tide away from dependence upon bureaucracy and back to personal responsibility now. Since government nannies are a major part of the problem, we should begin by ridding ourselves of some of the most redundant nannies—those in the U.S. Department of Education. Much of the educational control exercised by local, state, and federal departments duplicates the already needless, and possibly destructive, efforts of the other bureaucratic layers. Dismantling the U.S. Department of Education is being discussed and promoted by a number of educational political leaders, with the most

visible proponent being Michael Farris, president of the Home
School Legal Defense Association.

Tom Tancredo was appointed to the U.S. Department of
Education in 1981 and given the position of director of the
Region 8 office. When he assumed that position, he had 222
employees, 22 of them his personal staff. By October of 1988, he
had reduced the office to 64 prople, with only 3 personal staff
members. He spoke to more than a hundred groups around this
time, explaining what he had done. Then he asked the audiences if anyone had been able to tell the difference now that
there were far fewer regional staffers to serve them. Not one of
the thousands in his audiences could tell the difference.[18]

As restructuring efforts become more and more expensive
and fruitless, the forced demise of the U.S. Education
Department sounds more and more practical. But we must
reognize that this is only the first step. While the return of
educational control to the state level would satisfy many,
because it is easier to confront officials in your state capital
than in Washington D.C., the basic problem of government
assuming an inappropriate role still exists.

Some would prefer to see "local control," meaning no government control beyond the school district level. This
improves the situation more than does state control, but we
are still left with a socialistic system. The majority in the
school district can still vote to impose objectionable outcomes
or curricula. We are then back to the same situation as
Littleton, Colorado, and Vista, California, where school board
meetings serve as a worldview battlefield.

The only viable solution is to restore control to the most
local level of all—parents. They must be the ones to determine what their children learn. Most would respond to this
authority by enrolling their children in schools that operate

from a compatible worldview. However, they can also home educate their children. They can opt for a combination of classes from various providers. They can hire private tutors, use correspondence courses, or take advantage of the myriad of educational options that are open to those not bound by the government's system.

This solution requires that government remove itself from any control over education at all levels. The idea is similar to the decision our founding fathers made in early days of our country to remove government control over churches and religion. They saw nothing but endless turmoil if the government tried to influence religious beliefs.

While we do not have government-dictated religion, we do have government-dictated belief systems, courtesy of the government schools. It is impossible to educate without working within some value-laden system, yet we cannot agree on a common set of values. Within a government-controlled school system, we can only do what the schools are already doing—impose one set of values at the expense of others. The only solution is the one that saved our country from two centuries of religious warfare. Just as the founding fathers chose separation of church and state,[19] we must now choose separation of school and state.

Freedom to Risk

Certainly there is risk involved with such a solution. However, true freedom includes freedom to fail.

Early pioneers trudged over the Appalachians searching for that perfect piece of land for the new homestead. They often took wives and children with them. They weren't trailed by social workers clucking over educational "opportunities" or medical care. Families were trusted to take responsibility and obtain what assistance they could when it was needed. Government was not waiting in the wings to rescue those who failed, so the responsibility was heavy. Yet, so many of these families did so well that thousands more followed them.

We need to return our society to one where people accept both personal responsibility and the risk that goes with it.

What about the Underprivileged?

The major stumbling block to separation of school and state is the justifiable concern for underprivileged children who might be overlooked because of poverty, parental neglect, or lack of opportunity.

Parental neglect is the most difficult issue to address when educational enforcement through compulsory schooling laws is removed. However, we must keep in mind that these very same parents are also those most likely to turn a blind eye to truant children under today's system. They are also the parents most likely to be unsupportive of the best of the school's agendas. These are the children who are not getting an education now.

Often, such attitudes are symptoms of government-driven dependence because these families have learned that there is no need to accept personal responsibility; after all, the government is there to provide for their basic needs. In effect, the problem of neglected children is itself another good argument for discarding some of the welfare programs that unintentionally foster these attitudes.

Parents in any social milieu are never homogeneous in their attitudes; some will be responsible, some irresponsible. But if we return the responsibility for parenting and education to parents, the result will almost certainly be an increase in the number of parents who choose to be responsible.

Sociologist Charles Murray writes:

> It is not a desire for purity that pushes me toward radical conclusions, but the stubborn characteristic of human nature that used to lead Henry Stimson to say that 'the only way you can make a man trustworthy is to trust him.' It is the dilemma of the reality test: If humans *really are* making their own decisions and *really are* reliant on their own resources, then their behavior will be importantly guided by that reality. As soon as that reality is compromised, people know it. We observe this reaction in ourselves in dozens of trivial ways in everyday life (if my wife were to announce that from now on she will not turn down the thermostat before retiring then I would remember to do it, whereas now I tend to forget).[20]

The huge majority of parents care about their children and want them to be educated. As long as the state assumed responsibility, the tendency existed for many parents to forget about sharing that responsibility. When parents are treated with disdain, or even when they are simply ordered what to do by schools, they quickly abandon efforts to be involved. Trusting parents enough to give them back authority over their children can change parental attitudes.

The problems of poverty and opportunity are more easily solved. There are a number of possibilities for providing educational opportunities for those unable to afford it. Before describing solutions, we need to accurately assess the extent of the need. Separation of school and state will change the financial status of many families, particularly those in lower-middle and upper-lower classes. These are families who are carrying a huge tax burden to support our present school system. If that system is privatized, the government will no longer need to collect taxes to pay for it. (If they cut welfare programs, there are huge additional savings.) In California, over half of the state budget goes to education. While the mix of local and state monies varies from state to state, the overall percentage of the tax take that is spent on education is fairly close to 50 percent in all states. At the federal level, around 7 percent of the budget is spent on education.

When the federal Department of Education shuts down and government shuts off the money spigot, billions of dollars will be saved. If taxpayers can keep much more of their disposable income, the percentage of families who can then afford private education increases dramatically. The percentage of families who cannot afford to pay for their children's education will decrease significantly. While it is beyond the scope of this book to provide a definitive program for financing education for the remaining poor, we can offer a few practical suggestions. The actual solution will probably be a mix of these:

- Private charity. We have seen the large number of businesses, foundations, charities, and private philanthropists willing to invest in education. Given a decreased tax burden that lets them keep more of their own money, their generosity is bound to increase.

- School plant ownership transferral to scholarship foundations. Schools own an immense amount of property and buildings. These could be sold to private scholarship foundations which, in turn, could rent the property to private school operators. The rental funds can be used to provide scholarships for poor children.

- Alternative schooling. A vast array of alternative educational opportunities will arise. Computer learning has the potential to redefine education, cutting teaching costs with individualized, computer-monitored instruction. Part-time school might be the solution for parents who want to home school part time and send children to school for some classes. Classes might be offered by people from various professions, retirees, or others interested in teaching. The cost for such classes might run the gamet. Parents might be able to trade out labor for educational services. For example, Dad provides school grounds maintenance on weekends to offset part of the tuition costs.

We have barely begun to explore true educational alternatives. Yet, it would be foolish to claim that such a radical change in education as separation of school and state would be without risk. Some children will fall through the cracks. There will be a time of transition while parents learn to again accept their responsibility for their children.

But consider the alternative. Countless children are failed by the present system. Antagonism between conflicting worldviews might well become violent as factions fight for control over the values that will be taught to all of our children. As parents have less and less control over what happens in their local schools, they will become less and less responsible for their children. As government agencies begin to dictate parenting policies, health care, and family relationships, we are a short step from simply turning our children over to the state at birth so that it can have complete control over future citizens.

We are faced with two choices. We can choose the security of the government womb and pay the price of freedom. Or, we can choose a challenging future that holds both risks and responsibilities.

What Next?

No sensible person believes that repaving the road to freedom will be an easy or quick task. Government social programs are such a familiar part of the landscape that we do not even recognize them for what they are—redistributive, socialistic programs. The system itself, by robbing the private sector of so much money in the form of taxation, has limited the options open to the needy. Private charity is discouraged as the government claims responsibility and the resources for providing for the less fortunate. Apathy rises, and fellow citizens turn a blind eye, believing that government nannies have everything under control.

If we ever hope to escape the socialist web, we have to begin somewhere, and we have to begin now. The first and most easily accomplished step is the elimination of the U.S. Department of Education. They do nothing that cannot be done as well or better at the state, local, or private level (unless we accept the goal of redistribution of wealth from wealthier states to poor states!). And all of this duplication of effort and government meddling increases the cost of education substantially.

We can fight for immediate protection of parental and family rights by advocating The Parental Rights Amendment in every state and eventually at the federal level. The Parental Rights Amendment states, "The right of parents to direct the upbringing and education of their children shall not be infringed." This amendment or variations thereof have already been introduced in seven states[21] and legislators have committed to introduce it in nine more.[22] Such an amendment reduces arguments about condom distribution in schools, inappropriate tests, and numerous other educational flash points to the basic issue of who has primary say over the upbringing of children. Write to Of The People for information about The Parental Rights Amendment: 2111 Wilson Blvd., Suite 7000, Arlington, VA 22201.

The Grassley Amendment to Goals 2000 is a more complicated version of this amendment, and the Grassley language also deserves consideration for incorporation into state legislation.

We can support private voucher foundations that help provide scholarships for the needy. Many private businesses and organizations are working together to make private education a reality for thousands of children. Write to the National Scholarship Center, 1 Massachusetts Ave. N.W., Washington, D.C. 20001 for information and a list of organizations operating across the country. We can encourage churches and private organizations to start their own schools. We can encourage parents who choose to home educate their children. We can urge our legislators to let taxpayers keep more of their hard-earned money so that they have the wherewithal to be charitable. And, perhaps most importantly, we can each freely commit to helping others without waiting for government nannies to do the job.

End Notes:

[1] Robert Marzano, "When Two Worldviews Collide," *Educational Leadership*, Dec. 1993/Jan. 1994. Most of the articles in this issue deal with this problem.

[2] Lonnie Harp, "Kentucky Officials Announce 'Corrections' to Reform," *Education Week*, January 26, 1994, p. 13.

[3] Dr. Robert L. Simonds, *How to Elect Christians to Public Office*, CEE, Costa Mesa, CA, p. 35.

[4] *How To Help Your School Be A Winner!: A Manual for Starting and Operating an Effective Local Parents' CEE Chapter,*" NACE/CEE, Costa Mesa, CA, p. 5.

[5] "Who We Are," *Freedom Watch*, June-July 1993, Citizens Project, Colorado Springs, CO.

[6] "School Board Elections Nearing," *Freedom Watch*, Citizens Project, Colorado Springs, CO.

[7] Chester E. Finn Jr., *NASSP Bulletin*, March, 1982, "Public Service, Public Support, Public Accountability," p. 69.

[8] Richard Mitchell, "Voucher, Smoucher," *Underground Grammarian*, Vol. V, No. 2, Feb. 1981.

[9] John O'Neil, "Is U.S. Headed Toward a National Curriculum?," *Update Conference Report*, ASCD, Vol. 35, No. 5, June, 1993, p. 6.

[10] *Potential Strategies for Long-Term Indicator Development*, National Education Goals Panel, No. 91-08, Sept. 4, 1991., p. 52.

[11] Ibid., p. 44.

[12] Ibid., p. 48.

13 Ibid.

14 "Conformity on campus in the name of Diversity," *The Orange County Register*, Feb. 2, 1994.

15 Meg Sommerfeld, "E.D. Releases Regulations Designed to Strengthen Oversight of Colleges," *Education Week*, Feb. 2, 1994, p. 13.

16 Europe's cradle-to-grave welfare bill comes due," *The Orange County Register*, Feb. 1, 1994.

17 Marvin Olasky, *The Tragedy of American Compassion*, Crossway Books, Wheaton, IL, 1992, p. 76.

18 Personal conversation with Tom Tancredo, Aug. 26, 1994.

19 The use of this phrase is not intended as agreement with modern-day interpretations of that term which make Bibles contraband in the schools.

20 Charles Murray, *In Pursuit of Happiness and Good Government*, Simon and Schuster, NY, 1988, p. 246.

21 Kansas, Minnesota, Nebraska, New York, Pennsylvania, South Carolina, and Wisconsin.

22 Alabama, Arizona, Illinois, Michigan, Mississippi, Missouri, Ohio, Oregon, and Washington.

Bibliography of Suggested Reading

Arons, Stephen. *Compelling Belief, The Culture of American Schooling*, Amherst: University of Massachusetts Press, 1983.

Blumenfeld, Samuel L. *Is Public Education Necessary?*, Boise, I.D.: Paradigm Company, 1989.

Blumenfeld, Samuel L. *NEA, Trojan Horse in American Education*, Boise, I.D.: Paradigm Company, 1984.

Brovard, James. *The Destruction of American Liberty*, New York: St. Martin's Press, 1994,

Carlson, Allan. *Family Questions*, New Brunswick, USA: Transactions Books, 1990.

Eakman, B. K. *Educating for the New World Order*, Portland, O.R.: Halcyon House, 1992.

Gatto, John Taylor. *Dumbing Us Down*, Philadelphia: New Society Publishers, 1992.

Glenn, Charles L. *Choice of Schools in Six Nations*, Washington, D.C.: U.S. Department of Education, 1989.

Hall, David W., ed. *Welfare Reformed*, Franklin, T.N.: Legacy Communications, 1994.

Klicka, Christopher J. *The Right Choice, The Incredible Failure of Public Education and the Rising Hope of Home Schooling*, Gresham, O.R.: Noble Publishing Associates, 1992.

Lieberman, Myron. *Public Education, An Autopsy*, Cambridge, M.A.: Harvard University Press, 1993.

Murray, Charles. *In Pursuit of Happiness and Good Government*, New York: Simon and Schuster, 1988.

Murray, Charles. *Losing Ground, American Social Policy 1950-1980*, New York: Basic Books, 1984.

National Education Goals Panel Reports from the various goals panels, 1850 M Street, N.W., Suite 270, Washington, D.C. 20036

Olasky, Marvin. *The Tragedy of American Compassion*, Wheaton, I.L.: Crossway Books, 1992.

Patrick, James R., ed. *Research Manual, American 2000/Goals 2000-Moving the Nation Educationally to a "New World Order,"* Moline, I.L.: Citizens for Academic Excellence, 1994.

Price, Kevin J. *Empowerment to the People, An Economic Agenda for the 21st Century*, Washington, D.C,: Free Congress Foundation, 1993.

Pride, Mary. *The Child Abuse Industry*, Wheaton, I.L.: Crossway Books, 1986.

Richman, Sheldon. *Separating School & State*, Fairfax, V.A.: The Future of Freedom Foundation, 1994.

Roche, George. *One By One, Preserving Values and Freedom in Heartland America*, Hillsdale, M.I.: Hillsdale College Press, 1990.

Scott, Brenda. *Out of Control: Who's Watching Our Child Protection Agencies?*, LaFayette, L.A.: Huntington House, 1994.

Sowell, Thomas. *Inside American Education, The Decline, The Deception, The Dogmas*, New York: The Free Press, 1993.

West, E.G. *Education and the State, A Study in Political Economy*, Indianapolis: Liberty Fund, 1994.

ORGANIZATIONS:

(This list is not intended to exclude others who are working to further individual freedom, the rights of families, and freedom in education, but it should be a starting place for those wishing to make contact with such organizations.)

Family Research Council, 700 13th St. N.W. Suite 500, Washington, DC 20005, (202) 393-2100. Researches family issues and publishes *Washington Watch* and *Family Policy*.

The Future of Freedom Foundation, 11350 Random Hills Rd., Suite 800, Fairfax, VA 22030, (703) 934-6101. Presents "an uncompromising moral, philosophical, and economic case for individual freedom, private property, and limited government."

The National Scholarship Foundation, 1 Massachusetts Ave. N.W., Suite 330, Washington, DC 20001, (202) 842-1355. Serves as a clearing house for information about private scholarships and voucher programs.

Separation of School and State Project, 4578 N. First, Box 310, Fresno, CA 93726, (209) 292-1776. Provides information about issues relating to education and the state.

Social Renewal Foundation, Inc., P.O. Box 6, Philmont, NY 12565, (518) 392-7382. Private scholarships.

Of The People, 2111 Wilson Blvd., Suite 700, Arlington, VA 22201, 703-351-5051. Parental Rights Amendment.

The Rockford Institute, 934 North Main St., Rockford, IL 61103, 815-964-5819. Researches family issues and publishes *The Family in America*.

INDEX

"all children can learn," 131
"Animal Farm," 246
"Brave New World," 18, 183
"Harrison Bergeron," 77, 99
(CEE), 123-124, 233-234, 258
Abbeville-Greenwood Library Project, 34
Abortions, 158, 249
   Abortion referrals, 159
Absolute standards, 232
Abstinence, 233
Academic performance, 20, 103, 112
Academics, 9-10, 20, 47-48, 85, 114, 171
Accreditation, 107, 180, 242
Achieving Necessary Skills, 172
Ada Schools, 86
Adams, John, 51
Administrators, 55-57, 62, 64, 94, 98, 123-124, 126
Advanced Training Institute, 90, 100
Advisory Committee on Head Start Quality and Expansion, 17
Affective outcomes, 48, 85, 112, 133
African culture, 146
African proverb, 9

AFT, 95
Age-segregated classrooms, 69
Aid to Protestant denominational schools, 52
AIDS, 113, 154-155, 158
Alabama, 212, 217, 260
Alternative governance, 209
Alternative learning environments, 180
Alternative lifestyles, 112, 158
America 2000, 26, 30, 34-35, 45, 73, 127, 197
   Community Notebook, 34-35, 45, 127
American Association of University Women (AAUW), 140-141, 151
American Enterprise Institute, 166
American Federation of Teachers, 76, 98, 183
Amish, 139-141
Apprenticeships, 177, 181, 187-188
Arkansas, 141, 151, 173
Ashbrook, Congressman John M., 64, 223
Assessment, 19, 32-33, 63, 78-83, 96, 99, 105, 111, 126, 138-139, 173, 199, 201, 207, 209, 216-218, 228, 230, 239

Association for Supervision and Curriculum Development, 135, 150, 190

At-risk, 1, 3, 5, 7, 9, 11, 13-17, 19-23, 25, 32, 36, 38, 40, 43, 45, 225

ATI, 90

Attitudes, 18, 23, 48, 70-71, 84-85, 118, 133, 138, 142-143, 145, 156, 178, 201, 252-254

Attitudinal goals, 70

Authority, 11, 24, 29, 31, 37, 47, 54, 60, 64, 70, 92-93, 110, 130, 138, 159, 163, 165-166, 184, 232-233, 240, 251, 254

Ayres, William H., 223

Baker, Eva, 238

Ball, William B., 140

Baltimore, Maryland, 162

Before-school experiences, 8

Behaviors, 17-18, 138, 156

Beliefs, 17, 44, 47-48, 71, 84-85, 91, 133, 137, 143, 149, 178, 223, 232-233, 251

Bethlehem, Pennsylvania, 137

Bettendorf Survey, 142

Big Brother, 64, 150, 199

Birth control, 126, 158, 161-162

Blumenfeld, Sam, 55, 67, 261

Bob Jones University, 241-242

Boone, Daniel, 218

Bowman, Zane, 86

Boysen, Thomas C., 211, 233

Briefing Book, 30-32, 45

Brownson, Orestes A., 53

Bruce, Donald C., 223

Bureaucrats, 7, 27, 65, 88, 117, 126, 169, 194, 218, 223, 241, 246

Business Roundtable, 95, 227

Business, 3, 40, 48, 61, 71, 95, 158, 162, 170, 181-182, 184, 186-188, 202, 206, 223, 227

Butler Area School District, 96

California, 14, 21, 28, 34, 39-40, 42, 46, 63, 68, 80, 84, 99, 115, 119, 125, 128, 133, 158, 161, 164, 174, 205, 212, 216, 228, 233, 239-240, 249, 251, 254

California at Los Angeles, 239

California Learning Assessment System, (CLAS), 63, 80-81, 249

California Learning Assessment, 63, 80, 216

California's Little Hoover Commission, 39

Carnegie Corporation, 224-225, 230

Carnegie units, 69, 84, 87, 96, 177, 190

Carnine, Douglas, 59, 68

Casey, Governor Robert, 215, 249

Catholic immigrants, 52

Center for Critical Thinking and Moral Critique, 80

Center for health education, 154

Center for the Study of Evaluation at the University of California at Los Angeles, 238

Centers for Disease Control, 156

Centralization, 62

Centralized computer systems, 198

Certificate of Advanced Mastery, 171, 177, 179

Certificate of Initial Mastery, 135, 171, 177, 180, 190

Certificates of Mastery, 133, 170, 173-174, 176-178, 190, 225-226

Champlin, John, 70, 98

Character education, 47

Chicago, 38, 86

Child Abuse
  Child Abuse Registry, 40
  Child abuse accusations, 38
  Child abuse in the classroom, 130
  Child Abuse Industry, 42, 46, 262
  Child abuse investigators, 36
  Child abuse prevention program, 36
  Child abuse, 13, 21, 36-38, 40-43, 46, 130, 262

Child care, 23, 25, 38-39, 43, 215, 224

Child Protective Services, 28, 39

Child welfare, 20, 38, 42

Child-care centers, 17

Children's Protective Services, 40

China, 43

Choice in Education, 235

Christian Coalition, 234

Christian parents, 91, 125

Citizens for Excellence in Education, 123

Citizens Project, 233-235, 258

Citizenship, 6, 103-104, 130, 137-139, 150-151

Cizek, Gregory, 76, 98

Claremont Institute study of California, 212

Index

Clinton's health care plan, 154, 159, 194-195

Clinton, Hillary Rodham, 180, 182-183, 191,225

Clinton, President, 5, 154, 214

Clipper chip, 194, 201-202

Coercion, 44, 132, 136, 139, 176

Coerced attendance, 133

Collective responsibility, 44

College preparation, 87, 172

Communities for Developing Minds, 62

Community organizations, 48

Community service, 29, 35, 104, 137, 150

Competency, 6, 75-76, 96, 103, 105, 107, 109, 111, 113, 115-117, 119, 121, 123, 125, 127

Comprehensive health education curriculum, 154-155

Comprehensive Services For Children and Youth Act of 1991, 19, 25-26, 154

Compulsory schooling, 48, 50-52, 54, 131-134, 140, 180, 252

Computer tracking, 194-195

Condom distribution, 233, 257

Congress, 51, 57, 65, 89, 113, 195, 208, 219, 221, 262

Congressional Record, 68, 192

Consolidation, 21

Control of local school districts from Washington, 65

Coordinated services, 18-19, 37

Copp, George and Gabrielle, 37

Council for Exceptional Children, 225

Council of Chief State School Officers, 197, 203

Cradle-to-grave, 5, 7, 73, 194, 245, 259

Creationism, 234

Critical thinking skills, 105

Cultural Literacy, 91-92, 101

Curriculum attacks, 124

Curriculum framework, 79, 239

Daniel Boone District, 218

Data tracking, 194, 237

Davis, Jayna, 85, 100, 127

Delaware, 66, 199

Delivery sites, 33

Denominational schools, 52

Department of Education at UCI, 133

Department of Education, 11, 18, 23, 25, 29, 67-68, 95, 97, 99, 110-111, 133, 144, 150-152, 156, 177, 190, 198-199, 203, 210, 228, 250, 254, 257, 261

Department of Education grants, 95

Department of Family Services, 36

Department of Health and Human Services, 25, 156

Department of Motor Vehicles, 198-201

Department of Social Services, 28

Developmental delays, 21-22

Developmental needs, 31

Developmental screenings, 43

Digital Telephony and Communications Privacy Improvement Act, 193

Dilution of the academic curriculum, 114

Disabled, 10-11, 134, 205

Disadvantaged, 7, 10-11, 32, 110, 208

Diversity, 99, 118-119, 139, 141, 214, 242, 259

Dobson, James, 124

Drugs, 6, 12, 31, 36, 149, 158

Drug-free schools, 155

Duche, Jacob, 51

DuPont de Nemours, Pierre, 51, 66

Early Childhood Family Education, 34

Education, 5, 8-11, 15, 18-20, 23-26, 28-29, 31-35, 43, 46-62, 64-75, 77-79, 81, 83, 85-101, 103-105, 109-111, 113-118, 122-123, 126-128, 130-135, 138-141, 144, 146, 150-163, 165, 167-170, 172, 174-179, 182, 185-187, 189-191, 195-203, 206-214, 216-223, 225, 227-243, 248, 250-255, 257-259, 261-263

Education and human service delivery districts, 33

Education reform, 5, 186, 206, 210, 217

Education Commission of the States, 35

Education Week, 20, 25-26, 67-68, 91, 98-99, 101, 127, 150, 154, 167-168, 190-191, 198, 203, 213, 225, 227-230, 258-259

Educational restructuring, 9, 74, 213

Edwards, Dr. Charles, 89

Eighth goal, 24, 58

Elders, Dr. Joycelyn, 154-155, 159

Elementary and Secondary Education Act, 15, 18, 24-25, 59, 146, 154, 206, 214, 227-228

England, 51, 213, 216
ESEA, 18-19, 206-207, 209
Essay-on-demand, 217
Euclid Avenue Elementary School, 56
Evans, Dennis, 133
Evolution, 91, 125-126, 233
Expanding preschool services, 19
Factory model of schooling, 71
Falwell, Jerry, 242
Family and Children First, 16, 29-30, 45
Family assistance programs, 9
Family centers, 21
Family Connection Project, 34
Family counseling, 19, 36, 38
Family income, 71
Family Law Quarterly, 44
Family privacy, 21, 163
Family rights, 10, 16, 46, 247, 257
Family screening, 21
Farenga, Pat, 185, 191
Farrell, Pennsylvania, 215
Farris, Michael, 250
Feder, Don, 44, 46
Federal aid to education, 64, 219-221
Federal control, 64, 111, 205, 220-221, 223, 240, 242, 249
Federal grant money, 19
Federal job-training efforts, 175
Federal role in education, 110
Feelings, 71, 80, 112
Fessler, Diana, 30, 34
Fifth national goal, 74
Financial incentives, 157, 165, 181
Finn, Chester, 238
First national goal, 7, 10
Florida, 34, 40
Focus on the Family, 124
Foreman, Mark, 120, 123-124, 128
France, 51
Fraud in a voucher system, 237
Freedom, 58, 93, 138-139, 141, 146, 184, 186, 188, 231, 234, 238, 241, 244-245, 249, 252, 256, 258, 262-263
Freeh, Louis J., 193
Fundamentalists, 63, 232
Funding, 14-15, 17-18, 25, 28, 43, 57-58, 95, 109-110, 135, 137, 157, 208, 211-214, 217, 228, 240-241, 243, 249

Garrett, Sandy, 86
Gatto, John Taylor, ix-xxviii. 55, 67, 178, 191, 261
GED certificates, 176
Georgia, 34, 173
German apprenticeship system, 183
Germany, 51, 171, 181-183, 187-188, 245
GI Bill, 241
Glean, Richard, 215-216
Glenmont School, 213-214
Global economy, 6, 69, 186
Goal 3, 7, 17, 78, 92, 103, 119, 137, 150-151, 153, 157, 239
Goal of education, 90
Goals 2000, 5, 7, 9, 11, 15, 17-18, 26, 34, 43, 49, 51, 53, 55, 57, 59, 61, 63, 65-67, 74, 80, 93-94, 97, 109-110, 131, 136, 144, 146, 153, 157, 159, 167, 169-172, 174, 176, 179, 184, 194-195, 206-210, 213-214, 224-228, 230, 235, 248, 257, 262
Government control, 48, 187, 224, 244, 250-251
Government dependency, 240
Government interference, 11, 88
Government Nannies, 1-2, 4, 6, 8, 10-12, 14, 16, 18, 20, 22, 24, 26, 28, 30, 32, 34, 36, 38, 40, 42, 44, 46, 48, 50, 52, 54, 56, 58, 60, 62, 64, 66, 68, 70, 72, 74, 76, 78, 80, 82, 84, 86, 88, 90, 92, 94, 96, 98, 100, 102, 104, 106, 108, 110, 112, 114, 116, 118, 120, 122, 124, 126, 128, 130, 132, 134, 136, 138, 140, 142, 144, 146, 148, 150, 152, 154, 156, 158, 160, 162, 164, 166, 168, 170, 172, 174, 176, 178, 180, 182, 184, 186, 188, 190, 192, 194, 196, 198, 200, 202, 204, 206, 208, 210, 212, 214, 216, 218, 220, 222, 224, 226, 228, 230, 232, 234, 236, 238, 240, 242, 244, 246, 248-250, 252, 254, 256, 258, 260, 262, 264
Government Nanny programs, 7
Government regulatory paperwork, 55
Government's takeover of parental responsibilities, 8
Governor's Conference on Children and Youth, 42
Graduation rate, 6, 176

Index

Grant money, 19, 209, 215, 218
Grassley Amendment to Goals 2000, 257
Great Britain, 51-52
Grier, George, 198
Griffith, Ben, 119-120, 128
Grove City College, 241-242
Hand, Kathy, 208
Hawaii, 5
Head Start, 17-18, 25, 32, 34
Health and Rehabilitation Services, 40
Health care, 10, 27-28, 31, 74, 155, 157, 159, 161, 165-166, 194-195, 225, 243-244, 256
Health curricula, 157
Health education, 28, 65, 104, 153-157, 159, 161, 163, 165, 167, 195, 202, 221-222
Health screenings, 18
Health security card, 194
Health services, 19, 28, 38, 41, 159
Healthy Students-Healthy Schools, 154-157
Healthy Tomorrows, 28-29, 45, 156
Hiestand, Edgar W., 223
High standards, 74, 77, 98, 127, 150, 186, 206-207
High Success Network, 70, 84, 98, 100
HIPPY, 34
Hirsch, Dr. E.D., 91
Hispanic families, 118
Home School Legal Defense Association, 38, 250
Home schoolers, 180
Home visits, 23, 43
Homosexual activists, 126
Homosexual lifestyle, 141
Homosexuality, 126, 143
Hornbeck, David, 92-93, 95, 101 206, 210, 227
Howard, Gene, 40
Hudson, Michael, 124
Idaho, 212
Illinois, 115, 260
Immunization, 25
Income tax law, 224
Indians, 118
Individual responsibility, 167, 172, 231
Individuals with Disabilities Education Act, 225

Infants and Toddlers Program, 34
Instructional practices, 93
Interagency Task Force,29, 156-157, 163
Iowa, 101, 142-143, 206, 210
Irish Catholics, 117
IRS, 38
Italy, 51, 245
Jamestown High School, 142
Jenkintown School District in Pennsylvania, 72
Job training, 20, 133, 171, 174-176, 187-188, 244
Jobs for the Future, 173
JOBSTART, 175-176, 190
Johnson City Schools, 71
Johnson City, 71-72, 86
Kansas Outcomes, 105-108
Kansas, 105-108, 112-113, 206, 260
Kassebaum, Senator Nancy L., 175
Kentucky Education Reform Act, 210
Kentucky's assessment, 79
Kentucky, 79, 99, 132, 141, 150, 152, 160-161, 163, 168, 200-201, 203, 210-211, 216, 227, 233, 258
Kindergarten readiness, 9
Klicka, Christopher J., 38-39, 46, 51, 55, 66-67, 262
Kunin, Madeleine, 131
La Paz Middle School, 14
Learning a Living, 173, 190
Learning centers, 84, 135, 180
Liberty University, 242
Lieberman, Myron51-52, 55, 60, 66-68, 262
Life Stress Inventory, 142
Literacy, 6, 31, 34, 51-52, 54, 76, 91-92, 101, 189
Littleton, Colorado, 86, 96, 251
Littleton High School, 96-97
Local autonomy, 208
Local control, 62, 75, 92, 163, 208, 212-213, 239, 250
Local education agency, 209
Local forum, 91
London, 141, 213
Lonthair, Jaime and Paul, 39, 42
Losing Ground, 59, 67-68, 168, 190, 262
Lucia Mar School District, 84, 100

Luksik, Peg, 85, 98, 100, 114, 117, 127-128, 229
Magaziner, Ira, 180, 182-183, 191
Maine, 173
Mainstreaming, 64, 226
Mangel, Claudia Pap, 44
Martin, Dave, 223
Marzano, Robert, 231, 258
Medi-Cal, 28-29, 164-165
Medicaid, 25
Meloy, Al, 62
Michigan, 62-63, 212, 260
Midnight Artists, 139
Mills, Richard, 101
Milwaukee, 237
Minnesota, 34, 86, 98, 126-127, 167, 260
Minorities, 48, 54, 118, 151
Missouri, 5, 11, 21, 24, 35-36, 260
Mitchell, Richard, 238, 259
Mobile medical van, 28
Money, 4, 14, 17, 19, 56, 61-62, 117, 157, 164-166, 172, 181, 185, 205, 207-209, 211, 213-215, 217-219, 221, 223, 225, 227-229, 236-238, 241-243, 248-249, 254-256, 258
Monitoring of private lives, 237
Multi-culturalism, 104, 112, 146
Murray, Charles, 59, 67-68, 168, 190, 253, 259
National Assessment of Educational Progress, 79, 83
National Association of State Boards of Education, 105
National Black Women's Health Project, 161
National Center for Education Statistics (NCES), 195, 197-198, 202-203
National Center on Education and the Economy, 182, 225
National Center on Educational Outcomes (NCEO), 75, 98, 104, 112, 126-127, 157-158, 167
National data banks, 95, 194,217
National Defense Education Act Amendment of 1961, 219
National Education Commission on Time and Learning, 113
National Education Goals, 8, 24-26, 69, 79, 97, 99, 103, 127, 150-151, 157, 196, 202-203, 206, 231, 259, 262

National Education Standards and Improvement Council (NESIC), 109, 207
National examination, 79
National Goals, 5, 29, 35, 72-74, 78-79, 91-93, 97, 105, 108-110, 136, 141, 154, 196, 199, 201, 207, 238-239
National Health and Nutrition Examination Survey, 22
National Household Education Survey, 23
National identity card, 194
National standards, 78-79, 111, 205, 207, 209, 211, 213, 215, 217, 219, 221, 223, 225, 227, 229, 239-240
National test, 79
National Women's Health Network, 161
Nationalized curriculum, 79, 240
Nationwide assessment system, 78, 239
Neglected children, 253
New Age content, 233
New American School Development Corporation, 73
New Hampshire, 212
New York Daily News, 185
New York State Community Schools Program, 20
New York, 20, 35, 71, 98-99, 142, 185, 190, 230, 260-263
NewsChannel 4, 85, 100, 127
Non-graded classrooms, 96
Norplant, 161-162, 168
North Carolina, 35
Nunnos, 164-166
Nutrition, 4, 10, 22-23, 27, 31, 38, 49-50, 153, 155-157
Objectives of the national goals, 35, 108
Ohio, 29-34, 45, 64, 76, 141, 152, 260
Oklahoma, 85-86, 100, 105-108, 112-113, 127
Olasky, Marvin, 247, 259
One-stop service centers, 218
One-stop shopping, 19-21, 25, 33, 37, 155, 166
Opportunity-to-learn standards, 94, 207
Oregon's Educational Act for the 21st Century, 135
Oregon, 59, 135, 173, 177, 179-180, 190, 206, 260

Orientations, 70
Orwell, George, 246
Outcome-Based Education (OBE), 69-71, 73, 75, 77-79, 81, 83, 85-91, 93-97, 99, 101, 114, 117, 127, 174, 178, 216, 234, 238, 240
Outcomes Driven Developmental Model, 71
Outcomes, 19-20, 56-57, 70-71, 75-76, 78, 82, 84-85, 87-88, 90, 98, 100, 104-109, 111-113, 126-127, 133, 141, 144, 151-152, 157-158, 167, 172-173, 177-178, 187, 190, 196, 199, 217, 225, 247, 251
Owen, Robert, 53
Parent education, 19, 29, 34-37, 43, 219
Parent involvement, 18
Parental and family rights, 16, 257
Parental concerns, 63
Parental consent, 159, 161, 163, 165, 200
Parental involvement, 6, 58, 61
Parental responsibility, 28
Parental rights, 28, 136, 160, 163, 257, 263
Parents and Professionals Involved in Education, 160
Parents As Teachers (PAT), 16, 18, 26, 34-37, 43, 185, 191, 195, 234
Partners, 5, 48
Partnerships, 6, 30, 58, 95, 180
Paserba, Robert, 96
Paternostro, Judy, 163
Paul, Dr. Richard, 80
Pell Grants, 241
  Pell Grant fraud, 237
Pennsylvania Educational Quality Assessment, 138
Pennsylvania, 72, 95, 101, 114, 137-138, 142, 151, 173, 199, 206, 215-216, 218, 249, 260
Performance standards, 152, 170, 207, 209
Perkins,Carl D., Vocational and Applied Technology Education, 209
Personal responsibility, 56, 104, 170, 249, 252
Personal values, 70
Philadelphia, 67, 95, 134, 150-151, 216, 261
Pierce v. Society of the Sisters, 116
Planned Parenthood, 126

Poland, 51
Political agenda for education, 72
Politically correct, 70, 89, 118, 137, 141-143, 146
Portable credentials, 170
Portfolios, 82-83, 217
Portugal, 51
Potts, Ray, 85
Poudre County Even Start, 35
Prenatal health systems, 10, 18, 22, 27
Preschool, 8, 10, 16-19, 23, 25, 32, 50, 201
Priscilla and the Wimps, 81
Privacy, 16, 21, 38, 64, 83, 140, 159, 163, 193, 198-202, 238
Private foundations, 215
Private school, 52-53, 83, 134, 179, 196-198, 236-238, 240, 255
Procrustes, 22
Progressive tax, 224
Property taxes, 211-212
Proposition 13, 212
Protestant bias, 53-54
Protestants, 54, 117
Prussian model, 115, 178, 179
Public housing agencies, 20
Public school curriculum, 54
Public schools, 9, 16, 52-55, 61, 73, 90, 115, 117, 134, 139, 146, 212, 234-236
Public's interest in providing education for everyone, 47
Purpose of schooling, 48, 114
Questionnaires about family habits, 83
Radical right fundamentalists, 63
RAND study, 82, 158
Readiness, 7-9, 17, 22, 30, 47
Reauthorization of The Elementary and Secondary Education, 15, 18, 24-25, 146, 154, 206, 214, 227-228
Regulation of Colleges and Universities, 241
Religious agenda, 234
Religious conservatives, 52
Religious right, 124, 234-235
Report cards, 69, 199
Restructuring, 9, 14, 26, 61-62, 73-74, 79-80, 83, 92, 95, 97, 100, 111, 130, 140, 159, 169, 178, 184, 187, 189, 206, 210-211, 213, 216-218, 249-250

Rewards and penalties, 210
Rhode Island, 21
Robertson, Pat, 234
Robillard, Donald, 214
Rogers, Laura, 35-36, 45-46
Role of government, 21, 126
Roots and Wings project, 73-74
Rugg, Dr. Harold, 221
Rush, Benjamin, 115
Russia, 51
Sales taxes, 212
San Dieguito Union High School District, 93, 101
San Fernando, California, 161
SCANS, 95, 171-174, 190
Schindler's List, 119
School administrators, 98, 123-124, 126
School agenda, 9, 48
School board, 29, 62, 64, 69, 72, 91-94, 96, 97, 120, 124-126, 218, 233-235, 251, 258
School District Data Book, 197
School Site Interagency Services Team, 29
School wars, 124-126, 233
School's mission, 9, 69, 111
School's responsibility, 10
School-based clinics, 74, 154, 158-160, 163, 165-166
School-linked services, 20
School-to-Work
  School-to-Work Opportunities Act of 1994, 170, 180, 209,229
  School-to-work legislation, 170, 173, 175, 225
  School-to-work transition, 132, 169, 171, 173, 175, 177, 179, 181, 183, 185, 187-189, 191
  School-to-work, 95, 132, 169-171, 173-175, 177, 179-181, 183-185, 187-191, 209, 218, 225, 229
Science standards, 91
Scott, Julia, 161
Screening, 12, 21-23, 32-33, 35-36, 38
Secular humanism, 54, 233
Self-esteem, 112, 130, 173, 232-233
Separation of school and state, 249, 251-252, 254-255, 263
Service delivery regions, 33

Sex education, 126, 128, 233-234
Sex Respect, 126
Shalala, Donna, 17, 156
Shanker, Albert, 76, 98, 183
Shapell, Nathan, 39
Simonds, Dr. Robert, 123, 233
Simplicity Survey, 143
Site-based management, 92, 213
Sixteenth Amendment to the Constitution, 224
Slavin, Robert, 73
Smith, Marshall, 207
Social democracy, 245
Social engineering, 114, 117, 210
Social objectives, 114
Social Security, 194, 198-199, 201, 243
Social service agencies, 34, 37-39, 42, 156, 164. 166
Social services, 18-21, 25, 28-29, 34-35, 37-38, 43, 74, 156, 163, 166, 198, 201, 210, 215, 245
Social workers, 5, 8, 11, 16, 18-19, 22, 28-29, 35, 38-39, 129, 165-166, 219, 252
Socialism, 54, 57, 123, 179, 182, 246-247
Socialist, 53, 57, 73, 221, 243, 247, 256
Socialistic programs, 256
Socialists, 52-54
South Washington County, 86
Soviet Union, 57, 60, 123, 133, 248
Sowell, Thomas, 67, 149, 152, 263
Spady, Dr. William, 70, 84
Spain, 51
Spanking, 12, 37
Standardized tests, 80, 83, 99
Standards voluntary, 206-207
Standards, 65, 70, 74-78, 82-83, 91, 94-98, 109-113, 127, 132, 136, 150, 152, 157, 170-171, 174, 186, 196, 205-209, 211, 213, 215, 217, 219, 221, 223, 225, 227, 229-230, 232, 238-240, 242-243
State curriculum-framework, 64
State family policy, 30, 43
State standards, 109-111, 208
Stealth candidates, 234
Sticht, T.G., 189, 192
Stimson, Henry, 253
Stokes, Karl, 162
Subjective indicators, 112

Success By Six, 35
Successful OBE implementation, 84
Supreme Court, 116, 140
Tancredo, Tom. 250, 259
Taxes, 89, 211-212, 217, 224, 236, 254
Teacher training, 18, 60, 223
Teachers College, Columbia University, 221
Teachers stand in opposition, 95
Teachers' union, 93
Teaching the Scans Competencies, 171
Tenth Amendment, 109, 127
Testing drives the curriculum, 78
Thatcher, Christopher, 213
The National Center on Educational Outcomes, 75, 104, 112, 157-158
The School-to-Work Transition, 132, 169, 171, 173, 175, 177, 179, 181, 183, 185, 187-189, 191
To Tell the Truth, 98, 100, 229
Tolerance, 119, 128, 141
Totalitarianism, 114
Tracking, 187, 194-195, 199, 237
Transformational OBE, 71, 88
Troy, Frosty, 124
Tucker, Marc, 182-183, 191
U.S. Department of Health, Education, and Welfare, 110, 195, 202, 221-222, 250
U.S. Department of Labor's statistics, 185
U.S. News & World Report, 184, 191, 202, 229
Underprivileged children, 252
Uniform standards, 70, 77
Unitarian, 53-54
Utilitarian approach to education, 189
Vaccinations, 4, 8-9, 20, 195
Validity of outcome-based education, 94
Values, 17, 44, 47-48, 70, 85, 114, 120-123, 133, 136, 139-142, 144, 146-147, 149, 153, 178, 189, 201, 231-234, 251, 256, 262
    Values clarification, 232
    Values conflicts, 136, 146
Vermont, 82, 100
Violations of family and individual privacy, 83
Vista, California, 125, 233, 251
Vocational training, 177-178

Voinovich, Governor, 29
Voluntary nationwide standards, 109
Voluntary state standards, 208
Vonnegut, Kurt, 77, 99
Voter registration, 137
Voting, 105
Voucher, 116, 235-238, 240-241, 257, 259, 263
Waivers, 19
Wall Street Journal, 245
Washington Department of Social and Health Services, 41
Watt, Kelley, 125
Wattenburg, Ben, 166, 168
Webster, Daniel, 51
Welfare assistance, 19
Welfare programs, 59, 243, 253-254
Western European countries, 245
White collar jobs, 184
White House, 17, 25, 201
Wisconsin Educational Goals Committee, 88
Wisconsin vs. Yoder, 140
Wisconsin, 68, 88, 101, 139-140, 173, 212, 229, 260
Worldview, 54, 90, 120, 122-123, 148, 231-233, 235, 251,258
Young, Linda, 96-97, 101
Youth Centers, 180